THE GUINNESS BOOK OF HISTORICAL BLUNDERS

THE GUINNESS BOOK OF
HISTORICAL BLUNDERS

GEOFFREY REGAN

GUINNESS PUBLISHING

For Alan and Anita

Published in Great Britain by
Guinness Publishing Ltd
33 London Road, Enfield, Middlesex EN2 6DJ

"Guinness" is a registered trademark of
Guinness Publishing Ltd.

First published 1994

Reprinted 1995

ISBN 0-85112-785-1

A catalogue record for this book is available from the
British Library

Designed by Cathy Shilling

Typeset by Ace Filmsetting Ltd, Frome, Somerset

Printed and bound in Great Britain by
The Bath Press, Bath

Front cover illustration: The Bridal Night, by James Gillray (The British Library, London)

Picture Acknowledgements

The publishers wish to thank the following for permission
to reproduce pictures in this book:

Archiv für Kunst und Geschichte, Berlin
The Hulton-Deutsch Collection
Mary Evans Picture Library
Popperfoto
Ann Ronan Picture Library
Topham Picture Source
The Kobal Collection

CONTENTS

INTRODUCTION

A television newsreader recently made a plea for 'better news'. He was apparently disturbed by having to read about bad news, night after night, and felt that somewhere something 'good' must be taking place. Of course, he was right. Most of what every human inhabitant of the planet does on a daily basis is at worst neutral in its effects and at best good and life-asserting. But it is not newsworthy. It may seem perverse, but it is frequently the bad and life-threatening stories that attract the attention of the public rather than their opposites. The tabloid newspapers are full of stories about the serial killer, the politician involved in sex scandals, the thuggish rock star or footballer involved in a fracas at a wine bar. Bad news makes good news in the media. Nor is this merely a passing phase, a reflection of modern cynicism. As one looks back into history one finds this same pattern recurring – the interest that the majority of ordinary people found in the activities of the extraordinary. Saints were admired, but sinners – the bigger the better – were feared, and fear was always the stronger emotion. Thus to investigate the blunders of history is to do no more than people have always done, namely to study at a comfortable distance extraordinary activities or events, closer contact with which would have proved both uncomfortable and dangerous.

It has never been my intention to sneer at the failures of ordinary people in the past. Each age can only be assessed by its own standards. Yet by those very standards it is still possible to single out the stupid, the corrupt and the evil. Lope Aguirre would have stood out in any age as a symbol of evil, while Titus Oates might have flourished during the French Revolution or the Reformation, or indeed in the service of Josef Stalin or Adolf Hitler. Idi Amin or Nicolae Ceausescu might have been emperors of Rome, in succession to Caligula or Nero. Such men are appalling both within their own historical periods and when judged from a modern perspective.

But blunders were not always made by blood-crazed dictators. Sometimes decisions that resulted from the best efforts of committees were equally disastrous. The Aswan Dam, for example, has proved to be as damaging an ecological error as the less well-intentioned activities of Soviet nuclear planners, who dumped nuclear waste in Soviet arctic lands and polluted not only their own territory but parts of northern Scandinavia as well. Such irresponsible actions did not even have the excuse that they were motivated by the greed which fuels the demolition of Brazil's rainforests. Communist planning disasters are represented in this book by examples both from the Soviet Union and China. In the former, Nikita Khrushchev 'raped' the Virgin Lands of Kazakhstan and watched the wind blow away the profits. In China, Mao Zedong made strenuous efforts to surpass his capitalist enemies by making steel in back-yard works. In doing so, he brought China closer to economic collapse than ever before. Not content with this, less than a decade later he incited China's young people to 'rub out' the past in an act of philistinism unparalleled in history.

History's blunders can be amusing as well as shocking. The saying 'there's nowt so queer as folk' is well illustrated by the extraordinary lengths to which people have gone in order to improve on what nature intended. Make-up that rotted the skin, corsets that damaged the internal organs, lotus shoes that crippled the feet, food that poisoned you, doctors who killed you – all of these appear in our first section entitled 'The Human Condition'. And when people were not damaging their physical selves, they were frequently frittering away their life's savings on farcical projects like houses with towers as high as Salisbury Cathedral that had the awkward habit of falling down, or tulip bulbs that cost a king's ransom, or trips to the Arctic in search of gold.

That there have been many crimes committed by religious leaders throughout history will come as no surprise. The eradication of heresy in the lands of southern France in the thirteenth century makes grim reading, and the behaviour of Crusaders as they passed through Christian lands on their way to Jerusalem brings into question the whole notion of Christianity as a religion with love and forgiveness at its central core. The persecution of witches in the sixteenth century shows us the dark side of human nature reflected in mass hysteria.

And yet my intention in writing this book has been to entertain more than to instruct. Most of the blunders contained within these pages have resulted from foolishness, a human frailty but not an evil. For every Idi Amin or Saddam Hussein, there are Martin Frobishers or William Patersons, good men overtaken by events which they could not control. And as for poor chauvinist John Knox explaining his sexism to that arch-feminist Elizabeth Tudor – one cannot but sympathize with the old bigot in his distress. But who feels pity for the Roman soldier who killed Archimedes, the Greek inventor, during the siege of Syracuse in 211 BC? The skill of Archimedes had kept the Romans at bay for two years, but when the city eventually fell their soldiers burst into the houses, killing and looting. Strict orders had gone out from the Roman commander, Claudius Marcellus, that Archimedes was not to be harmed. However, the soldier who entered the house of the great man found him working out a scientific problem and far too busy to concern himself with soldiers and battles and sieges. The soldier ordered him to come with him to Marcellus but Archimedes did not reply. He probably did not even hear him, so intense was his concentration on the scientific proof on which he was working. Baffled out of his wits by the Greek's eccentric behaviour he did what he did best – and killed him. In return the Roman soldier was severely punished by Marcellus for he, at least, realized the enormous loss to the world that the death of the Greek genius represented. 'Just doing my duty', would have been the soldier's reply to criticism. If it was the inventor's duty to invent then it was his duty to kill: his conscience was clear. But in the court of history he was not just a murderer but a blunderer. He had slain that irreplaceable ingredient in human life – genius. This was bad news for the human race, but it must have filled the daily papers in Rome the next day.

CHAPTER ONE: THE HUMAN CONDITION

The more faults human beings find with the conditions in which they live, the more they try to change them for the better. Unfortunately, in pursuit of this 'improvement' they can sometimes make errors of judgment that can be positively harmful to their health and happiness. Yet throughout history, even when the evidence of their own senses has suggested that they were misguided in their search, they have persevered and suffered the consequences.

A tight fit

While the straitjacket was invented to stop the mentally disturbed hurting themselves and others, the corset now appears to have been a much more dangerous device, through which those deranged by fashion inflicted greater harm on their own bodies. The health aspects of the corset controversy became a matter of public concern after about 1840, when tight lacing became the norm. In spite of evidence suggesting that women were endangering their health in pursuit of the fashionable 'wasp-waist', most fashion-conscious ladies were unconvinced and continued to endure agonies from their leather or whalebone corsets.

There was nothing new about the pursuit of the wasp-waist. In the Middle Ages, one French queen decreed that her ladies should try to achieve waist sizes that seem to us today to be unbelievable: ten to thirteen inches. How these were achieved we can only guess at, but certainly early corsets were barbaric. During the Renaissance a Medici duchess reputedly acquired a thirteen-inch waist by employing an iron corset, and even as late as the early nineteenth century corsets were made of leather, half an inch thick, like the stocks worn by British soldiers in the eighteenth century to keep the head erect. Women wearing these early corsets have been described as resembling 'an ant with a slender tube uniting the bust to the haunches' – not the sort of description to set fashionable gentlemen's hearts thumping.

The effect of such tight corsets was that women's back and stomach muscles atrophied so that they could not sit up straight without corsets and even had to wear them in bed. Women assumed that very slender waists would make them sexually more attractive to men. This is a moot point. What corseting did do, however, to enhance female sexual characteristics was to force the breasts up until even the most modest of them were amply positioned beneath the lady's chin.

That wearing corsets was a cult cannot be denied; but that it was a self-imposed one by women is perhaps more surprising. Unlike Chinese foot-binding (see p. 6) with which it is sometimes compared as an element in the suppression of women's rights by a cruel and oppressive male sex, it was, on the contrary, a harmful habit imposed by women on themselves in the name of fashion, and with the aim of winning husbands.

The harm women suffered from corsets was both physical and psychological. Victorian autopsies apparently confirmed that in a few cases the dead woman's liver had been severely damaged by corsets – some reports even claimed that the liver had been virtually cut in two. In addition, other organs were forced out of their natural alignment. In 1837 a book was published on the deformities of women's chests and spines as a result of tight lacing. It clearly showed that those women who used the tightest lacing were injuring their organs and damaging the vertebrae of the spine. In spite of the clearest evidence of the damage done, women continued to wear tight corsets and even increased the tightness of the lacing. Frequent examples appear in prints and books of the period of maidservants – even husbands – putting their foot into the middle of the woman's back in order to get more leverage for pulling the laces ever more tightly. In 1850 Doctor Copeland in his *Medical Dictionary* offered the warning that not only did women endanger their spine by wearing tight stays, but also their uterine organs. The future generation was being endangered by the folly of the fashion-conscious female. As a Frenchman wrote, corsets were 'the assassins of the human race'. A German scholar even claimed that corsets were the cause of numerous diseases among women, including tuberculosis, cancer, epilepsy and melancholy.

At the Great Exhibition of 1851, Britain showed a full range of her wares, including – of course – the British corset. Pride of place went to the *Corset Amazone*, which featured elastic lacings, and which 'yields to every respiration or movement of the equestrienne'. Even during pregnancy and childbirth some women insisted on wearing corsets, with the result that there were numerous cases of inverted nipples, in which the nipple was forced backwards into the breast rendering it impossible for the victim to feed her child.

With due reverence to Doctor Bowdler, the Victorians had a way of catering for every shape and size of lady. How relatively unembarrassing it must have been for the obese and hunched matrons of the time to demand of the assistants in the new department stores a 'Self-Adjusting Symmetrico Restorator Corporiform' – a corset for fat women with a curved spine. Even the sloppiest girl, with the unfashionable habit of slumping forward with her weight on one foot, could find salvation through the use of the 'Riverso-Tractor Hygienic Corset'. The merely fat could get by with the 'Self-Regulating Corporiform', but those ladies liable to collapse under the weight of their own excesses were offered the 'Self-Adjusting Corporiform with invisible props'. There was even hope for the flat-chested girl, with the 'Invisible-Scapula Contractor'.

One certain danger of tight corseting was its effect on the lungs and breathing habits of Victorian women. Of the normal kinds of breathing, from chest and

The famous wasp-waist, popular among fashionable women in the latter part of the nineteenth century, was achieved by the tightest possible lacing of their corsets. The actress portrayed here c. 1890 had little to smile about as the lacing was in all probability seriously damaging her health.

abdomen, it soon became almost impossible for women to breathe other than from the chest. The result was that medical opinion began to regard such breathing as normal for women. The shallowness and rapidity of the breathing of tightly corseted women contributed to something that has always puzzled twentieth-century commentators on Victorian history – the fashionable lady's propensity to faint. Corseting rather than affectation contributed to the 'delicacy' of the Victorian female. One American female writer wrote that the corset, 'pretending to be a servant is, in fact, a tyrant – that aspiring to embrace, hugs like a bear – crushing in the ribs, injuring the lungs and heart, the stomach and many other internal organs'.

Blunders in bloomers

The Great Exhibition of 1851 introduced the British public to bloomers – a form of ladies' clothing which originated in the United States. It developed from a mountain climbing costume named after Mrs Amelia Bloomer, publisher of a ladies' magazine known as *The Lily*, and devoted to the propagation of women's rights. The garment's most original feature was its skirt which opened out and reached to the knee, with the rest of the leg to the ankle enclosed in a frilly legging. So popular were bloomers among liberated ladies that they became almost a symbol of the women's movement. On 6 October 1851, a grand Bloomer Ball was held at the Hanover Square Rooms to popularize the new garment, but the occasion had the direst consequences. Only ladies dressed in bloomers were admitted to the meeting, but those ladies who turned up were predominantly prostitutes, and this gave the garment the worst possible association. The meeting broke up in disorder, with men breaking into the buildings and indulging with the 'ladies of the town' in a fantastic 'orgiastic brawl', requiring the attentions of the metropolitan constabulary. From then on, bloomers were condemned by ladies of the better classes and became associated only with 'loose' or 'fallen' women, notably after the magazine *Punch* went on the attack against them. Mrs Amelia Bloomer would have been shocked if she had seen the fate of her novel garment in London, but there was no way back for the 'bloomer' after its first catastrophic association with the sins of the flesh.

The Lotus élite

Of all the extraordinary ways in which women have changed or enhanced their appearance to win the admiration of their menfolk surely the most cruel and incomprehensible has been the Chinese tradition of footbinding. Women in some African tribes have elongated their necks with rings, or broadened their lips with plates, or stretched their ear-lobes to an amazing degree to better display their jewellery, yet nowhere else but in China have women consented deliberately to

Bloomers originated in the United States of America and were briefly popular in Britain among
more liberated young women. But their association with loose morals, though undeserved,
limited their general acceptance.

cripple themselves – to a point where walking becomes almost impossible – in order to please their menfolk. Whatever the sexual predilections of their male admirers, permanent disablement seems a high price for women to pay in order to satisfy them.

The practice of footbinding in China lasted for at least a thousand years. Its origin is shrouded in mystery, though there are a number of possible explanations for it. Its development was based on the Chinese male's search for status. To have a wife with bound feet was a symbol of economic standing. Since it would be impossible for her to work in the fields or in the house it was a way of demonstrating to neighbours that a man was rich enough to support her without needing her help. Moreover, it was a form of chastity belt. A crippled wife could not walk far from her house and therefore her husband would know where she was at all times.

It was during the age of Confucius that the Chinese first exhibited their preference for small feet, large feet in either sex being a sign of lower-class origins. Even today it is not unknown for Chinese mothers – in defiance of strict government prohibitions – to confine the feet of young children in tight socks to inhibit natural growth. But it was probably in the tenth century that the process of footbinding really started. The Southern Tang emperor Li Yu (961–75) apparently became enamoured of a concubine with the name of Lovely Maiden, who was both slender-waisted and small-footed. He loved to watch her dancing and in her honour he built a six-foot-high lotus out of pure gold and asked her to dance within it. But first he asked her to bind her feet with silk cloth to resemble the points of a moon sickle. He then saw her dance in the golden lotus with all the grace of a 'rising cloud'. His imagination – or his love – must have been very great, as Lovely Maiden's dance with bound feet was probably not one of her best. Nevertheless, so impressed was the emperor that he decreed that all women of the higher classes should emulate Lovely Maiden and bind their feet, so that in future their steps would be small and elegant. Henceforth, women would not go out alone but only be carried in sedan chairs, concealed by screens. Women with rich husbands would no longer need to use their feet. In addition, it would greatly enhance male feelings of superiority to see even young women hobbling or walking only with the aid of a stick. Men would feel more protective towards such obviously helpless creatures.

Although footbinding traditionally originated in such a poetic way, its effects on the young girls who had to endure it were unpleasant in the extreme. The suffering they underwent at the hands of their mothers has no parallel in human history in terms of parental mistreatment. A western friar, Odoric of Pordenone, visited China in the fourteenth century and described the way in which Chinese mothers readily bound the feet of their daughters: 'With the women the great beauty is to have little feet; and for this reason, mothers are accustomed to swathe their daughters' feet so tightly that they can never grow.' The process involved winding a bandage two inches wide and ten feet long around each foot in turn. The purpose was to force the four smaller toes back under the sole, while the big toe was left unbound. The bandage was then wrapped around the heel so tightly that it was pulled close to the toes. The result was that the normal foot was reduced to a length of not much more than three inches and the finished product, a hideous and unsightly deformity, was then referred to as a

A Chinese noblewoman displaying her 'golden lily' feet c. 1890. The tradition of footbinding
in China was of great antiquity and was viewed by both men and women as an important
symbol of social status.

'lotus'. During this agonizing process the young girl was expected to remain silent and was beaten if she cried. From the first moment of binding she was not allowed to remove the bandages, even if the pain prevented sleep. After many months the big toe was then forced upwards to assume the shape of a new moon and in time the smaller toes became compressed into the sole or merely dropped off.

Chinese women took great pride in their 'golden lotus' feet and in the tiny shoes that they wore at their weddings, embroidered with good luck tokens and sayings like 'Wealth and Eminence until our hair turns white'. The size and shape of a bride's feet were considered vital. When she arrived at her husband's home and alighted from her sedan chair crowds of relations and well-wishers were there to inspect her foot size. The tiny-footed bride won great praise from the onlookers, pleasing the parents and delighting the groom, who was seeing his wife for the first time. But if the girl had feet that were larger than normal everyone laughed at her, her father in law was humiliated and her husband was shamed for the rest of his life. At the wedding festivities guests had the right to measure the bride's feet with a ruler and scorn her if the results were not satisfactory.

Throughout the country grotesque beauty contests took place in which the women displayed their lotus feet. On these occasions, lower class women with unbound feet – described as 'lotus-boats' or 'duck-feet' – hid themselves away in shame. In Shanxi province a famous contest took place known as the Assemblage of Foot Viewing or 'sunning the feet'. Women attached bells or silk butterflies with moving wings to their shoes so that as they hobbled and minced about on their crippled feet they created pleasing effects. Connoisseurs inspected especially small feet but were not allowed to touch them with their hands. As one Western observer wrote, 'It was just like going to a department store to see an exhibition.'

It was the influence of Western missionaries from Europe and America in the late nineteenth century that sounded the death-knell of footbinding. They were appalled at the oppression of Chinese women and felt that footbinding was a symbol of the inferiority they were brought up to expect. American missionaries described the way in which some women got around by putting their knees on stools and pulling themselves forward. Others died from gangrene or from amputation after having their feet bound. Many women had to be carried about on the backs of servants. Progressive Americans regarded the situation in China as scandalous. In the early years of the twentieth century missionaries joined Chinese reformers in pressing for the emancipation of women from the age-old ritual of footbinding, which symbolized their social inequality. Even after footbinding was made illegal in China the people still regarded it as a traditional part of Chinese life. When a Chinese lady went to France in 1936 with her children and charged Parisians one franc each to view her golden lotuses the Chinese expatriates in Paris complained to the Chinese ambassador that she was bringing an ancient Chinese custom into disrepute and the woman was immediately expelled from France.

The painted lady

HAMLET [to Yorick's skull]. Now get you to my lady's chamber, and tell her, let her paint an inch thick, to this favour she must come.

Hamlet's instructions would have had a special significance for his Elizabethan audience. Perhaps 'an inch thick' was a bit extreme, but not by much, for the make-up of the time had to cover a multitude of sins. The pale, often white, complexions of Elizabethan women were not only intended to arrest the ravages of time but to conceal the effects of smallpox or any number of other disfiguring skin complaints to which even the highest in the land were prone. But as with many 'medicines', even of the cosmetic kind, the 'cure' was frequently worse – and more dangerous – than the ill, and those who favoured Venetian ceruse merely hastened the moment when they shuffled off this mortal coil.

The spread of looking-glasses in the late Middle Ages gave a great impetus to the use and manufacture of facial make-ups. Although condemned by the Church as tools of the devil and symbols of the deadly sin of vanity, these glasses enabled women, for the first time, to examine closely their complexions in search of the dreaded 'sun spot' or freckle. It was to cover freckles, as well as more serious imperfections, that women painted their faces. Initially face creams might contain bizarre but harmless ingredients. Isabeau of Bavaria, later queen of France, for instance, bathed in asses' milk and coated her face in a lotion comprising boars' brains, crocodile glands and wolves' blood.

During the sixteenth century, Italy – particularly Venice – led the world in cosmetics as in so much else. Venetian ceruse was accounted the best in the world and held its pre-eminence well into the nineteenth century. It was the height of fashion to use it, but it was also the height of folly. Venetian ceruse was made from white lead and was extremely poisonous when absorbed through the pores of the skin. But this did not deter the leaders of fashion. Venetian women even formed a society – Isabella Cortese was president and Queen Catherine de' Medici of France an honorary member – for learning about and testing new cosmetics. They resisted efforts by the Church to denounce their vanity and by physicians of the time to warn them of the dangers of some of the ingredients they used. They applied white lead ceruse thickly to face, neck and bosom, and often merely added another layer rather than remove the previous application. The effect was sepulchral and in spite of criticism by their menfolk – one referred to the ceruse as a devilish invention to make women look 'ugly, enormous and abominable' – women carried on using it. A sixteenth-century monk complained that women painted their faces as if covering a wall with lime and plaster, not realizing that it 'wears them out and makes them grow old before their time, and destroys the teeth, while they seem to be wearing a mask all the year through'. The much-maligned physicians of the time – those that were not quacks – railed against the use of white lead and the equally deadly mercury sublimate to improve the complexion. As one pointed out, the poison stayed within the body of the woman and could be passed on to her children. But all the warnings

Queen Elizabeth I of England holding a miniature. In her later years Elizabeth used ever-increasing amounts of face paint to combat the ravages of old age. But the ceruse with which she coated her face contained white lead which had severe side effects and could lead to early death.

were to no avail and women continued to disfigure and kill themselves in their search for novelty and beauty. One physician, beside himself with anger at the stupidity of the female sex, raged, 'There are many who have so betard their faces with these mixtures and slubber-sauces, that they have made their faces of a thousand colours: that is to say, some as yellow as the marigold, others a dark greene, others blunket colour, others as of a deep red died in the wooll. Thus the use of this ceruse, besides the rotting of the teeth and the unsavourie breath which it causeth . . . doth turne faire creatures into infernall Furies.'

In Elizabethan England, the queen set the pattern for all her court ladies by painting her face thickly with white lead. The older Elizabeth got the more she painted until she resembled a ship's figurehead, worn from storm and battle, with the paint peeling off. The French ambassador was just one who commented on the appalling quality of her teeth, victims of the white lead make-up. In addition, Elizabeth used ochre and mercuric sulphide for cheek rouge. Some of her ladies-in-waiting swallowed concoctions of ash, coaldust and tallow candles in the belief that it would give them a pale complexion. Those who survived took on a greenish hue. Faint hearts who feared the poisonous paints sometimes tried washing in their own urine, though the peerless Diane de Poitiers in France was said to have used no cosmetics and washed in rain water. All sorts of curious concoctions were tried, including the distilled flesh of a young raven, fed for forty days on hard boiled eggs. A more successful potion – one destined to survive for two hundred years – was Soliman's Water, which was supposed to clear the skin of spots, warts and freckles. As its main ingredient was sublimate of mercury it cleared most faces of their skin, as well as corroding the flesh, causing the teeth to drop out and the gums to recede and making a young woman aged in a matter of a few years.

During the seventeenth and eighteenth centuries the curse of smallpox continued to persuade fashionable ladies to risk their lives for their complexions by using ceruse. Horace Walpole described its effects on Lady Mary Wortley Montague. By 1740, he wrote, 'Her face is swelled violently on one side, with the remains of a gummata, partly covered with a plaister, and partly with white paint, which for cheapness she has bought so coarse, that you would not use it to wash a chimney.' Walpole's vicious comment refers to the erosion of the skin caused by mercurial wash.

By the end of the eighteenth century painting or enamelling of the face was so widespread that even the clearest evidence of its dangers was simply ignored. When women were prepared to cut off their toes in order to be able to wear ever slimmer shoes, they were unlikely to be deterred from using such traditional beauty aids as ceruse. An author of the period wrote that white lead cosmetics, 'affect the eyes, which swell and inflame, and are rendered painful and watery. They change the texture of the skin, on which they produce pimples and cause rheums; attack the teeth, make them ache, destroy the enamel and loosen them. They heat the mouth and throat, infecting and corrupting the saliva, and they penetrate through the pores of the skin, acting by degrees on the spongy substance of the lungs.' And above all, they killed. In 1767 the famous actress-courtesan Kitty Fisher died of lead poisoning, occasioned by her use of ceruse. Another prominent fatality was Maria Gunning, wife to the Earl of Coventry. During the 1750s it became a matter of debate as to how long she could survive with the amount of ceruse she plastered on to her face. In 1760 her health declined, and she spent her waking hours staring into a mirror, watching for imaginary blemishes on her plaster-white complexion. So withered had her skin become that she finally had to order her room to be darkened so that nobody could see her haggard looks. She died, in popular parlance, 'a victim to Cosmetics'. Ten thousand people attended her funeral, but few of those who had known the beautiful Maria Gunning would have recognized her as the bald, toothless and parchment-skinned crone who filled the coffin.

Even as late as the present century women have risked ill health and disfigurement in pursuit of elusive beauty. Before the First World War paraffin injections were popular, but they resulted in unsightly lumps and strong allergic reactions. Other women underwent skinning processes that resulted in permanent disfigurement and near-fatal infections. In 1912 one girl, in search of a perfect bloom, had her cheeks injected with a carmine liquid that was supposed to assure her of a 'pale pink rose' complexion. Instead, it turned her face and neck bright red and brought her out in a rash of pimples. Her complexion was ruined and her fiancé broke off his engagement to her. In 1911, the makers of Klintho Cream, which contained mercury, were forced by the American government to remove the words 'Absolutely harmless' from its label. Once they had done so, the product was returned to the market, apparently with the government's approval. A lady whose face had been disfigured by the mercury in Klintho was treated with iodide ointment, which reacted with the mercury to turn her face bright red. A second doctor prescribed sulphur ointment which turned her skin black. There seemed to be no end to the absurdities and indignities that women were prepared to endure in their frequently fruitless pursuit of what Nature never intended.

Quack, quack

Medical quackery traces its origins back to ancient times. The streets of Rome in the days of her greatness thronged with charlatans of all kinds, while bogus medical practitioners – with elixirs of life, cure-alls and so forth – are frequently to be found in classical comedy. During the Middle Ages, when most medicine was a hit-and-miss affair, mountebanks were a regular feature of the fairs that were held throughout Europe. The derivation of the English word 'quack' to describe medical charlatans is uncertain, but one possibility is that it comes from the German word *Quecksilber*, meaning 'mercury' – a common ingredient of many medicines even as late as the nineteenth century.

The success of the quack doctor may be cynically ascribed to ignorance on the part of the general public. An eighteenth-century anecdote forcefully supports this view. It describes a meeting between a famous doctor and a famous quack, both men foremost in their respective professions. But the doctor, for all his qualifications and medical successes, is still far less wealthy than his street-wise opponent. The doctor asks the quack to explain why this is so. The quack replies by asking the doctor how many of the hundred people who have just passed by possess common sense. The doctor answers that no more than one possesses real common sense. 'Well,' says the quack, 'that one comes to you for help and the other ninety-nine come to me.'

County Limerick was the birthplace in 1798 of John Long, who was to become one of the most famous 'specialist quacks' of all time. Without any formal medical training – he picked up what he knew from copying anatomical drawings – he set up as an expert on tuberculosis, or 'consumption' as it was more generally known at the time. His treatment was simple, being nothing more than a liniment that was rubbed into the chest. In the event that the patient was not seriously ill – and consumption was a fashionable disease among hypochondriacs – then Long's liniment effected a complete cure. If the patient suffered a skin reaction to his balm, Long responded by saying that it was clear evidence that the consumption had been forced to the surface and would be healed when the skin healed, after the application of cabbage leaves. Long was on to a winner provided that he avoided treating anyone who was in an advanced state of tuberculosis.

Long was so successful in his London practice that he was forced to move to larger premises in Harley Street, even then famous for its physicians, and there he spent the rest of his unprofessional life. In order to attract the most wealthy clients, Long provided himself with the most elegant and sumptuous consulting rooms and his business flourished to a point where he was earning more than £13,000 a year. Harley Street was regularly crowded with the carriages of rich ladies, desperate both for his liniment and a few minutes of the doctor's reassuring manner.

When Long was upbraided by his rivals for not possessing formal qualifications from medical colleges, his response was that of the scholar of the 'university of life'. As he said, he had not bought a degree from London or Edinburgh, but instead had 'pondered the dull page of science by the light of his own lamp and perfected his experiments by his own conviction in the solitude of private life'. For Long, the best form of defence was attack. He was not a 'bookish' practitioner, quick to operate on people or give them drugs, but earned praise as a practical man. It was quackery encapsulated – leave medicine to the medical men, but treat those who think they are ill and make them think that they are well. It is unlikely that Long treated many truly ill people at all. It was the safest way both for the quack and for the patient.

But of all quacks, Long came closest to hubris. In the treatment of Katherine Cashin he met his first setback. He had supplied the girl with his liniment and she had rubbed it on her back and chest. Unfortunately, she was clearly allergic to it and her back became very sore. A few days later she died and Long found himself facing a manslaughter charge. In spite of the evidence of his numerous rich supporters, who claimed that his liniment was harmless, Long was found guilty and sentenced to a fine of £250, a curiously light punishment for so serious a crime.

In spite of the court's decision – and this is one of the inexplicable aspects of quackery – Long became more rather than less popular, which perhaps endorses the theory that there is no such thing as bad publicity. Carriages clogged Harley Street and the great man's receptionists knew no peace as the wealthy besieged his consulting rooms in search of his chest liniment. They might have been less keen if they had known that the good doctor was already involved in another fatality. Incredibly, even while the Cashin case was being heard, a husband approached Long and asked him to treat his wife. Without seeing the woman, Long agreed. This was a bad mistake, for the woman was not only really ill with tuberculosis but had a throat complaint which may have been cancerous. Unaware of her true condition, Long used his liniment to disastrous effect. Her chest first turned red and then became blistered. Long applied cabbage leaves which were of no use whatsoever and the poor woman then refused any further treatment and consulted a real doctor. In spite of this, she died a month later and Long found himself facing a second manslaughter charge. Long was perhaps unlucky in this instance, for the woman clearly died from a condition that had nothing to do with his liniment. But mud sticks, and although he was acquitted, this latter case dealt a heavy blow to his business. He was even forced to publish testimonials in the newspapers, signed by nine members of the nobility, ten generals and admirals, an ADC to the king and the Mayor of Hertford. However, his business never recovered its former rude health. Fate had a final trick to play on John Long, for at the age of just 36 he himself died of tuberculosis, perhaps contracted from one of his 'real' patients.

One of the most effective of all quacks was Joshua Ward, who came from a privileged background, his parents being the wealthy owners of Wolverston Hall in Suffolk. In 1716 Ward began to 'gull' society when he was returned as MP for Marlborough, an amazing result as it appears that none of the voters had actually voted for him. However, before he could begin his irresistible march to Downing Street he was halted in his tracks by the inexorable hand of public rectitude. The real mayor of Marlborough had correctly recorded Joshua Ward's score as 'no votes', but one of Ward's friends – Roger William – impersonated the mayor, obtained the returning officer's sheet and inserted enough votes to win Ward the seat. This rather obvious fraud, once discovered, resulted in Ward having to flee to France, where he remained for sixteen years, until he received a pardon and permission to return from King George II.

From that point onwards, Ward's fortune rose as a result of his 'cure all', which came in two forms, the 'drop' or the pill. He had invented this elixir while in exile in France and once back in his native land he apparently effected some remarkable cures with it. In the household of the Lord Chief Justice, Baron Reynolds, a maidservant, one Mary Betts, was taken ill with a 'dead palsy', and her life was despaired of. Other physicians failed to effect any improvement in her condition. After two months the patient was emaciated and so weak that when she wanted to sleep her nurse had to pull down her eyelids for her. The Baron's wife heard of Ward's wonderful 'drops' and decided to try them on her maid. The result of the 'drops' was amazing – and alarming. The patient was violently sick, sweated profusely, and almost died. However, a couple more doses of Ward's drops effected a complete cure.

However, Ward's triumphs were matched by occasional setbacks. In 1734, it was

A French charlatan selling quack remedies in an 18th-century engraving. Quack doctors ranged from street pedlars selling ointments and elixirs to men like John Long and Joshua Ward, who worked from impressive premises and counted noble and even royal personages among their patients. What all quacks had in common, however, was the absence of any medical justification for the treatment they offered.

reported that Mrs Gilbert, who ran an ale-house, had taken one of Ward's pills, causing her 34 'vomits' and 22 'purgings'. She called in professional medical advice, which reported that she was continually retching and very weak. Only hours later she died. The death of Mrs Gilbert was just one of ten fatalities directly attributable to Ward's pills or drops. Ward was quick to defend himself against the accusation of 'quackery', claiming that his victims had been either too ill to save or too stupid to follow the correct instructions for taking his elixir. For example, Hester Straps, a barmaid from Charing Cross, died almost immediately after taking Ward's drops, but was described by her employer, Richard Haddock, as being in a 'languishing condition' through alcoholic abuse. One of Ward's sternest critics, a Doctor Turner, wrote in the *Grub Street Journal* that the famous 'drops' were no more than antimony salts that purged the body most severely. Another of that paper's correspondents hinted that Ward's reputation was higher among the city's undertakers and coffin-makers than it was among his patients, and that Ward had the 'art to kill' with a single drop of his potion, while others 'had to fill phials and sometimes quart bottles' with which to murder their patients.

But Ward had one ally who could protect him from all the shots of his enemies – King George II himself. Apparently the king had dislocated his thumb and Ward had been on hand to offer help. The king had kicked Ward 'sharply on the shin for his pains', but had thereafter been rather impressed with him, giving him an apartment in the Almonry Office at Whitehall, where he 'ministered to the poor at his majesty's expense'. The king also gave Ward a carriage and pair and the privilege of driving them through St James's Park. With such royal patronage Ward was made. He bought three cottages in Pimlico and expanded them into a hospital for the poor. Ward died a wealthy man, but the secret of his drop and pill died with him. If, as suspected, they consisted of antimony taken internally, they were damaging to the liver and resulted in dangerous purgings of the stomach. Larger doses could – and did in the case of some of Ward's unfortunate patients – result in colitis and even death. One of Ward's unofficial epitaphs ran, 'Before you take his drop or pill, take leave of friends and make your will'. It was probably a just verdict on this prince among quacks.

Five minutes with Venus and a lifetime with Mercury

The origin of syphilis is still uncertain. Whether it came to Europe from Africa as a mutated form of the skin complaint yaws, or came from the New World with Columbus's sailors and spread via the French army in Italy after 1494, experts are still undecided. What is certain, however, is that during the sixteenth century there was a sudden outbreak of virulent syphilis in Europe which physicians were initially helpless to control. The more prosperous among them simply ignored the problem, refusing to be involved with a disease 'that begins in one of the most degrading and ignoble places of the body'. As a result, the treatment of syphilis and allied venereal diseases was left to barbers and quacks, the latter probably earning their name from peddling quicksilver (mercury). These 'pox-treaters' chose mercury as the best cure for syphilis and by so doing established a precedent that was to hold sway for more than 300 years. The reason why they turned to mercury was because the metal had been used in the treatment of skin complaints like leprosy and scabies for generations. Whether it had actually done any good, however, is a moot point. Nevertheless, mercury became the acknowledged treatment for syphilis and countless patients incurred the dreadful side effects of mercury poisoning in their search for a cure to the price that Venus exacted of her votaries.

Barbers and quack doctors employed mercury in two forms. After mixing the mercury with pork fat, butter, vinegar, myrrh, turpentine and sulphur in an iron mortar they rubbed the mixture into sores that were often open to the bone. Some quacks, eager to establish their own individual style and reputation, mixed live frogs, chicken's blood, snake venom and even human flesh to the unction that they rubbed into the affected parts. Frankly, only the mercury had much effect, and this was because its toxicity caused people to salivate in bowlfuls. Having rubbed the unction into the wounds, the barber or physician wrapped his patient in towels and then left them in an extremely hot tub or oven to make them sweat copiously, in the belief that only copious salivation could rid the body of the venereal disease. Yet even if the patient actually was ridding himself of the syphilitic germs he was certainly dying of mercury poisoning. Some experts demanded that the patient fill a four-pint container with saliva each day, while others extended the mercury treatment to as much as four weeks, producing a prodigious quantity of saliva. Even those who survived this debilitating treatment were not guaranteed immunity from the second and third stages of syphilis, as these were far more difficult to detect than the initial ulceration and rashes. Most patients died well before the month was up, of heart failure, dehydration, suffocation or mercury poisoning. Other patients opted for suicide rather than being cooked for a month in an oven, all the time breathing mercury fumes. Those who did survive completed their cure in a hairless, toothless condition. Survivors also lost all their red blood cells, sank into a state of anaemia, were unable to keep down their food and usually succumbed shortly afterwards to the blessed relief of death. Rabelais, writing in the sixteenth century, described the appearance of syphilitics who were undergoing mercury treatment: 'Their faces shone like the keyplate of a charnel house, and their teeth danced in their heads like a keyboard of an organ or spinet under the fingers of a maestro and they foamed at the gullet like a boar at bay in the toils of a pack of bloodhounds.'

Some physicians tried to argue that the cure was worse than the ailment, but the majority insisted that mercury was the only substance that could get syphilis to relinquish its hold on the body. And there was never any shortage of patients willing to take a mercury cure. Whatever the views of learned and experienced doctors, the public was quick to purchase the mercury ointments of the quacks and charlatans who frequented every trade fair in Europe. This did not stop other quacks trying every kind of possible remedy for syphilis, including instructing patients to drink boiled ant's nest soup, stick earthworm plasters on their sores and even bind dead chickens to their private parts. It may sound comical to modern readers, but it must be stressed that the syphilis of the sixteenth century is believed to have been more virulent than today's strain of the disease.

The German soldier Ulrich von Hutten was one of the first syphilitics to try an alternative treatment to mercury. This was called gaiac, and was made from the wood of the gaiac tree, imported from Spanish America. It was first reduced to a powder, infused and a kind of decoction was then made. The patient was placed in a warm room, on a severe diet, and made to drink gaiac, after wrapping himself in blankets and sweating. This treatment also lasted for 30 days, after which it was claimed the syphilis was gone. This was not really surprising as the first stage of syphilis appears two to four weeks after infection and quickly disappears and the second and tertiary stages may not appear for some months, or even years. In any case, Hutten was a strong supporter of the gaiac treatment and certainly its side effects were minimal compared to the dreadful mercury regime. Unfortunately, many people felt that unless they were suffering their medicine was not working, and so most still opted for the mercury treatment. The result was that from the sixteenth century mercury was well established in every medical textbook for its therapeutic value in the treatment of skin diseases.

By the eighteenth century, syphilis was a less acute ailment, though its acolytes were still numbered in their millions and still accepted that mercury was necessary to their treatment. In Italy there were strange methods of applying the mercury, including a pair of underpants coated inside with a mercurial ointment. Fumigations were no longer fashionable, being increasingly replaced by frictions and ointments. By the end of the century physicians were administering mercury internally in the form of 'anti-venereal enemas' and calomel. The development of mercuric chloride or sublimate of mercury increased in popularity through the work of van Swieten, the court physician to the Empress Maria Theresa of Austria. His discovery became famous as 'van Swieten's liquor' and was widely used throughout Europe. It had the enormous advantage of allowing patients to treat themselves, rather than submit to lengthy and expensive sessions at the hands of physicians or quacks.

The true dangers of mercury as a medicine had been hidden from physicians since the sixteenth century, because its characteristic indications – skin eruptions, ulceration and neurological effects – were usually attributed to syphilis itself, whereas those who had always argued that the treatment was more dangerous than the disease had been right all along. By the mid-nineteenth century doctors were beginning to realize the severe limitations of mercury and its complete inability to cure anyone whose syphilis had reached the tertiary stage. Unfortunately, those who strove to replace mercury as a medicine frequently suggested arsenic as an alternative. But the quacks stuck by their mercury remedies, only making it appear more congenial to the patient. 'Aphrodisiac chocolate' became popular in France, even though it still contained sublimate of mercury. One quack claimed that his mixture spared people the shame of having their condition generally known, even by their own family. As he said, 'A husband can take his chocolate in the presence of his wife without her suspecting a thing: indeed, she herself can take it without realizing that she is swallowing an anti-venereal remedy; by this innocent means, then, peace and concord can be maintained in the household.'

The use of mercury as a treatment for syphilis inflicted suffering on a scale almost beyond computation. Thousands of patients died from mercury poisoning or from

From the 15th century onwards syphilis became one of the plagues of urban life in Europe. Mercury was regarded as the most effective cure, but its side effects were appalling. In this engraving from William Hogarth's *Mariage à la Mode*, a young man, having passed on the syphilis he caught from a prostitute to a young girl he has seduced, is complaining to a quack doctor that the pills he has prescribed for the young girl are ineffective.

the associated effects of the various mercury treatments used through the centuries. It is difficult to avoid the conclusion that the syphilis sufferer would have been no worse off if he or she had left the disease to run its full, terrible course, even to its conclusion in death. There were other 'cures' available whose inventors claimed did not contain mercury, notably Laffecteur's mercury-free nectar which, according to its inventor, contained honey, marsh reeds, aniseed and sasparilla. Unfortunately, Laffecteur was less a homeopath than a shrewd businessman. When his mercury-free nectar was tested it was found to be quite effective and he was given the contract for supplying the French navy – presumably a large and profitable order. But later investigations showed that the nectar sent for testing *had* contained mercury and that Laffecteur had added the metal to get the contract. Once this was achieved, he was prepared to supply the Navy with harmless – and cheap – honey-water. A generation of French sailors must have heaved a sigh of relief, but girls in every port must have dashed for cover at the first sighting of *les matelots*.

Thou shalt not commit adultery

Traditionally bread has been regarded as the staff of life, and in western societies it has always been the staple food. However, its effects have not always been beneficial, especially on the peasants and poorer townspeople who were far more dependent on it than the richer classes, with their easy access to ample supplies of meat and dairy produce. On occasions, either through accident or – more probably – through the practices of disreputable bakers, medieval Europeans suffered severe illness and death from the very bread they ate. Recent research has shown that much social and political unrest in medieval Europe had its origin in the effects that bread, tainted with ergot (a cereal fungus) or with darnel grass, had on the mass of the common people.

In 1383 at the church of San Piero in Faenza, the extraordinary effects of contaminated bread led to men and women trembling and dancing, 'hurling themselves to and fro inside the church' as if in the grip of a devilish spell. A contemporary chronicler already had his suspicions as to the cause: 'It is believed that the cause of many illnesses of which numerous people even die, is the bad breads that the people eat, namely that of beans, cabbage and plain oil.' Two centuries later, at Modena in 1592, it is recorded that one of the judges responsible for food quality was himself arrested 'for having had forty sacks of bay leaf ground to be put in the wheat flour to make bread'. Its effects were to poison many people 'sick enough to go crazy'. Unscrupulous dealers added darnel to the flour to create 'dazed bread', which was known to have stupefying effects on its victims, in which they danced about like madmen, beat their heads against walls or even killed themselves in a frenzy. St Vitus's dance, which was common among medieval peasantry, almost certainly stemmed from the presence of ergot containing lysergic acid (LSD) in their bread.

There is nothing new about adulterating food. Throughout history food producers and retailers have tampered with the food they sold, either to improve the flavour of the dish or else to reduce the cost of its production. To increase the quantity of rare or scarce foods retailers often 'bulked them out' with cheaper ingredients. Bread was sometimes bulked out with ashes or sand, and dangerously adulterated with zinc and copper sulphates. Naturally, with the widespread ignorance of the effects of food additives, this resulted in much harm to the public. During the seventeenth century, Francis Bacon claimed – extravagantly – that not one man in a thousand died a natural death. He was particularly hostile to the strong beer which was made of 'Thames water taken up above Greenwich at low water where it is free from the brackishness of the sea and has in it all the fat and sullage of this great city'. It was a wise drinker who knew what was in his beer in those days, or through how many people it had already passed. In the eighteenth century rogues coloured tea with copperas (ferrous sulphate), whitened veal with chalk and added vitriol to beer. One commentator claimed, 'I have seen a quantity of lime and chalk in the proportion of one to six, extracted from bread.' But the most terrible accusation, one confirmed in the old rhyme 'Fee, Fi, Fo, Fum', where the giant claims he will grind the bones of the 'Englishman' to bake his bread, is that bakers bought the bones of cadavers from charnel houses and powdered them to replace much of the flour in their bread.

The quest for improved food hygiene in the nineteenth century was greatly aided by the development of the microscope. Armed with this tool, government officials began to inspect foods and prosecute those who adulterated their products with dangerous additives. The results of these first surveys into food hygiene were truly shocking. In 1820 a German-born chemist, Frederick Accum, published a *Treatise on the Adulteration of Foods and Culinary Poisons*, which revealed to the British public for the first time the fact that they were being poisoned by much of the food they purchased and consumed. He cited a case where one Chaloner, a dealer in tea and coffee, had been found guilty of having adulterated nine pounds of 'spurious coffee' consisting of 'burned pease, beans and gravel or sand' and a 'portion of coffee'. He also had prepared coffee containing seventeen pounds of vegetable powder and not a 'particle' of genuine coffee.

According to Accum, cheese was particularly liable to adulteration and its effects were often dangerous or even fatal. Gloucester cheeses were frequently found to contain poisonous red lead, which was part of the annatto (yellowish-red dye) used to colour the cheese. Accum cited one case where a man was seized by violent stomach cramps on each occasion that he sampled a particular Gloucester cheese. Investigations revealed that a druggist had given the manufacturer of the cheese vermilion containing red lead to 'paint the exterior of his property'.

Pickles, according to Accum, depended for their sale on being of a 'lively' green colour. This, unfortunately, usually meant that they had been artificially coloured by the use of copper. Other vegetables including gherkins, French beans and green peppers were all subject to 'poisoning' by the addition of copper. Accum was informed of numerous deaths caused by the use of this metal in food production. Unscrupulous manufacturers often boiled the pickles with halfpenny pieces or left them to soak for long periods in brass containers. Cucumbers were sometimes adulterated by pouring boiling water on them from copper vessels, or mixing them with 'powdered verdigrise the bigness of a hazelnut'. Horrifyingly, vinegar was often rendered more acidic by the addition of sulphuric acid.

Poisonous confectionery must have cost the careless Victorian parent many a tear. According to the tireless investigations of Frederick Accum, sugar plums and comfits, which were often sold in the streets to unwary children, were particularly dangerous. White comfits contained sugar, starch and Cornish clay, a kind of very white pipe-clay, while red sugar-drops contained vermilion colouring, often having a high percentage of red lead. Poisonous concoctions of sweetmeats were rendered more attractive and more colourful by the addition of copper, which gave them a bright green colouring. Custards, creams and blancmanges were often found to contain leaves of the cherry laurel, which gave a 'kernel-like flavour', but which were poisonous. In one boarding school, it was reported to Accum, four of the children were taken severely ill after eating custard flavoured with cherry-laurel berries. Two women in Dublin died from drinking cherry-laurel water. William Cornfield of Northampton died on 8 June 1848, as a result of eating a blancmange at a public dinner which contained arsenite of copper, added to the ingredients by a grocer named Edmund Franklin 'with the full knowledge that it contained a deadly poison'.

Professor Queckett, writing at the time, also detected particles of sheep's brains in the milk that Franklin sold. This is not to suggest that Franklin was a simple murderer. Almost certainly he was no worse than many other food suppliers of the time, more concerned with his profit levels than with his reputation as a supplier of wholesome foods.

Coffee was probably the foodstuff that suffered most adulteration. In low coffee houses amazing mixtures of substances were frequently included in the drinks of the unwary. Apart from relatively harmless roasted carrots, roasted beetroot, scorched beans and peas, and acorns, some customers found themselves served with mahogany sawdust or even baked horse liver. A coffee dealer in Glasgow in 1851 received a hundred tons of lupin seeds from Egypt which eventually, one suspects, found their way into his premium blends.

As late as 1900 the deaths of many people in Lancashire was traced to the glucose that was supplied by a Liverpool firm and used in the local ale. A Royal Commission reported on the tragedy and concluded that arsenic had been added to the glucose. In the last few years evidence has come to light to suggest that the adulteration of food and drink can be as dangerous as ever. The revelation in the 1980s that some Austrian wine producers were using anti-freeze in their vintages produced a substantial consumer backlash, while an Italian purveyor of grated Parmesan cheese was forced to admit that his cheese was in fact made from ground umbrella handles. *Caveat consumptor!*

The man who loved chocolate

The Spanish conquistadores found more than gold and silver in South America in the sixteenth century. They also found what millions of the world's children would regard as an equally valuable commodity – chocolate. This luxurious product was greatly appreciated in Spain when it was first sampled there, but the inhabitants of other nations were significantly slower in taking up the chocolate habit, particularly the English. In fact, so plebeian were English tastes that when English privateers were able to seize the rich cargoes of Spanish ships travelling home from the Caribbean or South America, the English sailors tipped the chocolate beans overboard, thinking them no better than 'sheep's dung'. This blunder prevented chocolate reaching the English market for many years. In an attempt to wean his fellow Englishmen away from their irrational contempt for chocolate, the seventeenth-century English sailor Thomas Gage, who had been a prisoner of the Spaniards for a number of years, instructed them to serve the chocolate with a variety of flavourings including sugar, cinnamon, rose water and even pepper. Gage himself had a portable chocolate-making kit, and became the forerunner of a whole industry of British chocolate makers. Gage's other recommendation to his English readers – hedgehog and iguana savouries – did not catch on so well.

A bas les pommes de terre

It is a common misconception that potatoes were brought to Britain by Sir Walter Raleigh from Virginia. Nothing – or nowhere – could be further from the truth. If anyone can be credited with the discovery of the potato – and its carriage to a British public waiting to find a partner for its fried cod – it was that other Elizabethan sea-dog, Sir Francis Drake, who brought it from the coast of Peru via Virginia to Elizabeth I's court.

But across the English Channel the French regarded this English invention – the potato – as little less than a criminal assault on their national cuisine. Better by far to die of starvation than to succumb to the siren cry of the English 'spud'. The potato was banned in Burgundy in 1619 and other parts of France soon followed suit. It was said that eating potatoes caused leprosy and for more than a hundred years the French remained convinced that this earthy tuber was alone responsible for the dreadful disfiguring disease. The fact that the potato had only arrived in Europe in the sixteenth century – while leprosy was one of Europe's oldest diseases – seems to have eluded even the deepest thinkers. In Switzerland the dreadful potato was thought to cause scrofula, while even as late as 1774 the citizens of Colburg preferred to starve rather than eat the poisonous potato, which had been sent them by King Frederick II of Prussia to relieve their famine. In 1795, when their harvest failed and they faced starvation, the people of Munich were adamant in their refusal to even sample potatoes. But it was the French who were most resistant to the potato. The frequent dearths of wheat during the eighteenth century resulted in hundreds of thousands of deaths from starvation. In spite of this, the majority of Frenchmen could not be convinced that the potato was not poisonous. It was not until, in 1814, Antoine Beauvilliers published a cookbook extolling the virtues of such English dishes as *Woiches Rabettes, Plomb Poutingue* and *Mache Potetesse* that the French came to understand the English predilection for potatoes. But a century or more of neglecting the vegetable had cost France the lives of many thousands of peasants who succumbed to starvation rather than risk the poisonous or leprous 'spud'.

LOVE POTION NUMBER NINE

In the seventeenth century marriages among the nobility were not always made in heaven. Sometimes they were hatched in the minds of cold and calculating politicians, or in the lascivious fantasies of 'sugar-daddies' like King James I. This was certainly the case in 1606, when the beautiful thirteen-year-old Frances Howard, the little jewel of James I's court, was married to the fourteen-year-old Robert Devereux, Earl of Essex, son of Elizabeth I's favourite. The marriage was a mistake and its consequences for all concerned disastrous.

As 'cold and calculating' politicians go, Henry Howard, Earl of Northampton, was in a class of his own. As he sat in his darkened study in Northampton House, hatching plans to advance the Howard family, even the spiders must have felt uneasy as they wove their webs in the corner where he sat. Northampton saw in his great-niece, Frances Howard, a vital pawn in these plans: perhaps not quite a wife for the king's eldest son, Prince Henry, but surely a mistress? That should be enough to tie in the Howard family to the heir apparent. But first it would be wise to marry the girl off to some uncomplaining nonentity – a good connection, of course, but not a husband who might later complain. Who better than the son of Robert Devereux, the 'Elizabethan Icarus' who had risen too high and had lost his head in the late queen's reign? All the reports spoke of young Essex as a dull fellow. He should be flattered to get a wife like Frances and if, later on, he were to prove to be awkward – well, his father's treason should be enough to convince him to keep his mouth shut.

At Whitehall, King James I presided over one of the most brilliant and corrupt of English courts. This 'wisest fool in Christendom' was no fool when it came to identifying a fair bosom or a fine pair of legs. He admired the young ladies who waited upon his queen, notably the 'heavenly' Frances Howard, but he liked little boys even better, and called on his pages and courtiers alike to warm his bed when the queen was indisposed or even, it is rumoured, when she was disposed. So when Henry Howard suggested young Essex as a match for his great niece, James thought nothing could be better than the wedding of two such young people, with himself presiding over the festivities and keeping the 'wee gal' at court until Essex was old enough to take her to his home. Until then Essex could continue his education abroad, while Frances would remain behind to decorate the royal court.

In the hothouse atmosphere of James's court the beautiful child grew to become a young woman of sixteen, blond-haired, slender-necked and with fashionably small, rounded breasts. But like some exquisite tropical flower her beauty concealed a poisonous nature. A world of flirtation and petty intrigue was all that she knew and, encouraged by her fatuous mother, the countess of Suffolk, she pursued pleasures for their own sake. Masques, costume balls, parties and other revels filled her days and she became precocious and self-willed, ungovernable in her rages and vindictive to those she imagined to be her rivals or enemies.

She had a brief affair with Prince Henry, but it did not prosper. For the prince it meant no more than the sowing of his wild oats, while for Frances it was more duty than pleasure. In any case, she had eyes for just one man at court, the handsome young Robert Carr, King James's new favourite. And Carr was proving to be no easy target. He was the rising star at King James's court and moved in a circle of admiring male friends. The king was notorious for his admiration of young men and, even though Robert had not yet occupied the king's bed, he knew that at any stage it might be required of him. And an affair with the young Countess of Essex might prejudice his hopes of advancement. But Frances was not deterred. She was not interested in a casual affair; she was infatuated with Robert Carr and would do anything to bind him to her. Then, just as her pursuit of the young Scotsman began to prosper, she got the worst possible news: her husband, Robert Devereux, was returning from France to claim her.

Devereux was not the only young courtier returning from France in 1609. Sir Thomas Overbury, Robert Carr's closest friend and adviser, reached England only a few weeks before young Essex and was immediately faced with the Scotsman's love affair with the Countess of Essex. At first he took the whole matter rather lightly, even writing Carr's love letters for him, as well as the sonnets which the lady believed contained her love's deepest feelings. For Overbury it was just one of the frivolous affairs that were an everyday event at court. But he was mistaken. There was nothing frivolous about Frances's desire for Robert Carr, and in the intensity of her passion she was prepared to go to any lengths to win the man she loved – even murder.

Three years on the continent had not helped to smooth Robert Devereux's rough edges and the dull boy that Frances had married was now a gloomy young man – 'grumbling Essex' to those who knew him well. Dressed in the austere garb of a Puritan, he had something of the stern nature of that sect. Yet it is difficult not to feel sorry for him; his marriage to Frances had been no less a tragedy for him than for the young Howard heiress. The betrothal of two children, at the whim of James I, and for the political advancement of the Howard family, had served only to make both of them bitterly unhappy.

Frances was accustomed to the brightly dressed gallants of the court, men like the glittering Prince Henry or the dashing Robert Carr, and she regarded Essex as a poor specimen. She resolved never to be

Frances Howard, Countess of Somerset (1594–1632), has been described as a 'Lady Macbeth' of the court of King James I. An adulteress and a murderer, Frances was also the victim of a disastrous arranged marriage.

a dutiful wife to him but to remain a virgin – at least in the world's eyes – until she could find a way of winning the man she loved. In the meantime, she would remain at court where she felt safe, and would try to ignore her husband as much as possible. Essex found his wife's behaviour first baffling and then intensely frustrating. He was impatient to leave court and take his wife back to his home at Chartley. There he felt at ease among the orchards and fields, playing the country gentleman and hunting with his friends. But Frances had no intention of mouldering away with her dull husband in the dreary isolation of rural Staffordshire, and used every excuse to delay their departure. Six months passed with their marriage still unconsummated, until Essex's forbearance cracked. After a stormy scene, Frances fled the court and went to her parents' house at Audley End in Essex. There she stayed, sulking for much of the summer, with Essex coming and going in an attempt to make her see reason. They quarrelled bitterly whenever they were left alone together. Voices were raised and the servants heard Essex 'pray God to damne me yf ever I offer you any kindness till you call for yt', to which Frances shouted back, 'I wish to be damned yf ever I do.' Frances's parents were shocked by their termagant daughter. In defiance of holy scripture Frances was refusing to sleep with her husband. They repeatedly pressed her to be a dutiful wife, but she flatly refused. Essex finally told her that unless she came to Chartley by the end of October, he would take her there by force. Frances, in hysterics and threatening to kill herself, fled again, this time to her great-uncle at Northampton House, where she knew she would be safe. Henry Howard, who had arranged the Devereux marriage in 1606, now had bigger plans for his great-niece. The pursuit of Prince Henry had been a mistake. Robert Carr was the 'coming man' and if Frances could make a conquest there, then the Howards would be allied to the king's favourite. He decided to befriend his young niece in her present difficulties with Essex, and ensure that her parents did not press her too hard.

While she was at Northampton House Frances heard news which gladdened her heart. Her husband had been taken seriously ill, confined to his bed at Chartley with 'a most violent disease of a poisonous nature, imputed to, but far transcending, the small-pox'. This stroke of luck would allow her to stay in London throughout the winter and attend court. It would also give her time to think how she

could get rid of her husband and win the love of Robert Carr. There were many experienced women at court who could advise her, and perhaps it was one of them who told her that if she were able to deny her husband his marital rights, she could secure a divorce on the grounds of non-consummation, leaving her free to marry the man of her choice. She therefore decided to tell the world that Essex was impotent. But how could she deter her husband once he recovered? She needed help and who better to give it than her friend, 'sweet Anne Turner'.

During the rehearsals for a court masque Frances had met Mrs Turner – a young and attractive widow – who soon became her confidante, and was later to be her accomplice in crime. Anne Turner was the court dressmaker, and was responsible for making the delightful costumes and backdrops for masques and court revels. She came from a good background, daughter to a substantial landowner in Somerset and widow of George Turner, a noted doctor of physic. To all appearances Anne Turner was a respectable lady. However, appearances were deceptive. In reality Anne Turner ran a number of bawdy-houses and had a network of contacts in the London underworld. Even before her husband's death, she had been mistress to Sir Arthur Mainwaring, and had hoped eventually to marry him. However, Anne waited in vain, bearing Sir Arthur three or four children, but never succeeding in getting him to marry her.

As a widow Anne Turner had needed to live by her wits. She was probably no more parasitic than many of the hangers-on at court, and she soon found herself indispensable in two ways. As the owner of fashionable bawdy-houses she catered for the young gallants and ladies from court who wished to pursue their dalliances out of the royal spotlight. Her houses at Paternoster Row and Hammersmith, with their garishly decorated apartments, were a perfect setting for these casual affairs. Yet this was only Mistress Turner's private face. Her public one was as a leader of court fashion. She had introduced from France a yellow starch for ruffs and sleeves which produced a saffron colour, against which fashionable ladies could set off their fragile beauty. So lucrative was the trade in the yellow starch that she kept its ingredients a closely guarded secret, infuriating her rivals and making her many enemies. (At her trial in 1615, Sir Edward Coke, the sombre Lord Chief Justice, even stipulated that Anne be hanged wearing one of her own yellow ruffs, the fact that her executioner also wore yellow cuffs and a ruff in addition to his black hood, served to add mockery to the horror of her last minutes of life.)

It might be supposed that there was little Anne Turner could do to corrupt the morals of Frances Howard. Yet in another – and more dangerous way – Mistress Turner was a bad choice as companion for the young countess. Frances, like most of the court ladies at this time, trusted the quacks and charlatans who claimed they could contact the spirit world through palmistry, fortune-telling and astrology; more significantly, she shared with them a belief in the efficacy of potions and philtres to promote love – or destroy it. Among Mistress Turner's nefarious underworld contacts there were some who had shown the widow the uses of magic – both white and black – and had introduced her to Dr Simon Forman of Lambeth.

It was the great age of magicians and astrologers, of men who claimed to be able to read the future with some certainty and also to influence it. One of the most famous of the occultists was Simon Forman, a heavy-bearded man with piercing eyes that seemed to 'strip a woman naked'. Forman had a house in Lambeth, outside the jurisdiction of the College of Physicians, which had banned him from practising medicine in the city of London. His fashionable clientele, which included bishops and peeresses, spanned the full range of Jacobean society. His enemies described him as a charlatan, but Forman was a remarkable man, whose reputation was second only to that of the great John Dee among English astrologers and necromancers. Ben Jonson even based his play *The Alchemist* on the character of Forman. In the play the character of Subtle, like Forman, issues love philtres and aphrodisiacs, most of which were as ineffectual as the one consisting of artichokes, oil and vinegar to be consumed at the 'growing of the moon'. To the noble ladies who visited him with problems of the heart, Forman dressed up his advice with all the trimmings of the pseudo-scientist. As he knew only too well, the value of his love potions was not in their ingredients but in the sympathetic magic associated with taking them.

Anne Turner knew Simon Forman very well, and the two had found that they had reciprocal interests. Anne would travel up the Thames by boat from her house at Paternoster Row, near St Paul's, to Forman's home at Lambeth, to keep him up to date with the latest developments at court, notably the gossip and scandal, which the astrologer would use to impress his clients. In return, Forman would supply Anne with spells, enchantments and love potions to satisfy the yearnings of the many young, and not-so-young, visitors to her apartments at Paternoster Row and Hammersmith. It was a profitable business.

In her desperation to win Carr's love, Frances confided in Mistress Anne Turner. She, in turn, was only too happy to help the young countess and, towards the end of 1610, she took Frances to meet Doctor Forman at Lambeth. This first visit was conducted in the utmost secrecy. Frances and Mistress Turner, heavily cloaked, made their journey from Whitehall through the dark and chilly streets of the capital, with just two of the countess's most trusted servants for protection. Forman welcomed them with an air of professional detachment, anxious to preserve the appropriate aura of mystery. The old man first questioned Frances and, learning of her absolute determination to bind Carr to her by fair means or foul, took her through the secret ceremonies of initiation into the black arts, so that she would be ready to play her part in the work ahead. Soon the young countess and her 'sweet father Forman' were on intimate terms. For several months Frances made regular visits to Forman's house. During this period the astrologer supplied her with a lead figurine of a man and woman in copulation, which he assured her would soon bring Robert Carr to her bed by sympathetic magic. In her excitement Frances grew less cautious with the astrologer. Driven by the feeling that she must win Carr's love at all costs she pressed him for even more certain ways to bring this about. Forman gave her love-potions, which would be administered to him in his food by servants whom Anne Turner had bribed.

But progress was slow. As a man of business in the king's service Robert Carr had much on his mind besides his affair with another man's wife, however beautiful and desirable she might be. He did not share Frances's obsessive nature and was content for a while to send her the letters and poems with which Overbury kept him supplied. As a result, Frances was tormented by the delay and longed for immediate success with her love potions. In fact, Forman's potions were having an effect. In September 1611 Carr was forced to call in the king's physician, Doctor Mayerne, for what was described as a severe attack of dyspepsia.

The famous astrologer and necromancer Simon Forman (1552–1611) assisted Frances Howard
in her marital problems by using 'sympathetic magic', but he was not involved in the death of
Sir Thomas Overbury.

So concerned was Frances with her pursuit of Robert Carr that she pushed the problem of her sick husband to the back of her mind. In the Spring of 1611 she learned that Essex was feeling much better and would soon be coming to London to collect her. Buoyed up by Doctor Forman's support and armed with potions and devices designed to cool her husband's ardour, she agreed to travel back with him to Chartley. She was confident that while she held her husband at bay, her trusty Turner would administer the love philtres to Carr to make his love remain true. But at Chartley her doubts returned and she became depressed, shutting herself in her room and keeping the curtains and shutters drawn. Servants tiptoed past her room and brought food on trays which they later collected uneaten. They gossiped about the way Frances rebuffed the master and how the two of them argued every evening. The maids whispered that the marriage bed never bore the imprint of two bodies. Frances took every opportunity to be uncivil to Essex, blaming him for her own unhappiness, while the young earl was ashamed to admit how much she was hurting him. Frances's parents continued to press their daughter to be more reasonable, and her brother even visited Chartley to instruct her in her wifely duty, but to no avail.

Meanwhile, Frances was regularly dosing her husband's food with Forman's potions and it was affecting his health; even his sheets were impregnated with noxious substances by her servants to disturb his natural sexual instincts. In addition, she was using black magic: she had a wax model that Forman had designed to resemble Essex, and had thrust a thorn into its genitals, which she remembered to twist and turn every evening. Another of Forman's devices – 'too immodest to express' – Frances inserted inside her to prevent penetration. So severe was the assault on Essex's virility that he became impotent towards her, though whether as a result of Forman's hocus-pocus or through simple hatred of his wife we cannot be sure.

Essex spent the winter of 1611-12 in London, deciding to return to Chartley for the summer and insisting that Frances should at least play the public role of a dutiful wife. Her luggage was sent on ahead but, after a bitter row, Frances got her own way again and stayed behind. With her husband out of the way she acted quickly. She leased Sir Roger Aston's house in Hounslow and there she and Robert became lovers at last. But their relationship

had to remain a secret; Essex must continue to believe her a virgin. At other times the lovers found a haven at one of Anne Turner's houses, with Robert slipping away from court, often disguised. Yet the illicit nature of their lovemaking frustrated Frances, and she looked for a way to solve the problem once and for all. She had worked hard to deny her body to her husband. It was time to ask her great uncle to press the king for permission to divorce. She had already told him that Essex was impotent and that the marriage had not been consummated. Surely that was enough. By Autumn 1612, both partners were agreed that a divorce was the only solution. Their marriage had been nothing but a sham. Essex wanted to be rid of Frances; even the shame that he would face when the full story became public could hardly be worse than the private humiliation he had suffered at his wife's hands. The matter must be put to King James.

The king was deeply disturbed when he heard that the two young people he had married now hated each other. Nevertheless, under pressure from Henry Howard and in order to please his favourite, Robert Carr, he agreed to assemble a commission of bishops and lawyers to investigate the divorce. They, in turn, agreed that if the countess could substantiate her claim still to be a virgin, they would agree to a divorce. A group of matrons and midwives were selected to examine Frances, but she claimed the right, through modesty, of being examined under cover of numerous veils. When the examination was due to take place she substituted a young virgin – Sir Thomas Monson's daughter – and slipped out of the bed before the midwives entered her bedroom. The ruse worked, the worthies were satisfied that she was still intact and, to Essex's public humiliation, Frances was given her divorce on the grounds that her husband was impotent towards her.

Meanwhile, Sir Thomas Overbury was growing alarmed at the idea of his friend Robert Carr marrying Frances Howard. He could see that once Robert was tied to the powerful Howards there would be no room for him at his friend's side. He already had plenty of evidence of Robert's affair with Frances and knew that the countess was no virgin, whatever she claimed before the commission. If he decided to make this known to the king the marriage to Robert would be impossible, Frances would be disgraced and the power of the Howard family broken. It placed Overbury in a powerful –

and a dangerous – position. For a start, he was measuring himself against the Machiavellian Earl of Northampton, who was not known for playing by any rules. Northampton therefore convinced Carr that it might be wise to have Overbury imprisoned in the Tower while the divorce commission was reaching its conclusion, after which he could be safely released. Carr was uneasy at first, for he still liked Overbury and wished him no harm. But Northampton assured him that his imprisonment would be temporary. Unknown to Northampton, however, Overbury had publicly called Frances a whore. The countess was not one to forget an insult. Once Overbury entered the Tower she would make certain that he never came out alive to threaten her future happiness.

Northampton and Carr, meanwhile, had persuaded the king to imprison Overbury on a trumped-up charge. From Northampton's point of view it was vital that while he was in the Tower Overbury should have no chance to send out letters to the king about Frances's forbidden affair with Carr. So he arranged for one of his cronies, Sir Gervase d'Elwes, to take over the post of Lieutenant of the Tower. While Northampton was tightening his hold on the wretched Overbury, Frances had also installed one of her own servants, Richard Weston, as the guard with special responsibility for the prisoner. Carr, meanwhile, oblivious to the terrible crime that Frances was planning, continued to write to Overbury in the friendliest fashion, assuring him that he was moving heaven and earth to get his friend out. Meanwhile, Frances, helped by Anne Turner, had been making her own preparations, visiting alchemists and purchasing poisons, including arsenic, catharnides and sublimate of mercury to be administered to Overbury in food sent into the Tower. Acting through Richard Weston, Anne Turner took the poisoned tarts and jellies to the Tower and left them with Sir Gervase d'Elwes. Ironically, at the very moment that Frances was trying to silence Overbury, Robert Carr had worked out a plan to win the King's pity and secure his friend's release. Carr decided that James was most likely to pity Overbury if his health seemed in danger and so he sent – unknown to Frances – enemas and 'vomits' into Overbury to make him violently sick and purge his stomach. Thus at the very moment that Overbury was eating poisoned food from Frances – supposedly enough to kill twenty men – he was being kept alive because the 'vomits' were constantly clearing his stomach.

As the days passed, Frances became frantic at the possibility that Overbury might be allowed out of the Tower to denounce her. How could her poisons not have worked? The man was more than human. And then she learned that Overbury was taking enemas as well as eating the tasty delicacies that she was preparing for him. This news gave her the idea of how to silence him for good. Instead of tarts and jellies, she decided to send Overbury an enema of her own concoction, but this time containing enough sublimate of mercury to kill him outright. Her plan worked, Overbury dying in terrible agony, his body wracked with spasms and his skin bearing all the marks of poisoning. Only now did Northampton and Carr, who had never intended any harm to Overbury, realize what Frances had been planning all along and they desperately tried to cover their tracks.

Meanwhile, under strict orders from the king, the divorce commissioners had found in favour of Frances, who was given the divorce she had been plotting. The magnificent wedding of Robert and Frances now took place in the Chapel Royal, with Carr elevated to the earldom of Somerset to make him worthy of his bride and Frances allowed to wear her hair loose to demonstrate that she was a virgin bride. James financed the whole wedding and Frances received jewels which, by today's values, would be worth upwards of half a million pounds. Ben Jonson wrote the wedding masque and John Donne the epithalamium. The marriage marked the high point of Howard fortune, and the high point of King James's folly. For the second time he had blundered in arranging the marriage of the young Howard heiress. It was fortunate that Northampton died before he saw his plans for Frances unravel before his eyes and his family name exposed to public scorn.

For twelve months it seemed that the mysterious death of Sir Thomas Overbury had been hushed up. Yet all was not well with Frances and the man for whom she had committed murder. Now that Carr was openly an ally of the Howards he found that he had many new enemies at court, some of whom had previously been his friends. And these enemies believed the only way of breaking the power of the Howards was to oust Robert from the king's favour by finding a new favourite even more handsome than Robert. Even the archbishop of Canterbury joined the search for the new favourite. Eventually, Carr's enemies found what they were looking for: the young, 'long-legged' George Villiers, later to be

The 16th and 17th centuries were the great age of alchemy. In England men like John Dee and Simon Forman combined scientific experiment with magical incantations in their attempts to unlock the secrets of the universe. This engraving – *The Alchemist* – is based on a painting by David Teniers.

Duke of Buckingham, whom the king adored at first sight. It was a shock for Robert to find himself ousted from his favoured position and he grew furiously jealous and increasingly morose. The king, unaccustomed to finding Robert such poor company, warned him to mend his ways if he did not want to lose the royal friendship completely.

While Carr was undermining his position as the king's main minister, there were startling revelations from an apothecary's boy named William Reeve, who had taken the final, fatal enema to Overbury and who had been hustled away to France during Northampton's attempts at damage limitation. Taken seriously ill and believing that he was dying, the boy wanted to relieve his soul of the great sin he knew that he had committed by taking the poison to the Tower. News of the boy's story reached the English ambassador in France, who returned to England to report to the Secretary of State, Sir Ralph Winwood, what he had heard about the murder plot. The king was at first unwilling to believe that Carr and Frances could possibly have been involved in the poisoning. Yet so horrid were the details of Overbury's death that he felt obliged to call on his chief justice, Sir Edward Coke,

to investigate the whole affair. The series of trials that followed rocked the entire court. First Robert Weston and Mistress Anne Turner were examined, found guilty as accomplices to murder and executed, followed by Sir Gervase d'Elwes and the apothecary Franklin, who suffered the same fate. Finally Frances and Robert were indicted and tried by Sir Edward Coke and Sir Francis Bacon. The aggrieved Earl of Essex attended both trials, revelling in the humiliation of those who had harmed him. Frances pleaded guilty and threw herself on the king's mercy, but Robert defended himself stoutly. Nevertheless, there was too much evidence against him, he was found guilty and both husband and wife were sentenced to death. It came as no surprise when James pardoned them both and confined them in the Tower.

Robert Carr had been innocent of his friend's death and yet he had lost everything through his relationship with the dangerously unstable Frances Howard. Now scarcely talking to each other, the two lived out their lives in bitterness in Rotherfield Greys in Oxfordshire, each, it is reported, inhabiting one end of the house and never meeting except when separated by the length of the dining table placed in the central hall. Carr watched as George Villiers became both favourite and lover to King James, and dominated royal policy for the rest of the reign. While Robert watched his power and pres-tige wither away, Frances's fate was perhaps more terrible. She lost her looks and for the last decade of her life suffered from an agonizing cancer of the womb that eventually killed her.

MURPHY'S LAW

The Irish Potato Famine of 1845-6 was a terrible demonstration of the fatal results of too great a dependence on a single crop. At the start of the blight in 1845 two million acres of Irish land were planted with potatoes, mostly in labour-intensive plots of less than an acre each. The Irish economy at that time was entirely agrarian and the rising popu-lation had resulted in a relentless pressure on the available land. Landowners, often English absen-tees, let their land to middlemen, who sub-let at exorbitant rents to the peasant labourers. As a result, the vast mass of the population was entirely depend-ent on the land system, working casually for poor wages and subsisting on potatoes alone. Failure to pay the high rents led to eviction which was often tantamount to a death sentence, for without land the family could not grow the potatoes on which they depended. It was a vicious system that seemed to benefit nobody but the landlords.

Potato-dependence had started in the seven-teenth century, which was a bitter period for the Irish people. By 1660 they had seen their usual crops – oats, turnips and wheat – trampled down by successive English armies, so the arrival of the potato from the New World had seemed like a godsend. The potato supplied all their dietary needs and soon became their basic food. It was so much associated with the Isle of Erin that, in spite of its origin in the Americas, it became known as the 'Irish potato'. Probably never before in history had a single food become so much associated with one nation. Ire-land adopted the potato nearly 150 years before the rest of Europe, where it was accused of causing such diseases as scrofula, typhus and leprosy (see p. 25). The Irish must have laughed behind their hands. By the start of the eighteenth century the potato was Ireland's king and the peasants held it in awe. Rich in vitamins B1 and B2, as well as a host of essential minerals, the potato kept Ireland's poor well-nour-ished in even the harshest times. Its ability to store vitamin C ended scurvy in Ireland, and when mixed with milk, the resultant mashed potato also offered vitamins A and D. It was the complete food and Irish men and women ate potatoes for breakfast, lunch and dinner.

The potato certainly maintained a high level of fertility among the Irish people. From two million in 1780, the population had increased to five million just twenty years later, and to eight million by 1841. Such a rapid rise was the result of a booming birth rate rather than a significant reduction in mortality. At the time that the potato blight struck, in the mid-1840s, the population of Ireland topped nine mil-lion, making it one of the most densely populated areas in Europe, approaching in places the density found only in parts of China. A British observer commented in the 1840s that the potato 'had begotten millions of paupers who live but are not clothed, who marry but do not work, caring for nothing but their dish of potatoes'.

In 1845 the blight struck the Irish potato crop with all the devastating power that had marked the passage of the Black Death through Europe in the fourteenth century. In that single year half the crop was ruined and the following year the entire crop was destroyed. In the next two years – 1847 and 1848 – the blight struck again. Deprived of their staple diet, the peasants began to starve. Further-more, their lowered resistance left them prey to diseases like typhus and scurvy. The bitterly cold winter of 1846–7 consolidated the work of the potato blight and the typhus epidemic, resulting in thousands of deaths. Many children suffered blind-ness from xerophthalmia, which was caused by a lack of milk and vitamin D. Ireland was a blighted land and looked for help to her neighbours, but in vain.

Food rioters at Dungarvon try to break into shuttered baker's shops. The famine that followed the Potato blight in Ireland in 1846 was one of the greatest natural disasters to hit the British Isles. The inadequate response by the government at Westminster left many Irish with no option but to emigrate.

The inept British reaction to the Irish famine contributed much to the bitter hatred that the Irish felt for the English for the rest of the century and afterwards. As a result of the famine and the subsequent migration to America the population of Ireland fell by nearly fifty per cent in little more than twenty years. In the words of Fintan Lalor, the famine was the sort of event that 'did the work of ages in a day'.

Just across the Irish Sea, England was the richest country in the world, with food surpluses that should have enabled her to come to the aid of the suffering Irish. Instead, the English view was that accounts of the catastrophe were much exaggerated. In addition, in an age when Samuel Smiles was stressing the virtues of 'Self-Help' and 'Thrift', it was believed that a government should not interfere with either Providence or food markets. In simple terms, it was Ireland's bad luck that they had been struck by a potato blight. But it was their problem and it was best if they tried to solve it for themselves. Such smugness may appal us today, but in the 1840s few provisions existed, even in England, to care for the poor. In Ireland social welfare was even less developed than in England and poorhouses were few and far between. Thus when, at the height of the famine, the English decided to withdraw relief grants and place the burden of maintaining the starving Irish masses on the Irish Poor Law authorities, it was a death sentence for thousands.

The obvious answer was for England to export her surplus corn to Ireland, but this plan was slow to achieve acceptance and even slower to be implemented. Incredibly, when the corn did reach the Irish, many of them did not even know how to cook it. Prime Minister Sir Robert Peel tried to relieve distress in Ireland by importing maize, but the Irish dismissed it as 'yellow dust' or 'Peel's brimstone'. English economists, regarding the famine as an act of God designed to reduce Ireland's excessive population, felt that even a million deaths would scarcely suffice to solve the island's economic problems. The English politician, Charles Trevelyan, did eventually organize soup kitchens in Ireland for some three million people, but still felt that it was money wasted. In his opinion, 'The great evil with which we have to contend is not the physical evil of the famine, but the moral evil of the selfish, perverse and turbulent character of the people.'

Facing certain starvation at home, millions of Irish people emigrated to America, often in 'coffin ships', where they faced death from dysentery and typhus. On arrival in Canada or the United States, they were unwelcome. Many were herded together in 'fever sheds' on Grosse Island, in the mouth of the St Lawrence River. Here hundreds of Irish women and children died and here their menfolk vowed to take revenge on the English landlords who had forced them to leave their country and die in a strange land. Those who settled in New York had only enough money to live in ghettoes, where they existed in the poorest and cheapest accommodation. The ghettoes were a breeding ground for the Fenians, who committed atrocities in England and Canada in their search for vengeance. Those who had lacked the fare to cross the Atlantic went instead to England, coming ashore at Liverpool. As in New York, the Irish could only afford to live in the poorest areas of the city or in nearby Manchester. The bitter legacy of the Irish famine can be seen even today in the violent attempts of the Irish Republican Army to rid Ireland of what they see as eight hundred years of alien oppression.

A LATE PARROT

At moments of personal crisis Elena Ceausescu would remind her husband Nicolae, the dictator of Romania, that the Romanian people did not deserve him, that he was 'too great' for them. With unconscious irony Elena was speaking for the nation: the Romanians did not deserve Nicolae Ceausescu; nobody deserved to be ruled by such a monster. Even a nation steeped in the lore of werewolves and vampires, whose national hero – Vlad the 'Impaler' – was regarded by the rest of the world as the original Count Dracula, had never before suffered from such a pitiless regime. Yet, in spite of every evil he inflicted on his suffering people, he was highly regarded abroad, fêted by a dazzling array of international leaders, from General de Gaulle to Margaret Thatcher. President Richard Nixon spoke of Sir Nicolae Ceausescu as 'One of the great leaders of the world'. Ironically, when the Romanian leader figured in a British series of books on foreign heads of state, the volume about him entitled *Nicolae Ceausescu: Builder of Modern Romania and International Statesman*, was edited by Robert Maxwell. In it Maxwell praised him for his 'tireless activity for the good of [his] country'. There are few people today not themselves insane or irredeemably bad who would share this verdict. For by his experiment in socialist planning, he imposed unparalleled suffering on his people.

Most terrible among Ceausescu's blunders was his policy on birth control and population growth. Ceausescu launched his campaign to boost Romania's population in 1966. His methods were simplicity itself: he simply banned divorce, birth control and abortion. All women were required to give birth to a minimum of four children and were liable to monthly gynaecological checks to ensure that they were not using contraceptive devices. For those who did – or for the doctors who connived at abortion – the penalties were severe. Many desperate women perished trying to swim across the River Danube at night, often under machine gun fire, trying to find sanctuary in Hungary. In the space of twelve months, as a result of Ceausescu's policy, the number of babies born doubled. Unfortunately, Ceausescu gave absolutely no thought to the need for double the quantity of maternity facilities and baby care. Consequently there arose a severe short-age of gynaecologists, obstetricians and paediatri-cians, not to mention maternity beds in hospitals, baby clothes and baby milk. The Romanian infant mortality rate increased by 145.6 per cent in a single year. It was a modern 'Massacre of the Innocents'. To hide the consequences of this insanity, Ceausescu ordered that no birth certificates should be issued until a baby was a month old. How many babies died in that first month, and therefore never ap-peared on the infant mortality statistics, we will never know. As one Romanian writer put it, 'The infant who has never been born in the sight of the law cannot die.' The consequences of this policy were only too apparent in the hospitals, children's homes and asylums of Romania, which were filled with unwanted or physically and mentally handi-capped children, living in appalling conditions. Furthermore, the Ceausescu regime simply refused to accept that Romania had an AIDS problem and as a result of a further medical error hundreds of newborn babies were given blood transfusions at birth in order to strengthen them. Tragically, the blood used was contaminated with AIDS which, combined with the lack of fresh needles, gave rise to an epidemic among Romania's young. Since the death of Ceausescu, television cameras have shown the world the true horror of his social policies in the wasted and pitiful children known as the 'irrecuperables' abandoned in homes and orphan-ages throughout the country.

In 1971 Nicolae Ceausescu and his wife paid state visits to China and North Korea; it was a turning point in the careers of these two profoundly limited individuals. As a result of what he saw in North Korea Nicolae Ceausescu seemed to lose his hold on sanity. North Korea's capital, Pyonyang is designed as a monument to a living legend – Kim Il Sung. The cult of personality is so claustrophobic in Pyongyang that one lane of every street is set aside for Kim's use, and pictures of the great man and his son appear on every wall, public or private. As if that was not bad enough, every North Korean carries a badge with Kim's likeness on it. In every way, Kim Il Sung has outdone George Orwell's Big Brother. Whether it was the shock of such megalomania that affected Nicolae Ceausescu or the excitement of possibilities unfulfilled in his own country that turned his mind we can only guess. But one thing is certain – the Ceausescu who arrived in North Korea was not the same man that left it. Nor was his wife Elena the

same woman. The simple peasant woman he had married became a 'Lady Macbeth' driving him to unimaginable excesses.

After his return from North Korea Nicolae Ceausescu began a social experiment in his country that was based on the use of terror. Opponents of the regime disappeared only to join the swelling num-bers in the Doctor Petra Groza Hospital for the treatment of 'political paranoia'. Anyone who sug-gested that there were civil rights abuses was rushed into intensive care suffering from 'senile dementia'. Journalists fell to a variety of mental ailments, including 'persecution complexes', 'self-preserva-tion drive' and 'discordant character structure'. In the hospital the sane inmates were locked into wards with genuinely insane patients until nobody could tell one from another. At this stage a ghoulish charade was enacted: inmates made their own coffins and then were reported to have succumbed to fatal diseases, although it is more likely they were subjected to drug overdoses by the staff.

Ceausescu's actions were as mad as those of the Emperor Caligula. In 1978 the 'hole that was not a hole' incident occurred. A new underground sta-tion was being constructed in Bucharest and a vast hole – at least 12,000 cubic metres in extent – had been excavated as an entrance to the station. How-ever, one morning the civil engineer in charge of the project turned up for work only to find that his hole had disappeared. It had been there the night before when he clocked off and went home at 7 p.m., but now there was no sign of it at all. Instead of the vast chasm he had left the previous night, there were trees and park benches on open park-land. Thunderstruck, the engineer first doubted his sanity and then asked one of the dictator's aides what had happened. Apparently, Ceausescu had been planning to make a welcoming speech to new students at Bucharest's polytechnic, as he sometimes did, and wanted to use the park which was being disturbed by the work on the underground station. So Ceausescu ordered the hole to be removed until after his speech. All night hundreds of labourers, whole units of special troops with tractors and mechanical diggers, and specialists in landscaping worked at fever pitch to fill in the hole and return the park to its pristine condition. Trees were up-rooted from other parts of the city and parkland stripped of its turf. The job was finished by 6 a.m., thirty minutes before the civil engineer in charge of the project returned to work.

In 1981 the World Reformed Alliance of Churches reached the accurate but unwise conclusion that Romania needed the help of Christianity and sent Ceausescu 20,000 bibles to be distributed among the country's churches. Some 200 reached their destination intact but the others were sent to a factory in Braila in Moldavia, where they were turned into toilet paper. Romanian pulping being no better than other Romanian industry at the time, words like 'Esau', 'Jeremiah' and 'God' remained visible.

As a means of censorship Ceausescu introduced the Great Romanian Typewriter Decree in 1983. By this order the renting or lending of typewriters was outlawed, and the ownership of such machines required police permission. Would-be typists were ordered to report to police stations to give samples of their typing and a full account of why they needed the machine. If the typewriter was repaired it needed a new certificate as did its user. Any Romanian who inherited such a dangerous machine had to surrender it to the authorities or seek to qualify in its use. Defective machines could not be disposed of without the keys being handed over to the requisite authorities.

In a state where such decrees were possible it is not surprising to learn that suicide was the only form of self-expression permitted by the regime. When the old city of Bucharest was laid waste by the dictator in his construction of the Boulevard of Socialist Victory, many old people were thrown out of their houses and left to starve on the pavements. Their response was to kill themselves. By a cruel twist of some bureaucrat's mind, the dispossessed houseowners of Bucharest were obliged to sign documents requesting demolition of their homes, and some were even charged the cost of the work. So thorough was Ceausescu's destruction of buildings that stood in the path of the Boulevard of Socialist Victory that soon just a single building – the Brancovenesc Hospital – obstructed the route. Its fate was sealed by Ceausescu's dog – a black labrador known as Colonel Corbu. The hospital basement was infested with rats and in an attempt to wipe these out the staff kept a number of cats. On one of the dictator's visits to the hospital, Colonel Corbu saw a cat and gave chase. After a furious battle, in which both the colonel and the cat sustained some damage, the animals were pulled apart and Ceausescu furiously drove away. The doctors were aghast. Their cat had presumed to

assault a colonel in the Romanian Army and there would be repercussions. Sure enough, within days the order was sent for the hospital to be demolished. The previous year over 50,000 Romanians had received treatment there. But Colonel Corbu's nose had been bloodied and so the hospital had to go.

All this time, visitors continued to flood into Bucharest from the West. As well as British prime minister Harold Wilson and Conservative leader Margaret Thatcher, Ceausescu met former prime minister Edward Heath and luminaries from both right and left in British politics. Edward Heath even sent a card wishing the Romanian dictator 'congratulations and best wishes' on his 60th birthday. It was David Steel, leader of the Liberal Party in Britain who, in order to thank the dictator for the hospitality he had shown when Steel visited Romania in 1978, arranged for one of his black labrador's puppies to be sent to Ceausescu. The dictator was delighted and named the dog Corbu, which in Romanian means 'raven'. So pleased was Ceausescu with the dog that he took it everywhere with him and soon Romanians were referring to the animal as 'Comrade Corbu'. Unfortunately Corbu became a part of the dictator's own fantasy world and soon the dog was to be seen being driven through Bucharest in a limousine, with its own motorcade. As the British ambassador described, 'I saw this black dog sitting all on its own in the back of a Dacia, looking rather pompous with its nose in the air, as black labradors often do.' In case Corbu was lonely, Ceausescu arranged for a black labrador bitch named Sherona to be delivered to his palace. As one of the maids later explained, 'The Securitate [secret police] told us never to feed the dogs. There was a special doctor who checked the food – it was the best sort of meat. Only when this doctor had tasted the food could they be fed. Corbu always slept with the Comrade [Ceausescu] at night. During the day the dogs slept in Villa 12A, complete with bed, luxury furnishings, television and telephone.' Apparently the Romanian ambassador in London was under official orders to go to Sainsbury's every week to buy British dog biscuits and Winalot, which were then sent back to Bucharest in the diplomatic bag. Corbu was soon given the rank of colonel in the Romanian Army. All this might have been put down to an amiable obsession on Ceausescu's part, to an eccentricity that was engaging rather than dangerous. Unfortunately, it was merely the accept-

President Ceausescu of Romania with Queen Elizabeth II, during his state visit to Britain in 1978. Ceausescu was awarded an honorary knighthood by the Queen, but when the true nature of his appalling regime was realized by the West it was hastily withdrawn – just days before his assassination.

able side of a bizarre megalomania that was both frightening and deeply damaging to the Romanian people.

As Ceausescu's mental disturbance worsened during the 1970s he became dangerously paranoid. Convinced that he would be poisoned by his enemies or would contract some deadly disease from shaking hands with the world's leaders, he – and Elena – took to washing their hands in alcohol after each session of hand-shaking. On a visit to Buckingham Palace in 1978, British court protocol was shattered when the Romanian dictator was seen to disinfect his hands after shaking hands with the Queen of England. He also employed a food-taster during the state banquet and held all his meetings with his entourage in the middle of the palace gardens, assuming that his suites would have been bugged. The Queen must have felt that she was entertaining a madman. In spite of this – or perhaps because of it – she awarded the Romanian dictator

an honorary knighthood. Just days before Ceausescu's final overthrow and death, the British foreign secretary, Sir Geoffrey Howe, acting for the Queen, withdrew the honour.

After a meeting with Fidel Castro, at which he told Ceausescu that he had only recently survived a CIA plot to assassinate him by poisoning his clothes, Ceausescu took to wearing his own clothes once only and then discarding them in case they were tampered with. From that point onwards all his clothes were made by the secret police and a year's supply of them stored in a temperature-controlled warehouse outside Bucharest. He and his wife took their own bed linen and towels everywhere with them, even to Buckingham Palace.

The reasons why so many apparently intelligent world leaders indulged a raving lunatic, as it was quite obvious Ceausescu had become, were twofold. In the first place, Ceausescu was fervently anti-Russian and that made him little less than saintly in the corridors of power in Washington and London. Secondly, he was an avenue to trade deals which might prove beneficial to the economies of the West. In this respect the western leaders were fooling themselves. When Britain tried to secure a £300 million aerospace deal with Romania, she found that Romania's promises of cash were misleading. Having dangled the bait until the British had taken it, Ceausescu then tried to pay for the technology with Romanian products. At British Aerosopace and Rolls Royce the negotiators could barely believe the news that they were exchanging high-tech equipment for ice-cream, yoghurt and strawberries. The British were not alone in their embarrassment. After Canada had promised Romania a billion dollars' worth of nuclear reactors, she found that payment was being offered in perishable fruit.

Perhaps it is wrong to laugh at such a man. A parrot, the pet of one of the dictator's servants, was arrested by the secret police after being heard to repeat the words 'Stupid Nicu', with reference to Ceausescu's son. The bird was interrogated by the Securitate but refused to say who had taught it the phrase. The parrot was throttled and took its secret to the grave.

CHAPTER TWO: THOSE WHO PRESUMED TOO FAR

The poetic licence of Gabriele D'Annunzio

Many poets in history have been eccentric, but few have been more so than Gabriele D'Annunzio, once called the John the Baptist of Italian Fascism, more one suspects for the numerous times he lost his head over nubile Salomes than because he paved the way for Mussolini as Italy's Messiah. D'Annunzio found inspiration for his poetry in many unusual ways, including writing with a quill pen on paper balanced on an upturned umbrella, and keeping stillborn babies pickled in bottles on shelves in his study. Furthermore, he loved to shock the Italian establishment, which he regarded as inimical to the progress of his country. Daredevil womanizer, pilot and racing driver, D'Annunzio was unable to carry out the meanest task without revealing the showman inside him. On 9 August 1918, in the last months of the war, the skies of Vienna were filled with pieces of coloured paper – red, white and green – dropped by planes of the Italian Air Force. The squadron responsible was – need one say – led by Gabriele D'Annunzio. It was a propaganda coup, the text of the pamphlets reading, 'Viennese, we could now be dropping bombs on you. Instead we drop a salute.' Nobody died that night but poetry triumphed.

Born in Pescara on 12 March 1863, son of the flamboyant and lecherous mayor of the city, Gabriele D'Annunzio was the great soldier-poet of the First World War. He lost an eye in the fighting and, at the age of 52, charged the Austrian trenches in a flowing cloak, with a dagger held between his teeth and a pistol in either hand. On another occasion he sailed a torpedo boat into the middle of the Austrian fleet in the Bay of Bucari, and sank an enemy vessel. According to D'Annunzio, war was far too serious a matter to be left to the generals.

Peace brought nothing but frustration for D'Annunzio, who could scarcely bear to be out of the newspapers for a moment. In the port city of Fiume, on the the new Italo-Yugoslav border, he found a cause to fight for and to keep him at the centre of public attention. The Italo-Austrian armistice in November 1918 had not clearly established the ownership of Fiume. Although Italian troops had occupied the city, they were there only as part of a joint allied military force, along with British, French and American soldiers. D'Annunzio rightly assessed the mood of post-war Italy, which was that Fiume must become part of the Italian nation. As a result, backed by an army of enthusiasts who would have been better suited to carrying spears in a production of Verdi's opera *Aida*, the warrior-poet marched on Fiume. D'Annunzio's actions severely embarrassed the Italian government in the face of their allies. Italy had not been promised Fiume in the negotiations that brought her into the war in 1915 and had been hoping to win the city at the Paris Peace Conference in recognition of her great wartime sacrifices. D'Annunzio's unofficial action was likely to spoil everything.

On 12 September 1919 Gabriele D'Annunzio made a triumphant entry into Fiume. Typically the whole event was filmed for Italian cinema audiences. There was no resistance to his legions from the British and French troops who were still in the city, but the Italian troops, under General Pittaluga, were ordered to fire on the poet and his followers. Instead, D'Annunzio appealed to Pittaluga to join him. Ripping open his coat to show his war medals, he said 'All you have to do is to order the troops to shoot me, General.' It was pure theatre and the citizens of Fiume loved it. Soon, all the Italian troops in the city had gone over to D'Annunzio.

The government D'Annunzio established in Fiume was both cosmopolitan and radical. It included American journalists, poets, Belgian writers, Italian businessmen, trade unionists, anarchists and soldiers. In fact, D'Annunzio's government of Fiume was like one based on a Napoleonic Code written by Ezra Pound and acted out by the Keystone Cops. But it had its darker side. Behind the stage door 'Fiume had become a bordello, a refuge for criminals and prostitutes', and for drug addicts and louche barbarians. In spite of the theatrical posturings of D'Annunzio Fiume became a far cry from the 'Republic of Virtue' which had been the aim of Italy's 'First Duce'. Thousands of young Italians travelled to Fiume ostensibly to serve under *Il Comandante*, but more likely to indulge themselves in the forbidden world of free love and illegal drugs. They wore the black shirts of D'Annunzio's legionaries, with a skull and crossbones emblem, and swaggered about with daggers in their belts. It was better than school and infinitely more rewarding than sitting on street corners in Italy's cities with the rest of the unemployed. Once in Fiume they marched about in formation, giving Roman salutes and chanting 'Eia, Eia, Alala', which – according to D'Annunzio – had been the very words used by Achilles to spur his chariot horses forward.

As diplomatic pressure increased for Italy to remove D'Annunzio from Fiume, the poet himself was defiant, declaring that the England of Milton would never bomb a republic ruled by a poet. That was probably true, but she would have happily bombed Fiume. As one observer commented, 'it was a period of madness and bacchanal, ringing with sounds of weapons and those, more subdued, of love-making'. However much D'Annunzio tried to occupy the high moral ground, setting standards for the youth of Italy and making Fiume a symbol for all free-thinkers in Europe, he could not escape the fact that he was a sensualist rather than a man of high conviction, more Nero than Robespierre. While D'Annunzio claimed to be burning the midnight oil in solving the city's problems he was, in fact, entertaining Lily de Montressor, a singer from one of the port's seedy nightclubs, who was smuggled into *Il Commandatore*'s palace at night and left – five hundred lire the richer – each morning.

As D'Annunzio's legionaries indulged themselves in every kind of sensual pleasure, the administration of Fiume was collapsing, inflation was rampant, supplies of food low, and the drains needed attention. It was the everyday things that were annoying the warrior-poet, they were so mundane. Something had to be done to get people back to work and to persuade the legionaries to help administer the city. So a band of them, led by Guido Keller and known as the *sans-chemises* from their habit of marching around the town stripped to the waist, formed themselves into a vigilante group to improve public morals. They at once came up against the problem of D'Annunzio himself, who was at this stage deeply in the toils of an affair with the pianist Luisa Baccara. Keller and his men therefore decided to kidnap Luisa and take her as far away from Fiume as possible. To achieve this without *Il Commandatore* knowing was a problem, but they came up with a novel, even fantastic, idea: the 'Castle of Love'. This involved all the prettiest girls in Fiume being 'imprisoned' in a wooden castle, which was then 'besieged' by all the men, who pelted the castle with food, money and flowers. Luisa was to be the *Madonna Castellana* and at the high point of the 'battle' she would be kidnapped and spirited away, never to return. In fact, Keller planned to grab more than just Luisa. He had a boat strategically placed so that he could 'remove' all his political opponents as well, and strand them on a distant island. But the plan eventually failed when D'Annunzio put a stop to the festival at its height, saying the world would condemn it as 'too D'Annunzian'.

As everyone grew bored with all the fun they were having and found sporting was 'as tedious' as working, desertions from Fiume began to grow. Guido Keller got fed up, climbed in his aeroplane and flew high into the clouds, landing somewhere in Yugoslavia. Taking a fancy to a tiny donkey he saw in a field, he lashed the poor beast to the struts of his landing gear and took off, bringing the donkey – in what condition is not recorded – as a present for *Il Commandatore*. Most people were not so considerate and had simply become fed up with D'Annunzio's decrees. He instigated the worship of music in the following high tones: 'A great people is not only that which creates its own God in its own image' – the Fiumians were worried at the idea of a god in the image of the bald, one-eyed, bulbous nosed, fat and five foot six-inch D'Annunzio – 'but that which also creates its hymn to its God'. At a public meeting D'Annunzio announced plans for an enormous theatre to seat ten thousand music lovers. There was an enormous silence for no one was listening; the legionaries were too busy sleeping off the previous night's indulgence to worry about their leader's latest ideas. Groups of the legionaries had already taken over the protection rackets in the city and were organizing the prostitutes on the quayside. It was too good an opportunity to miss, with no police about and no proper government. To them D'Annunzio was just a 'soft touch'.

However, the end was at hand, in the shape of an Italian naval and military blockade which cut off Fiume from its food supplies. In November 1920 the Italians and the Yugoslavs reached an agreement at Rapallo to make Fiume an independent city under League of Nations jurisdiction. There was now nothing to stop the Italians putting an end to D'Annunzio's 'adventure'. Inside the city it was clear that the good times were over. The legionaries could not live on parades and uniforms and poetry, and increasing numbers simply deserted. On Christmas Eve a squadron of Italian ships closed in on the port and opened a bombardment. D'Annunzio left Fiume declaring that the inhabitants had not been worthy of his great ideas, though the truth was that most were looking forward to a return to normality.

D'Annunzio's loss was Mussolini's gain. The legionaries who left Fiume flocked to join the Fascists, complete with their black shirts, armbands, Roman salutes and castor oil, for dosing political opponents. D'Annunzio had written the script but Mussolini was going to direct the picture. Comic episode though the whole Fiume saga may seem to us, to D'Annunzio and his fellows it was intensely serious and significant. With hindsight one can see the occupation of Fiume as the forerunner of Mussolini's later – and successful – March on Rome in 1922. And the fact that the Italian authorities allowed D'Annunzio to indulge his fantasies and thumb his nose at the world for so long, merely showed Mussolini how feeble they really were.

The dark lord

The *enfant terrible* of the Crusading movement was Reynald de Châtillon or Reginald of Kerak as he was more commonly known – a knight at times mischievously inventive and at others brutally rapacious. No other Christian warrior – not even King Richard the Lionheart of England – was as feared and hated by the Saracens as Reynald, whom they referred to as 'Satan'. From his great castles in Moab, notably the impregnable fortress of Kerak, Reynald preyed upon Muslim caravans, descending on them like an eagle on a flock of doves, pecking and killing for his pleasure, and then taking prisoner the survivors, whom he would hold to ransom in the dark dungeons of his castles. Reynald acknowledged no overlord and would serve the Christian cause as the mood took him, sometimes as a cohesive force but at other times as a divisive factor in an already splintered command.

Reynald had first come to Palestine in the entourage of King Louis VII in 1147. When the French army returned home he remained, eager to establish a princedom for himself. As a younger son of the Sieur de Châtillon-sur-Loing, he could expect little back in France other than the right to a small landholding from the lord that he served. But in Outremer – the name given to the Christian colonies in the Middle East after the conquests of 1099 – he had a chance to exploit his undoubted talents as a fighter and as a ruthless and courageous leader. First he served as a soldier of fortune under the king of Jerusalem, Baldwin III, and in 1153 he made a brilliant marriage to an heiress, Princess Constance, which brought him the princedom of Antioch. It was an astonishing rise for a penniless knight, but Reynald took it in his stride. Although he was unpopular with the people of Antioch, who viewed him as a low-born upstart, he soon showed them his mettle, winning fame in battle against the Saracens. But Reynald was no perfect knight, no Lancelot or Galahad – he was a ruthless killer, with the manners of a goat. Nor could he always tell his friends from his enemies, or his co-religionists from the Muslims. In 1156 he attacked the Christian island of Cyprus, where his soldiers showed such ferocity to the Greek Christians there that it was said 'the Huns or the Mongols might have envied him'.

No lover of the Church, Reynald ordered all the nuns and women to be raped, while he cut off the noses and ears of all the priests. So thorough were Reynald's soldiers in finding treasure that it was said that there was not enough money left on the whole island to ransom a single man. This disappointed Reynald, who had intended to get a good price for his noble prisoners. Only news that a Byzantine fleet was coming to the rescue of the Cypriots persuaded him to let the survivors go and return to Antioch in triumph.

However, in 1160 Reynald's fortunes took a tumble. During a cattle raid on the herds of his fellow Christians in Armenia, he was ambushed by the Muslim governor of Aleppo and dragged off to spend the next sixteen years in prison. When the matter of his ransom was raised the people of Antioch were not keen to buy him back and so he languished, almost forgotten, in a Muslim dungeon. The years of captivity merely served to embitter him. When he was released in 1176 – during a Muslim–Christian truce – he was eager to make up for lost time. He had a score to settle with the Muslims whose current leader, Saladin, would soon wish that he had never agreed to release him. Wifeless and homeless, Reynald seemed to be back where he had been in 1147 when he had first left France. But, within months of his release, he had insinuated himself into the affections of a rich widow, Stephanie de Milly, through marriage to whom he gained control of much of southern Jordan, including the fortresses of Montreal de Shaubak and Kerak, the latter probably the strongest – and certainly the grimmest – castle in the entire kingdom. From these strongpoints he was able to overlook the Muslim caravans crossing from Egypt to Syria. By agreeing to release Reynald, Saladin had opened a Pandora's Box. Yet, unwittingly, he had also sown the seeds of his final victory in the holy war against Christendom, for Reynald's blunders were to pave the way for the final triumph of Islam in Palestine.

Reynald's Red Sea expedition in 1182 was certainly the most outrageous action ever undertaken by Christian forces against the Muslims. Its aim was nothing less than the seizure of the body of the Prophet Muhammad from its tomb in Mecca and its return to Reynald's castle of Kerak. There it would be held hostage and all Muslims who wished to visit the burial place of the Prophet would have to pay the master of Kerak for the privilege. Had anyone else planned this they would have been regarded as mad.

For the previous two years, preparations had been under way for the Red Sea raid, with boats being built on the Mediterranean coast at Ascalon, which were then transported in sections on the backs of camels across the desert wastes to Aqaba, on the Red Sea coast of modern Jordan. Muslim spies would have simply thought that Reynald was planning a pirate expedition in the Red Sea, aimed at the valuable trade between Arabia and Egypt. This might have worried the Muslims on a material level, but not half as much as the sacrilege that Reynald was really planning. The seizure of the body of the Prophet would have ranked in Muslim minds with the seizure of Jerusalem as something so fundamental that words could not express its significance.

Reynald first secured his port of departure by leading his men to capture Eilat, the adjacent Muslim town to Aqaba. With this achieved, he was free to launch his warships onto the Red Sea without fearing an attack on his base. The five boats that

Gustave Doré's idealized representation of Sultan Saladin, the Muslin leader who recaptured Jerusalem from the Christians in 1187. Saladin was plagued for many years by the cruel and rapacious 'dark lord' of Kerak, Reynald de Chatillon, who even launched ships into the Red Sea in an audacious attempt to seize the body of the Prophet Mohammed from Mecca.

comprised the squadron were all painted black to reduce visibility and were crewed not by Crusaders sporting the emblems of their holy orders, but by freebooters and Mediterranean pirates. With the assistance of local pilots Reynald's fleet moved down the African coast of the Red Sea, sacking the coastal towns as they went and capturing the important Nubian port of Aidhab. As more and more merchant ships were captured panic seized the Muslim world. Never before had a Christian ship appeared in the Red Sea and the Muslims were defenceless against Reynald's rapacity. Having pillaged all that the coast of northwest Africa could offer, the Christian pirates now crossed over to the Arabian coast, burning dozens of small ports and approaching al-Rabigh, the port of Mecca, holiest of all Muslim cities. Reynald's pirates landed on the coast, seized horses from the Arabs there and rode off towards Mecca, capturing a rich caravan on the way and putting the merchants to the sword.

Reynald had found a Muslim weak point and his men were making the most of the fact that they were meeting virtually no resistance. The Muslims seemed too paralyzed with shock to react. It had never been thought possible that the Christians could penetrate into the Red Sea. The Arabs who lived there, with no experience of the Crusaders as warriors, found their ruthless barbarity profoundly shocking. And now these infidels were even presuming to attack the holiest of holy places – Mecca itself. Sultan Saladin, campaigning far away in northern Syria, could only cringe in disbelief when the news reached him, and hope that his brother al-Adil, his representative in Egypt, could cope with the crisis.

Because the Muslims had never expected to face Christian pirates in the Red Sea, they had few available warships of their own. Nevertheless, al-Adil acted promptly, undertaking the enormous task of transferring ships from the Mediterranean to the Red Sea overland. This took six weeks, during which time Reynald's men had a free hand in the Red Sea to burn and pillage. But once the Egyptian admiral Lu'lu got on their trail the game was up. Reynald was no longer with his ships, having returned to his castle of Kerak to prepare for the arrival of the body of Muhammad. It was just as well for him as nemesis now descended on the Crusader fleet. Lu'lu trapped Reynald's ships against the coast and burned them all. The Crusaders, retreating inland, were pursued by the vengeful Egyptians. It is said that Lu'lu forced the Bedouin tribesmen to guide him by riding with a purse of silver attached to his lance as a bribe. Eventually, all 170 of the Crusaders surrendered to al-Adil's men on the promise of their lives. But this was never going to be something al-Adil could guarantee. So enraged was Muslim public opinion and so frustrated was Sultan Saladin, a thousand miles to the north and quite unable to help against the infidels, that mercy was unthinkable. Ultimately it was Saladin's decision to kill Reynald's men not just in revenge, but because they had seen the weak spots in Islam's defences and had, moreover, threatened impiety towards the holy places. Reynald's pirates were executed, some in Cairo, others in Mecca or Medina.

Reynald's plan, like so many others of his, had failed, but it had been a close-run thing. However, from the point of view of the Crusader kingdoms in Outremer, Reynald's action had been a terrible blunder. It had drawn the attention of Saladin to the threat to his southern frontier and had focused his mind on destroying the

Christians rather than securing his own lands from his Muslim enemies. Saladin swore an oath to kill Reynald of Kerak with his own hand, and for the next five years the Muslim leader never let a day pass without reminding himself of the insult he had suffered at Reynald's hands.

Given the immense power of his enemy, many men would have gone to ground and tried to be as quiet a neighbour as possible. This was not Reynald's way. He continued to provoke Saladin, raiding Muslim caravans from his fortress at Kerak. But Saladin needed no provocation. He had a grudge to settle with the lord of Kerak and in November 1183 he besieged the castle with a great army. As it happened, Kerak was staging the wedding of the year, namely the marriage of Reynald's stepson, Humphrey of Toron, to King Baldwin IV's stepsister, Isabella, and Reynald was not going to allow the minor inconvenience of a besieging Muslim army to spoil the celebrations. While Saladin's siege engines and catapults sent great rocks crashing against the walls of the castle, Reynald played the perfect host, conversing with his visitors and passing round the drinks. If the war cries and groans of the wounded got too loud he ordered his minstrels to up the tempo and get everyone dancing. A chronicler of the time records the charming, and not entirely implausible story, of Saladin's generosity towards the young lovers, if not towards their incorrigible host. Apparently during the siege the mother of the bridegroom, Stephanie de Milly, personally prepared some dishes from the bridal feast, and sent them out to Saladin who received them in his tent. In return the great warrior enquired as to which of Kerak's towers was being used by the newly-weds, and promptly ordered his engineers to cease the bombardment in that area so that the honeymooners could get some peace.

In the meantime, by means of beacon fires, Reynald had signalled to the Crusader capital at Jerusalem the news of Saladin's attack and a relief army had set out led by King Baldwin IV. In a matter of days, the Saracens were forced to raise their siege of Kerak and withdraw as the Crusader army approached. But Saladin was back the following year, in 1184, beating at Reynald's walls with his great siege engines. Again a relief army forced the Saracens to retreat. These close shaves might have warned lesser men to conduct their affairs with Saladin more prudently, but Reynald was never prudent. At Easter time in 1187, the dark lord carried out his most foolhardy action yet – he decided to capture Saladin's sister, whom he had heard was travelling in a well-armed caravan through southern Jordan. At that time there was a general truce between Christians and Muslims. Reynald, however, acknowledged no truces: he led his men against the caravan, killed the guards and took prisoner all the Muslim merchants, whom he dragged back to captivity in Kerak. Whether or not Saladin's sister was with the captives we are not told, but had she been there the fact could hardly have made Saladin angrier than he already was. Reynald had broken the truce, attacked peaceful merchants and was holding them to ransom. There was no option now but to raise the banner of holy war against the Christian kingdom of Jerusalem. Only when the infidels had been driven from Jerusalem would there be any peace for Saladin and Islam. Saladin also renewed his solemn oath to kill Reynald with his own hand.

What followed in 1187 was a catastrophe for the Christian world. Saladin invaded the Crusader kingdom, defeated and destroyed the Christian army and occupied the Holy Land, regaining Jerusalem after a Christian presence of 92 years. At the battle of Hattin the biggest Crusader army ever raised was destroyed and all the leading nobles of the realm were taken prisoner, among them, naturally enough, Reynald of Kerak. In his tent, after the battle, Saladin entertained King Guy and his leading knights. He challenged Reynald with breaking his word repeatedly but the lord of Kerak was unrepentant, replying scornfully 'I did only what princes have always done. I followed the well-trodden path.' If Sultan hoped to see Reynald beg for his life he was disappointed and so, true to his oath and wasting no more words, he swung his sword, killing Reynald with one blow. The career of the dark lord of Kerak, 'Satan' to the Muslim, was over. In his own way Reynald had contributed more than perhaps any other man to the fall of the Christian kingdom of Jerusalem.

Lambert Simnel

England was still a far from stable kingdom in the aftermath of the thirty-year civil war known as the 'Wars of the Roses', which ended in 1485. For several years Henry VII's hold on power was threatened by pretenders attempting to usurp his throne. Two significant revolts took place, with the aim of replacing Henry with one of the leading Yorkist noblemen. Both were far-fetched in their aims and incompetent in their execution, and both failed. The one involving Lambert Simnel ended in fiasco with its leaders dead or imprisoned and its focus – the supposed earl of Warwick – reduced from carrying orb and sceptre to peeling turnips and washing the dishes. It was a Tudor soap opera.

The first pretender to the throne of England after 1485 was a young boy, not much more than ten years of age, who was known as Lambert Simnel. So obscure was this child's background that we cannot even be certain that either 'Lambert' or 'Simnel' were his real names as they were both distinctly unusual for that time. In any case, whoever he really was is less important than who he pretended to be. Lambert Simnel became a pawn in the hands of an ambitious Oxford cleric, named Richard Simons, who had decided that working long hours at his studies as a means of achieving high office was far less easy and reliable than winning preferment at the hands of some powerful lord. And who was more powerful than the king himself? Simons was looking for a chance to insinuate himself into the affections of powerful men and perhaps become a 'kingmaker' himself. According to one account Simons had been entrusted with the tutoring of young Lambert Simnel by the boy's father, an organ builder named Thomas Simnel. Other accounts give no details of Lambert's father or his occupation. Nevertheless, Simons found the boy quick to learn and unusually good-looking, and an idea came into his head of how to use him to further his own aims. Simons knew of the rumours that Edward IV's son, Richard of York was still alive in the Tower (in fact, he was almost certainly dead). If Lambert Simnel could be so tutored that people believed he was Richard of York – and consequently heir to the throne – there would be many people who would reward Simons for his efforts, perhaps even with a bishopric.

Before Simons had gone very far with Lambert's training as a prince, a new rumour began to circulate that young Edward, Earl of Warwick and son of the Duke of Clarence had been murdered in the Tower. Simons decided to change his story and prepare his protégé as young Warwick, cultivating in the boy all the arts of the courtier and the great lord. Once Simons had perfected Lambert's training, he would circulate a new rumour that young Warwick had escaped from the Tower and was in his keeping. Simons undoubtedly had the backing of certain prominent Yorkists, probably including John de la Pole, Earl of Lincoln, who himself coveted the throne. It is likely that had Simnel's pretence proved successful, then the boy would have been disposed of in some way to open the way for Lincoln to ascend the throne.

When Lambert's 'education' was complete, Simons removed him to Ireland, where he felt confident in winning support for a Yorkist Pretender. On arrival, Simons and the boy were taken to the Earl of Kildare, who professed to believe the 'Warwick' story and was prepared to support an invasion of England designed to overthrow King Henry. The Irish people took Lambert to their hearts and promised to place him on the throne of England or die in the attempt. Lambert must have been an apt pupil and Simons a good teacher for the Irish to be so easily convinced that this organ builder's son was a royal prince. Lambert was taken to Dublin Castle, attended by all the pomp and ceremony due to a real king, and formally crowned as King Edward VI of England.

Across the Irish Sea, Henry Tudor was alarmed by the news from Ireland. His spies had kept him informed of the activities of his leading opponents but the appearance of this young boy was a complete surprise to him. He knew full well that he had the real Warwick imprisoned in the Tower and, after a meeting of the Council at Sheen on 2 February 1487, he decided to display the Earl of Warwick in public to scotch rumours that the impostor in Ireland was really Clarence's son. Warwick was taken through the crowded streets of London so that everybody could see him. Unfortunately, the plan backfired when the onlookers decided the real Warwick was the pretender and Lambert Simnel the true prince. Confusion was general, but the Irish were certain that they had the real Warwick and powerful Yorkist leaders like Lincoln, who planned to take the throne for himself anyway, did not much care who had the young earl.

Lincoln now openly joined the conspiracy against King Henry VII. In addition, the Dowager Duchess of Burgundy – sister to the late King Edward IV and a daughter of the House of York – promised to help the rebels with money and troops. The duchess had no faith in Lambert Simnel, but she hated Henry Tudor so bitterly that she was willing to go to any lengths to see one of her family take the throne of England. Lincoln collected 2000 Flemish troops under an experienced leader, Martin Swart, and shipped them to Ireland to join the main body of the rebels under Kildare. On 5 June 1487, the combined Irish and Flemish army landed near Furness, in Lancashire, where they were joined by English supporters, though in smaller numbers than they had hoped. It soon became obvious that the people of the north, exhausted by thirty years of civil war, were not turning out in great numbers to support the invaders. The Yorkist army consisted of just too many foreigners to be welcomed by the English onto their land. Not only did it steal and pillage as it went, its Irish soldiers were of doubtful quality, poorly armed and worse armoured; it was doubtful how useful they would be in a battle with armoured men-at-arms. At Stoke on 16 June, 1487, the rebels met the royal army and were overwhelmed. Kildare was taken alive, but Lincoln and Swart died in the fighting. Two important prisoners – Simons and Simnel – were taken to Henry Tudor's tent where the King's compassionate nature overcame all the arguments of his lords that the boy should die. Lambert seemed to Henry to be a complete innocent in the whole affair. He was an attractive, well-mannered child, who had been ill-used by scheming adults. Gazing at the wide-eyed boy, Henry called his head cook and asked him to find a job for the boy in the royal camp. After the return from Stoke, Lambert was employed in the royal kitchens, and later became a falconer in the king's service. He lived until 1534, but little is known of his later life. His tutor, Richard Simons, who deserved far worse of the king was granted his life perhaps because of his calling, though he was imprisoned for a while after the battle.

Henry's victory at Stoke did not bring down the curtain on the Yorkist claims to his throne. Although Henry had Lambert Simnel fully occupied in cooking his meals for him, a second, more dangerous – and equally oddly named – pretender was preparing his claim, Perkin Warbeck. But that is another story.

A DIRTY WHITE RAG

The search for the land of El Dorado obsessed the Spanish conquistadores during the sixteenth century, but in vain. They were in fact exploring the wrong continent. It was in the south of the 'Dark Continent' that El Dorado lay, or the closest thing on earth to it. Three centuries after the great Spanish explorers had lost their way either in the high Andes passes or in the misty rainforests of the Amazon, so much gold was discovered on the Witwatersrand, in the Transvaal Republic of South Africa, that it soon replaced silver as the standard for valuation. The goldfield at Witwatersrand, south of Pretoria, was easily the largest in the world – 170 miles long by 100 miles wide – yet, incredibly, the local white population seemed to show no interest in a discovery that was attracting prospectors to the site from all over the world. The Afrikaners of the Transvaal were pastoralists, sons of the soil, who had known about the gold for many years. So simple was their outlook on life that they had even used gold-bearing stone in the building of their farmhouses and it was possible to trace the gold seams in the stonework of their barns and sheeppens. Deeply religious, the Boers were not prepared to change their way of life in pursuit of instant wealth.

However, their deep conviction, or common sense, call it what you will, was not shared by the thousands of foreigners from throughout the English-speaking world and beyond who began to flood into their homeland in search of gold. These 'Uitlanders', as the Boers called them, were as unwelcome as the plague. The shanty-town that grew up and within months became known as 'Gold City' or Johannesburg, was regarded as an unholy place. Bars, brothels and cheap hotels sprang up catering for the worst sorts of riff-raff. The local Boers began to fear that their lifestyle was being overwhelmed by the English-speaking invaders. It seemed that what the British had failed to achieve on the battlefield they were attempting to win on the goldfield. The Boers had fought for their independence in 1881 – and won – and they would fight again if necessary.

British politicians had long wanted to create a federation in South Africa, drawing together the 'British' colonies of the Cape and Natal with the independent Boer republics of the Transvaal and the Orange Free State. The British had even annexed the Transvaal in 1877, but had been forced by defeat in the First Boer War to restore its independence. Nevertheless, Britain retained an undefined right of suzerainty over the Boer republics and, as more and more of southern Africa came under British control through the land-grabbing policies of Cecil Rhodes's British South Africa Company, the future for the republics seemed uncertain. Queen Victoria openly approved of Cecil Rhodes's actions, asking the great man at Windsor in December 1894, 'What have you been doing since I last saw you, Mr Rhodes?' Rhodes modestly replied, 'I have added two provinces to Your Majesty's dominions.' The Queen concluded, 'Ah, I wish some of my Ministers, who take away my provinces, would do as much.' In fact, Rhodes had won control of both Matabeleland and Mashonaland from their native rulers, and was administering the whole area as Rhodesia. But even this was not enough for Rhodes, who once said, 'I would annex the planets if I could.' Rhodes wanted the Transvaal and was prepared to go to any lengths to add it to the empire. He thought his mission divinely inspired: 'If there be a God, I think that what He would like me to do is to paint as much of the map of Africa British as possible and to do what I can elsewhere to promote the unity and extend the influence of the English-speaking race.'

The discovery of gold in the Transvaal and the 'invasion' of the Rand by the Uitlanders began to be seen by the British and the Boers as a prelude to a British take-over. However, the Boer republics had acquired an ally in the German Kaiser, Wilhelm II, who supplied the republics with German arms and seemed intent on thwarting the plans of Colonial Secretary, Joseph Chamberlain, and the Cape prime minister, Cecil Rhodes, to create a totally British South Africa.

To Cecil Rhodes, what could not be achieved by negotiation must be achieved by force. Using their grievances as a cover, Rhodes planned to foment an uprising of the Uitlanders in Johannesburg and then send in a military force, led by his friend and administrator of Bechuanaland, Doctor Jameson, to support the rebels. Although the Uitlanders were not to know it, all this was just a prelude to the raising of the British flag over the Transvaal. Yet one of the most curious things about the 'Jameson Raid' on 29 December, 1895, was that nobody – except perhaps for Jameson himself – actually wanted it to take place. The good doctor rode in the belief that he was going to the aid of the Uitlanders and that he would be welcomed with open arms. He was completely wrong. Just as wrong, in fact, was Cecil Rhodes who, for once, seems to have mislaid his shrewd common sense. How he supposed that Jameson with a few hundred men could overthrow the Boer government in the Transvaal which, just fifteen years before, had defeated and humiliated a British army of regulars under Sir George Colley at Majuba Hill, is a complete mystery. The Uitlanders were neither as strong nor as committed as Jameson thought and the Boers neither so weak nor distracted as Rhodes believed. They had painted a picture based on their own wishes and convinced themselves that things were as they wished them to be.

In fact, the Uitlanders were far too prosperous to bestir themselves to anything as risky as an armed insurrection. They had political grievances to be certain, but they were making money and that is why they had come to South Africa in the first place. They were not settlers, they were entrepreneurs. And if some more valuable commodity should be found in some far off part of God's earth tomorrow, many of them would have packed up and taken ship without a second thought. Their stake in South Africa was economic. They had spilled no blood on the soil as the Boers had repeatedly done in their struggles against the British and the Bantu tribes. All that really concerned them was that they should be taxed more fairly and that they should receive equal treatment with the local Boer inhabitants. In schools, for example, the Boers had insisted that English-speaking children should be taught in Afrikaans or not at all. Most Uitlanders, in fact, were not pre-

A cartoon of Cecil Rhodes, prime minister of the Cape at the time of the Jameson Raid.
Rhodes hoped for a rising among the Uitlanders of the Transvaal and it was to this purpose that
Rhodes sent his deputy, Dr Jameson, on his fateful mission. Rhodes was the imperialist *par
excellence* and added vast areas of central and southern Africa to the British Empire.

pared to give up their own nationality to become citizens of the Transvaal. Yet, hostile as the Boers were to the Uitlanders, they could not overlook the fact that the new people had brought enormous wealth into the Transvaal, so much so that in the period 1885–95, the revenue of the state had risen from £200,000 a year to more than £4 million.

By 1895 the population of the Rand goldfields was 100,000, of whom at least half were whites and the rest Bantus or Cape Coloureds. Of the 50,000 whites, nearly 90 per cent were Uitlanders and 75 per cent of British stock. As a result, it was impossible for Britain to stand by and watch her citizens being denied their civil rights by the Boers, who comprised a mere tenth of the total population. On

the other hand, President Kruger of the Transvaal realized that the only way to keep this vast influx of people from overwhelming the Boers was to deny them any participation in the politics or the administration of the Transvaal. He did not want to see the British flag hoisted in the Transvaal by the hordes of British prospectors pouring into the Rand. Before 1882 prospective voters had needed just one year's residence to qualify, but after that date the Boers restricted the vote to those born in the Transvaal or resident there for fourteen years. This inevitably disenfranchised all the Uitlanders. Kruger had made it clear that he would never allow the British to gain control of the Transvaal by the ballot box. In Cape Town, Cecil Rhodes noted Kruger's intention to deny the Uitlanders any rights in the Transvaal. He therefore put all the resources of his Consolidated Goldfields Company at the disposal of the Uitlander cause and sent his brother, Colonel Frank Rhodes, to the Rand to coordinate the Uitlanders' efforts to take control – by revolution if necessary – of the entire Rand. Once Frank Rhodes had organized the Uitlanders in a general rising, Rhodes planned to send in a military force to their aid and to achieve this he negotiated with a friendly Bechuana chieftain for the use of the town of Pitsani, situated in Bechuanaland just three miles from the Transvaal frontier.

The British Secretary of State for the Colonies, Joseph Chamberlain, had acquiesced in Rhodes's scheme for the Rand, but was unable to commit his government openly to supporting the uprising. In addition, the British High Commissioner in South Africa, Sir Hercules Robinson, was also apprised of Rhodes's plan. However, while Rhodes planned to support a rising of the Uitlanders, he received warnings from his brother that all was not well. It appears that in October 1895, the gold industry was booming on the Rand and hundreds of new prospectors were reaching Johannesburg daily. Everyone was entirely preoccupied with making money and nobody was in the least concerned with the idea of rising against the Boer authorities, except those who had failed to find gold. In any case, the Uitlanders may have been looking for the independence of the Rand, but the last thing they wanted was to win freedom from the Boers only to see the British take their place. The problem was that this was precisely what Cecil Rhodes wanted. Indeed, he had informed Joseph Chamberlain that this was his entire purpose in fomenting rebellion on the Rand.

Meanwhile, Doctor Jameson was assembling his forces at Pitsani. Leander Starr Jameson was a Scot and a romantic, reading little but the works of Sir Walter Scott, and taking as his model the eighteenth-century British soldier, Robert Clive. In later years Jameson was to be the model for Rudyard Kipling's famous poem *If*. Jameson was enormously popular with everyone who knew him and was given the supreme accolade for any Victorian gentleman: favourable comparison with animals. Lord Rosebury reached the heights when he described Jameson as having 'the eyes of an affectionate dog . . . and there can scarcely be higher praise'. To others he had 'the nostrils of a racehorse' and the

eager anticipation of a 'Scotch terrier ready to pounce'. Unfortunately, Jameson was also an impatient and arrogant man, who underestimated the difficulties that faced him. Easy victories with his Maxim guns over Lobengula's Matabele, and the disorganised Mashona, made him appear a 'Superman' to many people. But when dealing with the Boers he appeared a fool, saying 'anyone can take the Transvaal with half a dozen revolvers!'.

Rhodes's original plan had been for 5000 rifles and a million rounds of ammunition to be smuggled into Johannesburg for the use of the Uitlander rebels who, it was estimated, already had 1000 rifles of their own. To supplement these forces, Jameson would lead a further 1500 horsemen across the Transvaal from Bechuanaland. As a result, a full 9000 Uitlanders and their supporters would rise against the Boers and overthrow their rule in the Transvaal. Unfortunately, these figures were exaggerated. Just 3000 rifles reached Johannesburg and only half of these were even unpacked by the less-than-wholehearted revolutionaries. Jameson, meanwhile, had been able to muster just 500 Rhodesian policemen – the bulk of the Bechuana Police refused to ride with him as his actions conflicted with their loyalty to the British Crown – and with this depleted force he was planning to overthrow the Transvaal. In addition, the spare horses, forage and supplies that had been promised never reached Jameson because the man responsible for arranging them went on holiday instead.

In Johannesburg, the preparations for the Uitlander rising were conducted with as much secrecy as the local town crier usually employs in giving notice of a fire. Uitlanders drilled in the open, marching up and down the streets fully armed, in the full view of the local Boer population. Every club and bar hummed with news of the weapons that were being smuggled into the city ready for the rising. The Boers would have had to be drunk or stupid not to know what was being planned. The British – unable to rid themselves of their absurd interest in sporting affairs – used the language of polo and horse-racing for their 'secret' messages telegraphed between Capetown and Johannesburg, the rising being referred to as the 'polo tournament'. The rising in Johannesburg was never taken very seriously. When Jameson kept an appointment to meet Frank Rhodes in Johannesburg to discuss the distribution of weapons he found a message from Rhodes, apologizing for breaking the appointment but explaining that he was busy teaching a lady to ride a bicycle.

Back at Pitsani, Jameson was preparing to write himself – somewhat prematurely – into the history books. He had decided that he was to be a second 'Clive of India' and that his Maxim guns would 'draw a zone of lead a mile wide on each side of his column in which no Boer would be able to live'. It was stirring stuff and might have proved convincing if penned by Rider Haggard or G. A. Henty. In November, he asked the Uitlander leaders to send him a letter in which they would call on him to come to the rescue of thousands of unarmed British men, women and children whose lives were being endangered by the Boer authorities. Armed with this justification he could lead his men through the fires of hell to free his people from oppression.

In Britain, however, Joseph Chamberlain was faced with a difficult situation. Aware that the Uitlanders wished to govern themselves and had no desire to see the Union flag raised in Johannesburg, the Colonial Secretary was uncertain whether to encourage Rhodes and Jameson to carry out the planned rebellion at all. In the end, Chamberlain concluded that Rhodes's best chance of keeping the Uitlanders up to their promise of rebelling against the Boers was to launch Jameson sooner rather than later. However, some American Uitlanders made it clear to Frank Rhodes that they would join no rebellion intended to place them once again under the rule of their old imperial masters – Great Britain. In fact, so hostile were the Uitlanders to the notion of a British take-over on the Rand that it would have been far wiser for Rhodes and Jameson to call off the planned rebellion. Instead, Rhodes simply assured everyone that Jameson would not 'ride' until the moment was right.

Rhodes himself was in a cleft stick. On the one hand Chamberlain was telling him to expedite matters; on the other, his brother was telling him that the 'polo tournament' was postponed and that the Uitlanders were not ready to rebel. In the end, Rhodes chose the line of least resistance and sided with the 'big battalions', telegraphing poor Jameson at Pitsani that the rebellion would take place on 28 December 1895. The Uitlanders, however, were not prepared to be misrepresented in this way and they informed Jameson that under no circumstances should he ride until he heard from them again.

In London, Chamberlain had received a startling message from the German ambassador, informing him that Berlin was not prepared to countenance a change in the status of the Transvaal at that time and that Germany was prepared to support President Kruger against any such pressures. This came close to blowing Chamberlain's cover and the Colonial Secretary hastened to cover his own tracks, if necessary, by abandoning Rhodes and Jameson. He telegraphed Sir Hercules Robinson at Cape Town with the instruction that Jameson's proposed 'raid' should be stopped at all costs. But at Pitsani, Jameson was only too aware that each day brought desertions from his force. If he waited too long then the whole venture might prove impossible. He felt he had no alternative but to act straight away. After all, Robert Clive would not have waited for any man's orders. Jameson therefore decided to begin the raid, publishing the letter of invitation sent by the Johannesburg Uitlanders, and crossed into the Transvaal.

At the last moment Rhodes tried to stop Jameson from leaving Pitsani but it was too late – Jameson's men had cut the telegraph wires. Rhodes meanwhile denounced the pusillanimity of Joseph Chamberlain, commenting 'You cannot expect much of a product of the Birmingham workshop.' He was beside himself with emotion, claiming that if Jameson had started then he would have to resign as prime minister of the Cape. Chamberlain instructed Robinson to tell Rhodes that the charter of his company might be revoked as the penalty for Jameson's action, if it should lead to fighting with the Boers.

The Jameson Raid came as no surprise to President Kruger, who had long suspected that Cecil Rhodes would try something of the kind. Accordingly, he had his old white horse already saddled, and slept with his gun by his side. His spies had kept him fully informed of what was going on in the Uitlander movement and he was aware that there would be no rising of any significance in Johannesburg, so it was really a matter of 'arresting' Doctor Jameson when his raid had finally run out of momentum. He knew the path that Jameson was taking, mainly because Jameson's men had got drunk while they were supposed to be cutting the telegraph wires and had cut down a lot of fencing wire instead. The local Boer farmers had passed the message up the line to Pretoria and Boer commandos were called out, riding up and down the flanks of Jameson's column. The Commandant-General of the Transvaal, General Joubert, ordered Jameson to withdraw but the good doctor replied that he had

Doctor Leander Starr Jameson and some of his fellow-conspirators are pictured here aboard the British ship that returned them to England to stand trial at Bow street after the failure of their famous 'raid' in 1896.

come at the invitation of the Uitlanders and was there to maintain their rights. A light skirmish ensued, but it was not enough to worry an old Boer woman who wandered to and fro during the shooting, picking up used cartridge cases.

In Cape Town, Cecil Rhodes had one hope and that was that the Uitlanders would come out in support of Jameson should he ever succeed in reaching Johannesburg. But his hopes were without foundation. The Uitlanders had told Jameson not to cross into the Transvaal and they felt unwilling to risk their lives to rescue him now that he had ignored their warning.

Jameson, to his chagrin, now had to face opponents armed with 'weapons' supplied by his own friends. Commander de Wet met Jameson and showed him the order from the High Commissioner, Sir Hercules Robinson, ordering him not to invade the Transvaal. It was a cruel blow to Jameson's hopes, but he decided to ignore it and rode on. After three days and nights of riding, and with most of his men and horses thoroughly exhausted, Jameson's

column reached Doornkop, some thirty miles from Johannesburg. Here the Boers decided to stop the invading column and surround it. After a brief battle, Jameson's men were forced to surrender, using a white flag made from a Hottentot woman's dirty apron. It was a fitting end for a farcical operation. Just one Boer had been killed in the fighting but the invaders had suffered over a hundred casualties, including seventeen dead, from the accurate fire of the Boer riflemen. To compound the humiliation, Jameson and his men were first imprisoned in Pretoria and then handed over to British police in Natal, prior to being shipped back to England and put on trial at Bow Street, like common criminals. The Boers, not a people noted for their sense of fun, summed up their view of the Jameson Raid with sardonic humour. A Boer asked a British woman what was the colour of the English flag, to which she replied that it was red, white and blue. The Boer retorted, 'Oh, no, I have seen it twice: at Majuba and Doornkop. It is a dirty white rag.'

The Jameson Raid and its dismal denouement was a humiliation not just for Cecil Rhodes – who saw his dreams of painting the map red temporarily checked – but also for the British government and people, who suffered a quite unexpected setback in a region from which many disasters seemed to come. The Prince of Wales – later Edward VII – commented, 'The accounts from the Transvaal have been an unpleasant New Year's card.' The whole nation was plunged in gloom. And then came a stroke of luck. Onto the stage stepped that bungler *extraordinaire*, Kaiser Wilhelm II of Germany (see p. 71 and p. 91), and in a matter of moments the British nation pulled itself together, stood tall and felt a thrill of pride pulsing through its veins. The German monarch had sent President Kruger a telegram, dated 3 January, 1896, in which he congratulated him on overcoming the 'armed bands' that had broken into his country without the need to call 'on the aid of friendly Powers'. It was an amazing *faux pas* which was bound to bring a stinging reaction from the British government. The Kaiser's telegram had suggested that Germany would have come to the aid of Kruger had he needed it and this would have meant taking armed action within an area over which Britain still held suzerain rights. The British newspapers were soon ringing with headlines like 'Hands off Africa'. Queen Victoria gave her grandson a good 'ticking off' by telegram and 'Willy', the dutiful grandson, replied in an apologetic and crawling fashion. Kruger, partly amused and partly irritated by the collapse of stout party, told the German ambassador 'The old woman just sneezed and you ran away.' In Cape Town, Cecil Rhodes, who had been as depressed as a condemned man facing the gallows, was suddenly elated. Three years later he told the Kaiser, 'You see, I was a naughty boy and you tried to whip me. Now my people were quite ready to whip me for being a naughty boy, but directly you did it, they said, "No, if this is anybody's business it is ours." The result was that Your Majesty got yourself very much disliked by the English people, and I never got whipped at all.' Rhodes's words, however, could not disguise the fact that the Jameson Raid had soured relations between Britons and Boers in South Africa to such an extent that full-scale war could not be long delayed.

TITUS OATES AND THE POPISH PLOT

Rarely in history has an acute sense of smell been more necessary than it was in England in 1678. The fact that the English people failed to smell a rat when one presented itself in the shape of Titus Oates, exposed the country to one of its bloodiest and least comprehensible bouts of mass hysteria. Oates was without doubt one of the most loathsome rogues ever to impose himself on any civilized state. The failure of moderate men to remove him or of ambitious politicians to resist the urge to make use of him reflects badly on the morals of Restoration England.

The Popish Plot was 'discovered' in August 1678. The king first learned of it when he was walking in St James's Park and was accosted by one Christopher Kirkby, a man known to Charles as he shared the monarch's interest in chemical experiments. Charles listened to Kirkby's warning that there was a plot to assassinate him, possibly even that day, and that two men named Grove and Pickering were waiting in the park to shoot him. In the event nothing happened, but that evening the matter was brought to the king's attention again, this time by an eccentric clergyman named Israel Tonge. According to Tonge the plot was a complex one, involving the Jesuits, the English Catholics and even King Louis XIV of France. After Charles was assassinated, the story went, a French army would invade England. But the king was unimpressed and regarded the story as too far-fetched to deserve serious consideration. Israel Tonge was, at least on one subject, a dangerous madman. Eccentric in most things, he was positively vitriolic once the word 'Jesuit' was mentioned. He claimed to dream dreams and see visions, and in all of these the Jesuits figured prominently: doing harm, plotting against the lives of

Protestants, sanctifying daggers for killing the righteous, burning London to the ground, and pulling the tails of 'Protestant dogs'. It was the purest nonsense, but spoken with conviction much of what he said seemed possible to anti-Catholics everywhere.

Still, the story might have ended there had not Charles handed the whole matter over to the Earl of Danby for his investigation. Danby was more willing to listen to Israel Tonge than the king had been, as he was hostile both to the English 'papists' and to France. And at this stage Tonge received support from a man more rogue than eccentric – Titus Oates. In fact, there was nothing coincidental about Oates's sudden appearance, as he and Tonge had rented a room together and had been rehearsing their parts for some time. As a contemporary wrote, 'Tonge made the music all this while and Oates only drew the bellows. He, poor devil, swore to anything that came next . . . A false oath in his mouth was no more than an envenomed tooth in the mouth of a mad dog.'

Titus Oates was born in 1649 and had, apparently, enjoyed a good education at Merchant Taylor's School and Westminster, as well as at Gonville and Caius College, Cambridge. But the truth was rather different. Oates was, in fact, thoroughly disreputable and had been expelled from both schools and sent down from university. He had spent some time in Anglican orders, but had then converted to Catholicism, before seeing the error of his ways. He specialized in perjury and was such an established liar that it is incredible how many people's lives and fortunes came to depend on his word.

Oates was one of nature's mistakes. In appearance he seems to have closely resembled a pig, with a low forehead, small nose, tiny deep-set eyes, fat cheeks and a vast, 'wobbling chin'. As a child he was known as 'filthy mouth' as a result of his constantly running nose and was prone to convulsive fits. As he grew up he proved to be an unloving and unloved child, well known for his foul language and the abuse he heaped on his mother. As he grew rich on the suffering of others, he liked to wear fine clothes, but the effect was as ludicrous as dressing a warthog in court finery. His voice was high-pitched yet vulgar and his speech was very much 'that of the gutter'. He wailed in a 'sing-song' manner, but his words were only one part of the impression he made. Few of the men who met Oates ever forgot the experience. His capacity to influence apparently intelligent men against their better judgment has persuaded some historians to regard him as a mesmerist.

Oates's readiness to lie was observed at several stages of his early life. Whilst at Cambridge he bought a coat from a poor tailor, promising to pay him on a certain date. When the time came for payment Oates insisted that he had already paid. In fact, he had sold the coat to a second-hand clothes dealer. The affronted tailor regained the coat and took the story to Oates's tutor at Cambridge. When questioned, Titus swore on the Bible that he had already paid and that his mother had sent him the money by the hand of a well-known carrier. But when this man was summoned he denied Titus's story and said he had never even seen him before. Titus was sent down from Cambridge. But his disgrace did not last long. A few months later he had 'slipped into orders' and become first a curate and then Vicar of the parish of Bobbing, in Sussex. But even here he caused trouble and had to be dismissed. He was often drunk, stole his neighbours' pigs and hens and committed acts of 'gross indecency' – presumably the sodomy that had earned him dismissal from both Westminster and Merchant Taylors' schools.

Titus then turned his attention to schoolmastering. In order to obtain the mastership of a school in Hastings, he accused the young schoolmaster who held the post of committing unnatural acts with the boys in his charge. The schoolmaster, William Parker, was imprisoned because of Titus's accusation and, to make matters more certain, Titus accused the young man's father of treason and sedition into the bargain. Both father and son were therefore facing capital charges, for in those days sodomy was an offence punishable by death. In the event, however, Titus's evidence against them could not be substantiated. The younger man accused of sodomy had a clear alibi against the charge and so furious were the local people at Titus's perjury that he was forced to run away to sea to avoid being lynched.

How Titus got himself a job afloat is difficult to understand. Nevertheless, in 1677 he was appointed as chaplain aboard one of His Majesty's ships and was just as quickly 'run aground' for indulging in his usual sexual preference. Titus was 'sailing very close to the wind' and, as his captain observed, 'If his Coat had not Pleaded for his Neck, he might have stretch'd for Buggery while he was under my command.' One of his shipmates agreed: 'Caught in the crime of sodomy, he narrowly escaped a hanging at the yardarm.' Fleeing for his life, Titus found refuge with the Jesuits, who treated him kindly and then, for some reason too difficult to fathom, unburdened themselves to him about their plots to kill the king. And this man – perjurer and sodomite – was the man whose testimony, rejected on so many previous occasions in his life, was to cost so many good and innocent Englishmen their lives in the gruesome manner then laid down by the law for treason.

On the advice of the Duke of York, the king's council decided to interrogate Oates. On 28 September 1678 he made a series of apparently fantastic allegations, involving nine Benedictine monks, three Carmelites, two Franciscans, ten Dominicans, 51 Jesuits, fourteen secular priests and innumerable Catholic nobles. Oates painted a picture of a country teeming with blood-crazed Catholics, queuing for the right to take a potshot at their king. But so many of the accusations were obviously ridiculous and easily refutable that it is surprising that Oates was not thrown into the Thames. However, the council persevered with the interrogation and eventually got the 'names' that they wanted. Oates accused the queen's physician Sir George Wakeman and a secretary to the Duchess of York, Edward Coleman, of plotting to kill Charles II. Without knowing it Oates had hit the bullseye. Although Wakeman easily rebutted the charges, Coleman was found to have been in communication with the French. Oates was now in his element. With a warrant signed by Danby and with a squad of soldiers marching at his back, he began rounding up known Jesuits, dragging them from their beds in the middle of the night – even the men who had been so kind to him in the past and who had saved him from starvation. Oates loved to reward kindness with a kick.

It was at this point that a mysterious incident assisted Oates in his campaign against the 'papists'. The Anglican magistrate, Sir Edmund Berry Godfrey, who had taken Oates's sworn deposition against Coleman and Wakefield, was found dead on Primrose Hill. He had been missing for five days and his battered body bore the marks of a wound from his own sword, administered after he had died. At once 'the world was awakened', and the hunt for murdering priests and treacherous 'papists' took off. From his uncertain start with the council, Oates was swept into prominence on a wave of public hysteria. In the streets of London the talk was that Godfrey had been murdered by the Jesuits to silence him. So threatening were the signs of unrest that the king was forced to return to his capital and summon Parliament.

Charles was unhappy at the direction of events. In his view Israel Tonge was a lunatic and Titus Oates a knave and a perjurer. Their accusations against prominent men like Wakeman and Coleman were ill-disguised attacks on his Catholic wife – Catherine of Braganza – and his brother, the Duke of York. Yet public feeling was running so high after the Godfrey murder that he knew he would have to have the so-called 'plot' examined. But opponents of the king and the 'Catholic Court', led by Anthony Ashley Cooper, first Earl of Shaftesbury, saw Oates and his plot as a heaven-sent opportunity to embarrass Charles and possibly exclude his brother James from the royal succession. As Shaftesbury later observed, 'I will not say who started the Game but I am sure I had the full hunting of it.' And so a corrupt alliance of unscrupulous politician and lying fanatic was going to plunge the country into two years of terror.

The atmosphere in London in the last days of 1678 was one of scarcely veiled hysteria. Men who dared to venture into the streets at night went fully armed or in company, and the ladies of the court took to carrying pistols in their muffs. Houses were searched for hidden caches of weapons, resulting in such discoveries as: 'from the Widow Platt – one old gun'. So fierce was the hatred of Catholics in the capital that its like had not been seen since the days of Edward VI and the Smithfield burnings in the previous century. Some Catholic widows, in their terror, married elderly but respectable Protestant widowers. As in the days of James I, seventy years before, a search was made of the cellars of the House of Commons in case a new Catholic attempt was being made to blow up Parliament. The Spanish ambassador's house was closely watched and a special fence erected to cut him off from contact with susceptible Protestants.

Meanwhile, Oates had begun making some startling revelations. He indicted five Catholic lords on a charge of plotting to kill the king and lead a foreign invasion. When he heard the news Charles laughed. The men in question were either too elderly to lead anything other than a quiet life or too idle to kill anything other than their time in as pleasurable a manner as they could invent. Nevertheless, at Shaftesbury's instigation the five peers were arrested to await trial. Now the hare was running and Shaftesbury was in pursuit. His next step was to demand the exclusion of James, Duke of York, from the royal succession. This took the smile off the king's face and made him address the 'Popish Plot' more seriously. He advised his brother to stay away from the Privy Council and addressed both Houses of Parliament, assuring them of his wish to ensure the security of the Protestant religion. But it was not enough. The hounds wanted blood. On 5 November 1678, it was not Guy Fawkes who sat on top of the city's bonfires, it was the Pope. Hideously, the burning pontiff let out real screams produced by cats imprisoned in the papal effigy.

Titus Oates was enjoying his power to make people really unhappy. His new target for denunciation was the queen herself. On 24 November, he told the king directly that his wife was working with her physician to poison him. To help him in this latest accusation, Oates was supported by a rogue named 'Captain' William Bedloe, no more a military man than Oates was a doctor. Bedloe had been employed by the Jesuits and, in spite of their kindness to him, had decided they were easy targets. Bedloe was prepared to say anything at all to keep the 'plot' rolling and his own fortune in the ascendant. He said he could corroborate everything Oates had said against the queen and Sir George Wakeman. In defence of his wife, Charles interviewed Titus Oates and caught him out in a number of important details. Certain that the man was a fraud and a liar, he ordered him to be imprisoned, but after a few days he was released on the orders of Parliament. A dangerous constitutional crisis was beginning to develop, with Shaftesbury and his supporters playing the parts previously occupied by such worthies as John Pym, John Hampden and Oliver Cromwell. Charles had no wish to follow his father's path or else 'travel again' and so he was forced to give Oates 'his head'.

With the prison at Newgate packed with Catholics of all ranks and condition, preparations were being made for the state trials that would expose the full horror of the 'Popish Plot'. The Lord Chief Justice Sir William Scroggs was well suited to the grisly task ahead, being a man 'scandalous, violent and intemperate'. With such a judge presiding, with juries who were convinced of the prisoners' guilt even before the trial began and with witnesses and accusers who were expert perjurers, the Catholic

prisoners never had a chance. First Edward Coleman was tried for treason and, although the evidence of Oates and Bedloe was unconvincing, his letters to France were considered treasonable and he was found guilty and executed. While this good man suffered the full extremity of the law, being drawn on a hurdle to Tyburn, hanged on the gallows until insensible, revived only to be castrated, disembowelled with his intestines burned on a fire while he still lived, and finally hacked into quarters and beheaded, his accusers were rewarded – Bedloe with a small allowance, and Oates with a fine state apartment at Whitehall and an allowance of £1200 a year. It was more than he had ever earned honestly in his whole life.

Titus Oates was now the man of the moment. A contemporary wrote of him: 'He walked about with his guards, assigned for the fear of the Papists murdering him . . . He put on an episcopal garb, silk gown and cassock, green hat, satin hatband and rose, long scarf, and was called "the saviour of the nation". . . He had three servants at his beck and call, and every morning two or three gentlemen waited upon him to dress him.' Secure in his fame Titus began to elaborate on his previous lies. Even more fantastic plots were afoot. The assassins were going to kill the king with silver bullets of a special shape so that the wound they inflicted could not be healed. The public listened agog. Meanwhile, Scroggs was working overtime, condemning men to a traitor's death while Oates – like some crazed witch doctor pointing a bone at his victims – kept finding more Catholics involved in his plots.

In England in 1678 reason had given way to hysteria. Reports reached Shaftesbury that 'a great knocking and digging in the earth' had been heard 'in some cellars adjoining the House of Commons'. Soon nobody in London went abroad without keeping at least one ear close to the ground. Next came a story from Dorset, along with the sworn statements of men who had witnessed the episode, that a French army had landed on the Isle of Purbeck and had drawn up in line, with their officers at their head. The Earl of Danby, the lord-lieutenant of Dorset, spurred his horse towards Hyde Park, sword in hand and shouting to everyone to take arms as the French were coming. The truth was somewhat less stimulating and became apparent the following day. Apparently, the observers of the French landing had been mistaken – or drunk. The French line of battle turned out to be a hedge and the officers nothing more than some horses grazing in a meadow.

The City of London – always a stronghold of the opponents of the Court party – was carrying out its own purge. Any 'papists' or indeed any people suspected of being Catholic were driven from their homes and jobs and forbidden to return within ten miles of London. Chains were draped across the London streets to prevent charges by Popish cavalry and the Trained Bands were called out to place cannon in front of prominent buildings. Sir Thomas Player, the City Chamberlain, became so confused by events that he explained himself thus: 'I do not know but the next morning we may all rise with our throats cut!' City entrepreneurs seized their opportunities. Silk armour was produced for fashionable ladies and gentlemen in case there was a general massacre of Protestants. Presumably resistant to the most dangerous silk daggers, it apparently sold very well. Ladies had their fans decorated with gruesome scenes from Doctor Oates's plot, while playing cards were printed with key figures from the saga, including Titus himself with a normal sized chin. One can only presume that Israel Tonge was the joker, and Titus the knave.

One effect of the hysteria was that Jesuits were spotted everywhere, in the guise of shoemakers and coopers, and even the Frenchmen who entertained the children with their little marionettes were forced into hiding. London's disease soon spread into the countryside. Every unusual incident sparked a Catholic witch-hunt. Five sheep were found with their bellies ripped open and only the fat taken. Twenty cows were secretly milked by night, presumably by Jesuit storm troopers.

Throughout the country mothers echoed the words of one London lady with an eye to a fortune. 'Oh, Christ!' she said, 'That I had but a daughter to throw her into the arms of Oates or Bedloe.' The height of absurdity was reached when Titus decided that he wished the College of Arms to investigate his lineage so that he might have a coat of arms to match his importance. One is tempted to create one for him. The crafty heralds found a little known one of a family that had died out and foisted it on the rogue. Those who knew – and the secret soon spread – smiled every time the impostor referred to his 'blazon'. Nevertheless, a rumour was circulating at court that Titus was to be married to one of the Earl of Shaftesbury's daughters.

Meanwhile, the judicial butchery continued. Oates settled a number of personal scores, managing to implicate anyone in the 'plot' who had done him a bad turn and gleefully attending their executions at Tyburn to watch them hacked to pieces. But the public taste for blood was close to satiation and public opinion was turning against the inquisitors. Scroggs was quick to grasp this subtle change and Oates was astonished when those he accused began to be found not guilty and to be released. This was the moment that the king had been waiting for and he swooped on Titus Oates, like an eagle on a tiny rodent. On 31 August 1681 he was commanded by Black Rod to remove himself from his apartments at Whitehall. It was the beginning of the end. As Oates's fortunes waned, all those who had feared him began to take their revenge. Had Oates possessed a modicum of sense he would have left the country or at least adopted a low profile now that he had lost the backing of major politicians like Shaftesbury, but he was never known for his common sense. No sooner had he left Whitehall than he began denouncing the king for his perfidy, the Duke of York for his Catholicism and indeed anyone else who had crossed his path and had escaped unbutchered. He was promptly arrested on charges of sedition and thrown into prison. But it was the accession of James II – the Duke of York whom Titus had done so much to harm – that marked his final ignominy. James had a score to settle with the great Doctor Oates and it ended with Titus being led from his cell wearing a hat with the inscription 'Titus Oates, convicted upon full evidence of two horrid perjuries'. He was placed in the pillory at the gate of Westminster Hall, where he was pelted with eggs. A contemporary balladeer imagined what he must be thinking:

> From three prostrate Kingdoms at once to adore me
> And no less than three Parliaments kneeling before me;
> From hanging of Lords with a word or a frown,
> And no more than an oath to the shaking a crown:
> From all these brave pranks
> Now to have no more thanks,
> Than to look through a hole, through two damned oaken planks.

The following day he was pilloried in the City of London and on the third day he was stripped, tied to a cart's tale and whipped from Aldgate to Newgate, all the time making 'hideous bellowings'. Not content with this, James ordered Oates to be whipped again on the next day, during which he had to be dragged on a hurdle as he was too weak to walk. So

TESTIS OVAT

Titus Oates in the pillory after the accession of King James II in 1685. Oates was the moving force behind the 'Popish Plot' which condemned many Catholics to death as traitors in the years 1678 and 1679. Oates was in fact an inveterate perjurer.

severe was his beating that he almost died, yet sympathy for his plight was tempered with the thought that his perjury had cost the lives of many good and innocent men, who had died in far greater agony than he suffered. For the next three years

Titus Oates lingered in prison and, even though he was released with the accession of William and Mary in 1688, and granted a small pension, his fall was an established fact. He died peacefully in his bed in 1705, one of history's least lovable rogues.

SERGEANT, FIELD MARSHAL, PRESIDENT IDI AMIN

The career of Idi Amin may serve as a warning of the dangers of promoting a man beyond his abilities but not his ambitions, of appeasing bullies and of patronizing one's intellectual inferiors. Each of these common if inadvisable human traits played a part in the rise of a British Army cook to the presidency of a newly-independent African country and to a seat in the pantheon reserved for history's most brutal and loathsome tyrants. What deepens the sense of shock in learning of Idi Amin's misdeeds is the knowledge that so much human suffering was inflicted by a man with a broad smile and a ready, if heavy-handed, sense of humour. It is said that many of his victims died with the sound of his laughter still ringing in their ears.

Idi Amin had joined the King's African Rifles in 1946 as a cook but his phenomenal size – six feet four inches and nearly twenty stone (he was the heavyweight boxing champion of Uganda) – suggested that the Army might find a more active role for him than peeling potatoes. In fact, Idi Amin was exactly the sort of man that the British authorities were trying to encourage in their African colonies, as these approached the dates of their independence. As a result, corners were cut and men like Amin – 'big, uncouth, uneducated and willing to obey orders' were quickly promoted to sergeant and then to commissioned rank. This might have worked where European or experienced native officers would be available to set them an example, but in Uganda this was not so and Amin was promoted far beyond his ability. The British officers who knew Amin were not at all worried about the future. They called him 'a good chap' and 'a bit thick – a little short of the grey matter', but they trusted him to do the job, provided that somebody else was always

there to give the orders. The notion that one day Amin might be giving the orders himself would never have occurred to his British officers. In any case, by that stage they would be long gone, breeding horses for Newmarket or potting grouse in Scotland. The British officers concluded, if they had to choose the best native officers available, better the slow-witted but tough and loyal long-service men than those who were clever but inexperienced and possibly politically ambitious. However, this was their big mistake; they were underestimating Amin's own ambitions. Unintelligent he might seem to the British, with their public school and university backgrounds, but Amin had a ruthless cunning that might even have proved too much for them if the occasion had ever presented itself.

In fact, the British already had their suspicions about Amin, but they did not let these prevent them from recommending him for promotion. During military operations in Kenya in 1961, Amin – at that time a lieutenant – had ordered his men to shoot dozens of tribesmen, leaving their bodies to be eaten by hyenas. He also apparently used a technique of his own devising to extract information from cattle thieves: getting the suspect to lay his penis upon a table top and then threatening to sever it with a machete if he did not talk. Amin had personally cut off the genitals of eight tribesmen. The British authorities considered prosecuting Amin, but as Ugandan independence was only a matter of weeks away they decided not to rock the boat and the matter was hushed up. The British Governor, Sir Walter Coutts did inform Milton Obote, then Ugandan prime minister designate, about Amin's atrocities, but Obote decided to take no action either. After all, Amin would be the senior native officer in the Ugandan Army once the British left, and to have dismissed him would have thrown the country into disorder. But Obote was also making a dreadful mistake, one with terrible consequences for his own and his country's future.

Such had been the rush to give independence to Britain's African colonies – in the wake of the catastrophic Belgian transfer of power in the Congo – that Britain's prime minister, Harold Macmillan, took risks with the security of the administrations established in the newly independent states. Yet, with the Kabaka of Buganda as ruler and Milton Obote as prime minister, Uganda seemed to be well set on the path to a peaceful transition of power. In the fast-rising Idi Amin, however, the country was saddled with a dangerous psychopath. On Independence Day – 9 October 1962 – came further promotion for Amin, this time to major. Within a few months all the British officers had left Uganda for good and Amin had risen to colonel, with the additional rank of Army Chief of Staff, entitling him to play a part in the most secret councils of Obote's government. In 1966, with the help of the army and especially of his close ally, Colonel Amin, Milton Obote overthrew the Kabaka, forcing him to flee to Britain. As a reward, Amin received further promotions – first to brigadier and then general – but Obote, the socialist intellectual, was fatally underestimating the potential danger from the shambling giant, who always seemed so ready and willing to obey orders. It was the quality that the British had always valued in Amin, yet they had warned Obote not to trust him too far. Amin was a good NCO, but he was also a callous brute who should never have been left in command of anything bigger than a squad of new recruits.

Amin waited his chance and when Obote left the country to attend the Commonwealth Prime Minister's Conference in Singapore, he used his soldiers to seize power, at midnight on 25 January 1971. Significantly, there is clear evidence that British intelligence knew about what Amin was planning and may even have assisted the coup. Certainly the 'bluff' soldier who loved everything British seemed a better bet for the future than the socialist Obote, with his dangerous left-wing tendencies. Amin's coup was immensely popular in Uganda, where the merchant classes in particular feared that Obote had been moving towards a Communist state. Other African leaders – notably Julius Nyerere of Tanzania and Kenneth Kaunda of Zambia, friends and allies

of the fallen Ugandan leader – were shocked at the indecent haste with which Britain recognized the new regime. At first Amin played his hand with consummate skill, having the much-loved Kabaka's body flown back from Britain and staging a magnificent state funeral in Uganda. It seemed that the 'mindless brute' had out-thought Obote at every turn. A British observer commented, 'I have never encountered a more benevolent and apparently popular leader than General Amin.' But appearances were very deceptive. In the first place, Amin said he was going to call elections within a short period. Instead, he carried out a purge, killing 3000 Army officers and men and over 10,000 civilians, mostly from the Acholi and Langi tribes, which had been the main supporters of Milton Obote. Unable to identify all Amin's political opponents, his killers – named 'The Public Safety Unit' – simply murdered everyone whose name began with 'O', as did many of the names of the Acholi and Langi tribesmen. One of Amin's military rivals, Brigadier Hussein Sulieman, was also murdered and Amin kept his head, along with those of others of his enemies, in a refrigerator.

Abroad, Amin's successful coup was welcomed by both Britain and Israel. Britain preferred the strong, ex-British Army sergeant to the socialist Obote, while the Israelis were pleased to have a Muslim ally at a time when all other Muslim states were hostile to her. However, these friendships did not last long. Amin pushed his friends too far, asking Moshe Dayan of Israel to let him have 24 Phantom jet fighters. When asked why he needed them he simply replied, 'I need them to bomb Tanzania.' Both Israel and Britain refused Amin's request for arms and this resulted in his decisive switch to a new friendship with oil-rich Libya, whose leader Colonel Gadaffi denied Amin nothing.

Although Idi Amin had grown up under a British colonial regime and admired and imitated much about Britain, he could not resist ridiculing her on occasions. He enjoyed a state visit to Britain, when he met the Conservative prime minister Edward Heath and the Queen, and had a successful trip to Scotland, for which country he developed a special affection, loving everything from bagpipes to kilts and from Scotch whisky to Highland soldiers. On one occasion he contacted Queen Elizabeth and asked that he be provided with a plane, an escort of Scottish soldiers to carry him to the Commonwealth Games and a pair of size 14 brogue shoes. He was a great supporter of the idea of Scottish independence, writing letters of encouragement to the Scottish Nationalist leader in Britain, and raising the matter of Scottish devolution during discussions he had with with a puzzled Mao Zedong.

Unfortunately, he was constantly asking the British for weapons to attack his neighbours, including Harrier Jump-jets and Highland soldiers, which they were not prepared to supply. Amin once wrote to both the British and the American governments suggesting that they allow him to put a stop to their problems in Northern Ireland and Vietnam – presumably with his machete or his big, brown boots. During a moment of economic crisis in Britain, Amin sent a letter to Edward Heath 'offering to organise a whip-round amongst Uganda's friends if you will let me know the exact position of the mess'. He promptly ordered a plane-load of vegetables to be flown to help the starving in Britain and started a 'Save Britain Fund'. These may have been weak jokes but they had all the power of centuries of colonial oppression behind them.

It was Amin's decision to expel the Ugandan Asians on 5 August 1972 that condemned his country to utter economic ruin. The Asians were the backbone of the Ugandan economy, running 85 per cent of the businesses, and without their entrepreneurial skills there really was no future for Uganda. Economics, however, was not one of Idi Amin's strong subjects. He simply handed over Uganda's hotels and shops to his soldiers as if he was distributing the booty from a looted city. Photographs of the time show Idi giving shops away to his friends and senior officers, whether they wanted them or not or knew the least thing about operating them. They reacted in typical tribal fashion, inviting their kin to look over the place and take what they wanted. What was left after the party would be sold, for the highest price possible, if there were any buyers. The Ugandan soldiers knew nothing about contacting suppliers or restocking their premises. Soon the previously affluent shopping streets of Kampala were like those of a ghost town. Meanwhile, there developed a black market where the tribal 'freebies' found their way back into the trade cycle. Some products like sugar and butter were unobtainable for years, as were many vital drugs and medicines. To keep his troops happy, however, Amin organized the import of consumer goods and luxury foods for them alone, which were paid for by unfair taxation of the Ugandan masses, who lacked

even essential foods. The Asians were forced to leave Uganda without any of their possessions and with virtually no money, everything having been taken from them at Kampala airport.

The economic effects of the eviction were catastrophic. Just a few months after Amin took over the running of the huge Asian-owned sugar facilities, he was forced to buy sugar from Kenya. In 1973, 30,000 tons of sugar was imported into the country and the sugar factories in Uganda had to recruit workers from abroad to fill the technical and managerial positions vacated by the Asians. The black market swiftly seized sugar stocks and increased prices by 800 per cent, with not a shilling being paid to the government in taxation. Tourism stopped almost entirely and Uganda's hospitals closed for lack of trained staff. Along the shores of Lake Victoria the magnificent hotels stood empty, with thousands of local workers unable to find work. Idi Amin, however, compared the 'success' of his economy with that of Edward Heath's in Britain. As he pointed out, not a day had been lost to strikes in Uganda. Could the British match that? He offered bananas as a cure for Britain's ills. Somehow, it was symbolic.

Amin's growing hostility to Britain encouraged him to write patronizingly to ex-prime minister Edward Heath, after his election defeat in 1974, that he had heard Heath had been relegated from being prime minister and was now an obscure 'bandmaster'. He invited Heath to bring his band to Uganda, where he would be well paid with chickens and goats for his performances. He also wrote to Richard Nixon, telling him he was one of the most brilliant leaders in the western world and that he hoped he would soon recover from Watergate. Amin's sense of humour knew no bounds. He even claimed that some Asians had been painting themselves black with boot polish in an effort to stay in Uganda.

The Ugandan leader's link up with Colonel Gadaffi of Libya involved a switch away from his friendship with Israel. After the massacre of Israeli athletes at the Munich Olympics in 1972, Amin wrote to the UN Secretary General, Kurt Waldheim, praising the action of the Palestinian guerrillas. In the letter he extolled the virtues of Waldheim's fellow-Austrian, Adolf Hitler: 'Germany is the right place, where, when Hitler was Prime Minister and Supreme Commander, he burnt over six million Jews. This is because Hitler and all the German people know that the Israelis are not people who are working in the interests of the people of the world.' So astonishing was the letter that the Ugandan ambassador in New York hastily spread the word that it was merely one of his president's 'pranks'. After the Yom Kippur War of 1973 he declared that 'Arab victory was certain and that the [Israeli] prime minister, Mrs Golda Meir had better tuck up her knickers and run.'

By this time medical reports were suggesting that Amin was a victim of hypomania, resulting from a long-term syphilitic condition. Symptoms included attacks of violent and conflicting emotions and ideas, paranoia, acute schizophrenia and even general paralysis. In simple terms, Amin was as unbalanced as any major political or military leader has ever been for such a prolonged period. The schizophrenia might be seen in his choice of twin idols –

Queen Victoria and Adolf Hitler, statues of both of whom he had erected in Kuala Lumpur.

It is better to draw a veil – indeed several layers of veils – over the details of Amin's atrocious internal repression. As a mass murderer Amin must be figured among the most terrible, with a list of the dead running into hundreds of thousands. Yet it is not only the number of his victims that is shocking, but the manner of their killing – sometimes forced to execute each other with sledgehammers – and the perverse pleasure he took in carrying out many murders himself, jumping on the prone figures of his victims and crushing their chests with his huge booted feet. In order to pay his killers, Amin charged the relatives of the dead to collect their bodies for burial. Nobody was safe from Idi Amin. He himself shot Ugandan Archbishop Luwun, he killed his friend, the British renegade Major Bob

President Idi Amin in cheerful mood as he introduces his young son to British prime minister James Callaghan and Denis Hills. Behind Amin's smiling face there lurked an insane and blood-crazed butcher.

Astles, head of the 'Anti-Corruption' unit, and he gave another British ex-patriate, Bob McKenzie, a lion's head as a goodbye gift – no sooner had McKenzie's plane taken off than the head exploded.

Before he fell out with Astles, the two used propaganda to try to impress Uganda's African neighbours. At a session of the Organisation for African Unity held in Kampala, Amin announced that he was marrying a new wife – a 'go-go' dancer from the Ugandan Army, part of the the 'Suicide Mechanized Unit Jazz Band'. Then, to demonstrate the skills of the Ugandan Air Force pilots, Amin organized a bombing display for the OAU delegates. A stand was set up alongside Lake Victoria, looking towards a nearby island which Amin had named 'Cape Town' for the occasion. Unfortunately for the anti-apartheid cause, Cape Town escaped unscathed. The only damage done was to passing fish in the lake, for all the bombs fell there, not one hitting the target. The air chief responsible was soon dismissed and used as a target himself, this time successfully.

Amin and Astles took delight in hitting back at Uganda's ex-colonial masters. As a propaganda stunt, Astles arranged for Amin to be carried on a litter – all 300 pounds of him – by four European businessmen, while at the rear a ridiculous Swede carried a tiny parasol on a long pole, so that it shaded Amin's head from the sun. The whole scene was entitled 'The White Man's Burden'. Amin enjoyed the joke and had the scene reproduced on T-shirts, which he gave away freely to his foreign visitors. The blurb on the T-shirts read, 'Field Marshal Idi Amin Dada, V.C., Conqueror of the British Empire, King of Africa, Carried by the British'. One of the white bearers on this occasion – a British businessman named Robert Scanlon – later had a disagreement with Amin over business matters and was sledgehammered to death.

As president of the OAU, Amin took the opportunity to address the United Nations General Assembly in New York in October 1975. It was a truly embarrassing occasion. First, Amin strutted into the great hall, carrying a field marshal's baton, and with his chest so covered in medals that it must have been difficult for him to keep erect. Aware of his profound limitations Amin decided to let his UN ambassador read his speech, which was absurd and filled with outrageous nonsense of the kind that Amin thought very funny. The reaction of the delegates was either silence or embarrassed applause. The delegations of Britain, France and Israel simply got up and pointedly walked out of the chamber. The American delegation, on the other hand, launched a heated attack on Amin and the OAU. In a way this saved Amin's face, for the other African states were more hostile to the USA than they were even to Amin. The session ended with the African delegates cheering the field marshal instead of laughing at his preposterous performance.

The British reaction to Amin's regime was never as forthrightly hostile as it should have been. Having been at least partly responsible for the rise to power of the monster and having clear evidence of the atrocities he was committing in one of their ex-colonies, successive British governments failed to give a lead to his opponents, notably Julius Nyerere and Kenneth Kaunda. Even after the eviction of the Asians, Britain still preferred to try to placate Amin rather than condemn him. Perhaps it was the fact that 300 or more British citizens still lived in Uganda and might provide Amin with hostages, that persuaded the British government to react to events rather than mould them. However, there was a far more disreputable connection between Britain and Amin during the 1970s, one that undoubtedly helped to keep the dictator in power. Amin depended on his ability to keep his henchmen provided with the consumer goods that were unavailable to the rest of the Ugandan people. These were obtained mainly from Britain through the notorious 'Whisky Run' from Stansted airport to Kampala. The Foreign Office in Britain explained its failure to interfere with these shipments by claiming it was tied by EEC regulations which forbade the hindrance of trade, and insisted that its dispute was with Amin not the Ugandan people. But this convinced nobody. How many of the Ugandan people ever saw the luxuries being shipped from Stansted?

Eventually, Amin pushed the Tanzanian leader, Julius Nyerere, too far. He offered to marry him, saying that he loved Julius in spite of his grey hair and wanted to have his children. Nobody, however, was laughing when, in October 1978, Amin invaded Tanzania with 3000 troops, who raped and massacred as they advanced. The better-trained Tanzanian troops drove Amin's men back, only for the Ugandan president to offer to settle the war with a boxing match between himself and the diminutive Tanzanian leader, with Muhammed Ali as referee. Nor was this Amin's only prank during the conflict.

One wonders how many military commanders in history, while engaged in a battle, have deliberately spread false information to their own troops for the sheer fun of watching them panic? Amin did. He spread rumours that the Tanzanians were closing in on Kampala 'just for a joke'. In the ensuing panic, Amin enjoyed watching his ministers disappearing into the bush and his soldiers scurrying about like ants in a nest. However, reality was beginning to stalk Amin in the shape of real soldiers and real politicians. By March of 1979 the Tanzanians actually were closing in on Kampala, forcing Amin to try 'a Custer' – a last stand at the unsuitably named Jinja. Unfortunately ginger was exactly what was missing from his bully-boys by this stage and none of his troops turned up for their date with destiny. If his troops were no Seventh Cavalry Amin was no Custer – he did not turn up either. In fact, Amin had already made his escape to Libya, where Gadaffi harboured him until he tried to molest the Libyan leader's daughter and was promptly thrown out of the country. Last seen in the Ivory Coast, Amin has been fortunate to escape with his life after the full details of his atrocious behaviour emerged.

The rule of Idi Amin proved to be a disaster not just for Uganda but for the whole of Africa. When the country had gained its independence in 1962 it seemed to be a model of how African states might develop under democratic leaders like Milton Obote. Instead, some thirty years later, it offers a salutary warning for those who thought that the thin veneer of British customs and values left behind by the colonial power would prove enough to save the people from the unbridled ambitions of military dictators like Idi Amin. Uganda was particularly unfortunate to fall victim to both an ambitious general and a psychopath in one and the same person. Amin did not simply massacre hundreds of thousands of innocent people, torturing and maiming thousands more, he also broke the back of the Ugandan economy and revealed at a stroke that racialism – in the form of his expulsion of the Ugandan Asians – was not simply the white man's crime.

CHAPTER THREE: A BLUNDERING PROFESSION

An image problem

In a pre-photographic age, arranged marriages conducted between princes and princesses were always accompanied by much uncertainty. Lack of information about the temperament and personality of one's future spouse was one thing, but not knowing whether he or she was cross-eyed, dwarfish or shaped like a baboon was stretching things too far. Bride and groom had to either rely on the sometimes inaccurate descriptions of their spouses-to-be from courtiers trained in the art of diplomatic language, or else entrust their fate to a royal portrait painter, who depended for payment on satisfying his paymaster. It was as a result of Hans Holbein's famous painting of Anne of Cleves that a disappointed Henry VIII dismissed his chief minister, Thomas Cromwell, and later had him executed.

In June 1538, not long after the death of Henry's third wife, Jane Seymour, Cromwell proposed that the king should take a new wife from the House of Cleves, in Germany. The plan was tied up with the religious situation in Europe where England, fearful of a Franco-Habsburg alliance of the Catholic powers against her, wished to form an alliance with the Protestant League of Schmalkalden. Cromwell hoped that Henry's marriage to the Protestant Anne of Cleves would consolidate the alliance. One of Henry's courtiers, Christopher Mont, was sent to Germany to obtain a painting of the young lady. Unable to get such a picture Mont was thrown back on his own imagination, reporting back that he had heard 'praise of Princess Anne's person, that as well for the face as for the whole body she was incomparable and that she excelled the Duchess of Milan as the golden sun excelleth the silver moon'. Henry should have smelled a rat at once; the Duchess of Milan was simply awful and only resembled a moon in terms of her waning looks. Unfortunately, the Duke of Cleves wanted Henry to come to Germany to play the suitor and on bended knee ask for his sister and an alliance at the same time. This might have suited Cromwell, but Henry was not prepared to go on his knees to the ruler of a German 'dung-heap'. In any case, Henry now heard that Anne of Cleves had already been promised to the Duke of Lorraine.

Cromwell, however, was not deterred by this news and believed the matter of the duke could soon be overcome. As a result, he continued to press Mont to get a portrait of Anne. But the only local artist of note – Lucas Cranach – was too ill to carry out the commission. Mont was told by the Germans that he must make do with a painting done some time before which, in any case, was unavailable for the moment. Frustrated by these delays, Mont asked the Duke of Cleves if he could inspect Anne to see if her looks corresponded with the paintings he would – eventually – be allowed to take back to England. The duke was far from pleased: 'Do you want to see her naked?' he inquired. Mont was getting annoyed himself. The Germans seemed to be delaying the marriage negotiations for their own secret reasons. In frustration, Henry sent Hans Holbein from his court to paint a picture of Anne. In a matter of weeks the portrait was ready and was taken back to England. The king was apparently very pleased with what he saw and was prepared to go ahead with the marriage. It seemed that Cromwell was going to get his Protestant alliance after all.

On 24 September 1539, ambassadors from Cleves arrived in England to conclude negotiations for the marriage. The matter was settled and lavish preparations were made for Anne's arrival in England. While the king waited at Greenwich, Anne was held up for a fortnight at Calais by bad weather. On 27 December, she at last made the crossing and travelled to Rochester, where Henry, in disguise, got his first glimpse of his future wife. He was enormously disappointed. He railed against the courtiers who had sent him false reports: 'I am ashamed that men have so praised her as they have done and I like her not.' He had taken with him to Rochester a hamper of New Year's gifts but he did not give them to her.

When the king returned to Greenwich he summoned Thomas Cromwell and tore into him, bitterly accusing him of marrying his king to 'this Flanders mare'. Everyone had made a fool of him, Mont, Holbein and most of all Cromwell, who had pressed him to marry into the House of Cleves. He made it clear that although he would have to go through with the marriage ceremony, he regarded it as a farce and would look to secure a divorce as soon as possible. He told Cromwell that because of him he was having to put his 'neck in the yoke'. It was not a position that Henry enjoyed and one that Cromwell would soon regret. The ministers on the king's council, sensing that Cromwell was 'wounded' and that the king was prepared to abandon him, moved in for the kill.

Henry VIII's marriage to Anne of Cleves was never consummated. Henry's distaste for Anne increased after their first night together. He claimed that he found his new wife physically repugnant and had left her 'as good a maid as I have found her'. By Easter 1540, Henry believed he had found a reason to divorce Anne, namely her pre-contract to the Duke of Lorraine. This was clutching at straws, but Henry was desperate. He wanted to send Anne home yet, curiously, the girl did not want to go. She seemed unconcerned that her new husband was so eager to divorce her and appeared to like England, being willing to stay as one of the royal pensioners in an apartment of her own at Richmond. On 7 July 1540, Henry got his divorce and the marriage was declared null and void.

But the king did not let the matter end there. He blamed Thomas Cromwell for the humiliation he had gone through and claimed that Holbein's painting had completely misrepresented Anne's appearance. Others, like Nicholas Wotton, declared that the painting was 'a lively image'. We will never know who was right.

Anne of Cleves (1515–57), fourth queen of Henry VIII. Though a plain and rather dull girl, Anne was by no means as unattractive as King Henry claimed, and was certainly better-looking than the king's beloved third wife, Jane Seymour.

Probably the fault rested with Henry, who was looking for a degree of perfection unlikely in a dull girl brought up at a provincial court in Germany. In fact, it is clear that Anne of Cleves was almost certainly better-looking than Henry's beloved Jane Seymour. The point really was that Henry was growing old and found Anne uninspiring and lacklustre. She was a shy girl, who spent most of her time weaving and sewing. Yet her physical charms – of which he was so scathing – were probably a match for his. Certainly his next wife, Catherine Howard, found Henry repulsive. Perhaps the 'Flanders Mare' found that the 'English stallion' was no more to her liking than she was to his.

The affair of the Cleves marriage proved fatal to Thomas Cromwell. He lost the king's favour and, even before the divorce had been arranged, was under arrest and awaiting execution in the Tower. His enemies at court, notably Thomas Howard, Duke of Norfolk, had secured his overthrow. Howard had a beautiful niece, Catherine, who might be able to restore the king's taste buds after his plain German fare. Anne lived out a quiet life in England, while for the lack of a photograph – or an honest diplomat – Thomas Cromwell lost his head.

The Beer Hall Putsch

By 1923 the Weimar Republic in Germany was rent by internal division and was in danger of economic collapse. Hyper-inflation had ruined the savings of Germany's middle classes and the government was intensely unpopular. On the streets of Germany's cities right- and left-wing thugs fought for supremacy. In Bavaria, Adolf Hitler's NSDAP – the Nazis – were eager to stage a rising as a prelude to overthrowing the central government. However, when Hitler staged his famous 'beer hall' putsch, the revolt failed. Yet everything could have turned out quite differently but for the blunders of Hitler's henchmen, particularly the SA leader, Ernst Röhm.

In 1923 the Nazis were on a wave of success, with new members flooding to join the party and Ernst Röhm's SA or *Sturmabteilung* – a particularly thuggish Nazi paramilitary organization – growing stronger than ever. Hitler was convinced that the people were ready for revolution. In Bavaria the local authorities were lenient to the violent actions of the SA, and the Weimar Republic was scorned by militant nationalists. The mass of the people, while they might be shocked at Hitler's rhetoric and the violence of the brownshirts in the streets, still shared his dreams of a strong, rejuvenated Germany. Complaints from Berlin about Hitler's violence were received unsympathetically by the local commander of the army, General von Lossow, and many Bavarian officers renounced their oath of allegiance to the national government. Bavaria, ruled by a triumvirate of General von Lossow, Colonel von Kahr and the Chief of Police, von Seisser, teetered on the brink of a complete breakaway from the republic.

In early November 1923, Hitler was convinced that he should stage a putsch in

Munich. He told his supporters that there was a danger that the effects of hyper-inflation might drive the German people into the arms of the Communists. Before this happened he must seize power. At first he planned to stage his coup on 11 November, fifth anniversary of the armistice and the 'stab in the back' of the German army by the 'November Criminals', but events moved too quickly for him. He knew he would require the cooperation of the triumvirate and needed to find an opportunity to get them together at the same time and place. His chance came unexpectedly. On the evening of 8 November, the three Bavarian leaders were due to speak on the same platform at the Bürgerbraükeller and Hitler – in spite of suffering from a nervous headache and toothache – was determined to be there to meet them.

As evening drew on the brownshirts finished their day's work and began to get into uniform. They would be needed that night if things turned nasty. The SA were being directed to various points in the city, while Hitler and his immediate entourage moved across the River Isar to the beer hall, which was about half a mile from the centre of Munich. The Bürgerbraükeller was a large, rambling building, with space for as many as three thousand people in its main hall. By 8 p.m. the place was crowded with drinkers. But the officials, tipped off about potential trouble, had 125 policemen ringing the building, as well as mounted troops and a number of army officers

Reichsminister Ernst Röhm, head of Hitler's SA, pictured in his office in 1933. Ten years earlier, during the 'Beer Hall Putsch', Röhm's blunders ensured the failure of Hitler's attempted coup in Munich.

scattered around inside the main hall. Just a quarter of a mile away hundreds of special riot police were ready to come to the beer hall at a moment's notice. The atmosphere was tense as Hitler and his men arrived, the future Führer in his red Mercedes car. Hitler was alarmed at the huge crowds that had gathered and wondered whether his supporters would be able to come to his assistance through the seething mass of people. He ordered the police to disperse, promising that his own SA would guard the building. He then went inside, found a free table and began sipping a beer. By 8.30 p.m. the beer hall was surrounded by armed brownshirts and his own steel-helmeted bodyguard pushed through into the main hall. Meanwhile, an SA unit had set up a machine-gun in the balcony to rake the audience if necessary. Anyone who tried to leave the building was stopped, and beaten if they resisted. The time had now come for action. Hitler leapt onto a chair and bellowed for quiet, firing his pistol at the ceiling. He announced that the national revolution had begun and that the building was surrounded.

The triumvirate of ministers were standing on the stage but when they were ordered by Hitler to move into a side-room they refused to go. Hitler went up to them and waved his pistol, whereupon they obeyed. In the side room he told them of his plans and asked for their support. Significantly von Lossow whispered to his colleagues, 'Put on an act.' Hitler promised them all kinds of important positions if they supported the putsch, but he seemed to be unaware that these regular army officers had no respect for him, a lowly corporal, at all. Hitler was becoming embarrassed. He could not convince the triumvirate to help him and he did not know what to do next. He sipped his beer absent-mindedly. Outside the drinkers were getting bored and began jeering at the brownshirts, calling out that it was pure theatre and a 'Mexican Revolution'. The whistles and jeers were instantly stopped when Göring stepped forward and fired several shots into the ceiling. He shouted, 'You've got your beer, what are you worried about?' 'We don't like the cabaret,' someone shouted back. 'Do you support the revolution?' Hitler shouted. 'Ja, Ja', came the reply from hundreds of drunken voices. That was good enough for the Nazis – public approval.

The arrival of General Ludendorff in Hitler's red Mercedes changed the whole picture. The First World War hero was a man with whom all Germans could associate and if he was backing Hitler and his brownshirts that was good enough for most people. A drunken chorus of 'Deutschland über Alles' broke out as Ludendorff stepped out of the car, and when he entered the beer hall there was not a dry eye in the house. A wit – probably the last in Germany for a generation – observed that now everybody was there but the psychiatrist.

Meanwhile, on the other side of the river at the Löwenbräukeller, some 2000 people, many of them Hitler's supporters led by Ernst Röhm, were drinking and listening to two brass bands. In between songs, the scar-faced Röhm would bellow out that Germany needed revenge against those who had betrayed her in 1918. At 8.40 p.m. a telephone message from Hitler told Röhm that the revolt had started successfully. Röhm marched to the platform and told the assembled revellers that the triumvirate were deposed in Munich and that Adolf Hitler had declared a national revolution. Röhm then led everyone outside and began to march towards the Bürgerbraükeller. On the way Röhm received new orders, to occupy von Lossow's military headquarters. Brass bands played and crowds lined the streets cheering. It all went to Röhm's head – or was it the beer? Whatever caused him to blunder we shall never know, but his next decision condemned the entire putsch to failure and Hitler to prison. Röhm reached the military headquarters building and walked inside. The guards threatened to shoot but Röhm confidently outfaced them and climbed to the second floor, where he met the duty officer, a man he knew well. The duty officer opened the gates to the rioters outside and Röhm now proceeded to take over the building, placing his own guards in position, stringing barbed wire around the entrances and setting up machine guns. The only thing he did not do was to relieve the duty officer or remove him from his office, which housed the telephone switchboard. It was an unbelievable oversight that was to prove fatal to the putsch. From this room the duty officer was able to relay details of the putsch across Germany, calling in help from surrounding areas.

While Röhm was condemning the entire operation to failure, Hitler was also making mistakes of his own. Hearing that his men were having trouble at the engineers' barracks, Hitler decided to go there in person to sort matters out. This meant leaving Ludendorff in charge of the Triumvirate at the Bürgerbraükeller. No sooner had Hitler left than von Lossow told Ludendorff that he needed to go to his office to collect something. He swore on his oath as a German officer that he would return. Ludendorff allowed him to leave the beer hall, failing to notice that he was quickly followed by von Kahr and von Seisser. When Hitler returned from the engineers' barracks it was to find that Ludendorff had allowed the prisoners to escape. Hitler was as furious as an ex-corporal can afford to be with the ex-war lord of all Germany. He pointed out that von Lossow could sabotage the whole putsch, but Ludendorff was unrepentant. He would always trust the word of a German officer. Hitler, as a lowly corporal, would not understand that.

Von Lossow, meanwhile, reached his office and immediately contacted the duty officer at military headquarters. He ordered the man to send out orders to neighbouring military commanders, calling on them to march on Munich without delay. Loyal army units from Ingolstadt, Augsburg, Regensburg, Landshut and from other Bavarian cities, received von Lossow's SOS and hastened towards Munich. While Röhm and his men congratulated themselves on holding the military headquarters with a grip of iron, in the room next door to them the putsch was being sabotaged. Some four hours after they had taken control of the military headquarters, it occurred to one of Röhm's men that they had not yet got control of the switchboard, but by then it was all far too late.

Errors were taking place elsewhere, though none of them compared with Röhm's original mistake. Röhm's brownshirts decided to smash up the printing presses at the *Munich Post*, only for orders to come through from Hitler that he wanted to use the *Post* to publish his propaganda the next day. In other areas total confusion reigned. In one area municipal police could be arresting putschists, while no more than a street away putschists were arresting the police. Sometimes sheer embarrassment worked

Hitler's SA set up a road block in front of the War Ministry during the 'Beer Hall Putsch' of 9 November 1923.

against the Nazis. Many of their followers were very young and in some streets were chided by bystanders with statements like 'Do you have your mother's permission to play with such dangerous things in the street?' Some SA units actually retreated under the tongue lashings of the onlookers.

When Hitler realized that news of the putsch had been radioed to other areas, and that army units were closing in on Munich, he decided that he had no alternative but to stage a dramatic march through the city to see if he could force the people of Munich to back him rather than the triumvirate.

Ludendorff convinced Hitler that there was no danger in staging the march as no Bavarian troops would fire on any column in which he marched at the head. Hitler was convinced, his admiration for Ludendorff blinding him to the realities of the situation. The march began at noon, without a brass band at the head – the bandsmen, having received neither breakfast nor pay that day, had walked off in a huff. Some 2000 men followed the head of the column, where Ludendorff and Hitler marched, along with other senior Nazis, including Hitler's own bodyguard, Ulrich Graf. As the Nazis passed through the streets of Munich, they noticed that police and riot troops had moved into the city during the night and were cordoning off the streets. Each time the police tried to block the march, however, brownshirts with levelled bayonets pushed them back, saying 'Don't shoot at your comrades.' For a while Hitler's luck seemed to be holding. However, when Ludendorff ordered the column to march down the Weinstrasse towards the Odeonsplatz, it meant that the Nazis came face to face with the main police cordon. Here their bluff was called. As the column approached the road block they were ordered to stop but kept on marching.

A shot rang out, followed by a volley of fire. Hitler's bodyguard Graf leapt in front of his leader and took several shots in his body that had been meant for the Nazi leader. Hitler fell to the ground but he was not wounded, nor was Ludendorff who walked into the massed police ranks and was arrested. Most of the other Nazis took to their heels and ran. Eighteen men died in the brief exchange of fire, four police and fourteen Nazis. Hitler was later arrested and sent to Landsberg Prison. The putsch was over, its failure mainly attributable to the blunders of Hitler and his senior supporters.

Wilhelm the Hun

The European powers began dismembering China in the mid-nineteenth century, dividing it into various 'spheres of influence' and exploiting the Chinese people for their trade. The Manchu government seemed helpless to stop the gradual disintegration at the hands of European soldiers, traders and – worst of all in the eyes of the Chinese – missionaries. When Chinese resistance began it was spontaneous, stemming from the peasants themselves, the unconsidered millions who took matters into their own hands. In 1900 a popular movement known as the Boxers sprang up, aimed at driving out foreign influence from China. The Boxers, members of a secret society known as the Righteous Harmonious Fists, and identified by the red ribbons they wore round their foreheads and wrists, fought with traditional weapons, swords, spears and ancient muskets. What they lacked in firepower they more than made up for in numbers and fanaticism.

The spark which ignited the Boxer Rebellion was Germany's seizure of Kiaochow Bay and the city of Tsingtao in Shantung Province. Kaiser Wilhelm II had used the murder of two German missionaries as a pretext for seizing the bay for use as a German naval base and a port of entry for German goods. The Chinese particularly resented the way the Germans tried to 'Prussianize' the architecture of Tsingtao by erecting German-style buildings – notably a barracks – and an excellent brewery.

The Dowager Empress of China, Cixi, refused to use her troops to suppress the rebels as the Europeans asked her and instead ordered them to assist the Boxers, in the hope of annihilating all Christians in China. When the German ambassador, Baron Klemens von Ketteler, was shot dead in Beijing it was a signal for the Boxers to attack all the Europeans in the city. The European diplomatic community sheltered within the grounds of the British legation, where Sir Claude MacDonald had to organize its defence against both the Boxers and the Empress's troops. Sir Claude had to accommodate some 1000 European and American residents as well as an additional 2000 Christian Chinese, whom the Boxers had sworn to kill. He had at his command a mere 409 soldiers, sailors and marines drawn from all of the powers, with which to face the hordes of Chinese. A relief force of 2000 men, led by the British admiral Seymour – a force which incidentally contained both the young John Jellicoe and David Beatty of later First World War fame – was driven back by overwhelming Boxer numbers. For 55 days the Europeans held out until they were eventually relieved by a force of 25,000 foreign troops from eight nations commanded by the Russian general Linevitch. There was great rejoicing throughout Europe, along with a determination that the Boxers should be punished for their atrocities. Notable by their absence from the relief force were the Germans. Kaiser Wilhelm was distraught at the realization that Beijing had first been relieved by British and Japanese troops. His image as a great war lord was tarnished in his own eyes and he decided that German troops under his overall command must go to China immediately and help in the suppression of the Boxers.

As a result, the Kaiser made a speech demanding exemplary punishment for the Boxers in particular and the Chinese people in general. Taking no account of his ministers, Wilhelm ordered an expeditionary force of 30,000 soldiers and marines to be assembled, ready to sail at a moment's notice to China. He made it clear to his generals that this operation was his and his alone. He had no time for tedious military protocol. His soldiers were going on a mission of retribution, to teach the Chinese that they must never again dare to harm so much as a hair on the head of any European.

On 27 July 1900, Wilhelm reviewed his troops at Bremerhaven and made one of the most extraordinary — indeed infamous — speeches in modern history. So passionately did the Kaiser feel on the subject of the Boxers that he allowed his emotions to get the better of him and, as a result, he tarred the German nation with the brush of barbarism of which — nearly a century later — it still struggles to be free. Wilhelm announced, 'You must know, my men, that you are about to meet a crafty, well-armed, cruel foe. Meet him and beat him! Give him no quarter! Take no prisoners! Kill him when he falls into your hands! Even as, a thousand years ago, the Huns under their king Attila made such a name for themselves as still resounds in legend and fable, so may the name of Germans resound through Chinese history a thousand years from now. . . '. Wilhelm's Chancellor, Prince Bernhard von Bülow, who heard the speech, described it as 'the worst speech of this period and perhaps the most harmful that Wilhelm II ever made'.

But Wilhelm was unrepentant. He wanted German troops to take the lead in punishing the Chinese and he wanted a German officer to command all allied troops in China. But would the other powers agree? Surprisingly they did, with very good grace. Actually, nobody else wanted the job. The real fighting — where the reputations were made — was over and every soldier worth his pay was on a fast boat away from China. If the Germans wanted to do the 'mopping up' that was their business. In the end, Wilhelm got his way without a struggle and appointed Field Marshal Count Waldersee to head the international army as 'World Marshal'.

Waldersee arrived in China in mid-October 1900 and made a grand entry into Beijing, which was variously described as 'farcical' and 'absurd' by the French and British officers present. The German troops goose-stepped their way into the city wearing large straw hats, drawing from one British observer the comment: 'This must be some Berlin tailor's idea of an appropriate headdress for a summer and autumn campaign in the East.' In fact, it would have suited a band of Mexican desperadoes

A somewhat idealized representation of the role played by German troops during the Boxer Rising in China in 1900. In fact, the Germans behaved in an atrocious fashion, killing, looting and raping on the orders of the Kaiser.

far better. Waldersee insisted on wearing his Order of the Black Eagle everywhere he went, and carrying his marshal's baton, seemingly as a reminder to everyone he met that he was in charge. He had also brought with him an asbestos hut, the latest idea from the Berlin think-tank on what army commanders needed as their field headquarters. Waldersee soon got fed up with his hut and moved into the Dowager Empress's palace. Soon after, the palace burned down, killing Waldersee's chief of staff. Obviously the Berlin planners had known a thing or two when they sent the asbestos hut.

Incited by their emperor and supreme war lord to behave like a horde of barbarians, the German soldiers set about raping and murdering the Chinese, and looting what was left of their property. This could not have been much, since the light fingers of half the world's soldiers had had three months' start on them. It was even recorded, incidentally, that at the height of the looting after the relief of the British residency in June, Lady MacDonald had been observed in one Chinese palace up to her elbows in somebody else's property. Waldersee, in fact, was encouraging his men to behave badly. Eager to show his monarch that he could be as barbaric as any Hun, the count organized punitive expeditions into the countryside, ordering that every village headman within a hundred miles of Beijing should be shot. While he explained to the other allied commanders that he was 'exerting a moral influence of far-reaching importance', he was in fact committing atrocities against a helpless civilian population. Back in Berlin, Wilhelm was beside himself with fury when he heard that one of his warships had suffered seventeen hits from Chinese guns provided by the German arms manufacturer, Krupp of Essen. The Kaiser wrote to Fritz Krupp telling him, 'This is no time, when I am sending my soldiers to battle against the yellow beasts, to try to make money.'

While the Germans were enjoying themselves with their war games, everyone else was growing bored. The soldiers of other powers were needed elsewhere, to carry out more useful tasks like bringing in the harvest, directing the traffic or parading for the tourists, and one by one the foreign contingents left the international force until just the British remained for Count Waldersee to command. Even he had found better things to do than killing Chinese. Waldersee was enjoying a romantic liaison with the wife of a Chinese diplomat, who had served in Berlin. Alas, their love could not keep the 'World Marshal' from his duty and in June 1901, he left China to return to Germany.

The German expedition to China had been a disaster and in many ways a national disgrace. Without knowing it, the Kaiser had cultivated an image of his people as pitiless barbarians. Fourteen years later, during the German advance through Belgium in August 1914, public opinion throughout the world and notably in the neutral USA, would remember Germany's part in the suppression of the Boxer Rebellion and do what Wilhelm had hoped everyone would do – link Attila's Huns with Wilhelm's German soldiers. In the English-speaking world after 1900 the Germans *were* the Huns, and therefore unspeakably barbaric and militaristic. Thanks to the Kaiser the land of Dürer, Beethoven and Goethe had a lot to live down.

April in Baghdad

On 25 June 1990, just a week before Iraqi troops crossed into Kuwait and declared that it was henceforth a province of Iraq, the American ambassador in Baghdad, Ms April Glaspie, had a meeting with the Iraqi president, Saddam Hussein. At this meeting it is alleged that the Iraqi dictator was told by the American diplomat that the United States had 'no opinion on the Arab–Arab conflict, like your border dispute with Kuwait'. Saddam was probably surprised to hear this directly from an American source, but he was not slow to exploit his advantage. Convinced as a result of this that the Americans would never actually go to war to force him out of Kuwait, Saddam ordered his invasion to go ahead. Since that time, experts on the Middle East have scarcely been able to credit the enormity of Glaspie's blunder. It was nothing less than giving Saddam the green light for territorial aggression. Yet the truth is more complex than that April Glaspie made a slip of the tongue or was high on adrenalin or indeed anything other than tea and biscuits. The fact was that American diplomacy had placed Ms Glaspie in a 'no win' situation, from which it is difficult to see how she could have emerged unscathed. She was faced with the problem of conveying a dual message to Saddam: that the United States was in fact alarmed at the Iraqi threat towards Kuwait, and yet was still friendly towards Saddam's regime and wanted to maintain good relations. How American diplomacy had tied itself in such knots that it wanted to stroke the lion that bit its head off was the result of preferring the 'blood-crazed' dictator in Baghdad, for all his human rights violations, to the religious fundamentalism of Shi'ite Iran.

Since the overthrow of the Shah of Iran by the revolt that brought the Ayatollah Khomeini to power in 1979, American foreign policy in the Middle East had been forced to adjust to a new scenario. Iran had been the cornerstone of America's anti-

Communist policy in a notably volatile region. With Iran now dangerously unstable under an anti-American Shi'ite regime, the United States was quick to support Iraqi leader Saddam Hussein's opportunist strike against Iran in 1980. Overlooking what they knew of Saddam Hussein from their own and Israeli intelligence, the Americans made the fatal error of concluding that an enemy of their enemy must be their friend. For the United States' administration, Iranian fundamentalism was more of a threat to American interests than Iraq's aggression against her neighbours, notably Israel. As the Iran–Iraq war dragged on through the 1980s America became more open in her support of Saddam's corrupt regime. Blind to reports of human rights violations against the Kurdish people, the United States continued to keep Saddam well supplied with aid, especially in the form of military hardware and technology. Saddam was even allowed to use secret surveillance of Iran carried out by American satellites and spy planes. It was not until 1988 that the United States began to realize that she was backing the wrong horse. A weakened Iran offered no threat – except verbal ones – to American interests, whereas Iraq had by then accumulated a massive arsenal of weapons and had the world's fourth biggest army. Without realizing it, the United States had helped to create a Frankenstein monster than threatened the security of the whole Middle East region.

Furthermore, Iraq's economy had suffered severely from the eight years' fighting against Iran and by 1989 her annual expenditure was running at twice the rate of her oil revenue. National bankruptcy was staring Saddam Hussein in the face. Like Hitler, he decided to settle his economic problems by force. When Kuwait refused to grant him her entire oil revenue from the Ratga oil wells, he replied that it hardly mattered as the entire area was part of Iraq anyway. Faced with the unacceptable alternative of bankruptcy at home and humiliation in the eyes of his Arab neighbours, Saddam felt he must take over Kuwait entirely. The problem was, how would the United States react? And this is what he found out when he met April Glaspie on 25 July: the United States would fluff its lines and leave him to do what he liked. That Glaspie 'fluffed her lines' was not surprising, for her role was an impossible one. She had to flatter Saddam with words like, 'I admire your extraordinary efforts to rebuild your country', and yet warn him with phrases like, 'we can only see that you have deployed massive troops in the south'. In her own defence, Glaspie later insisted that she had said, 'We insist you settle your disputes with Kuwait nonviolently', but there is no record of these words in the interview and they are so curt and aggressive that it is impossible to believe she would have used them directly to a man like Saddam Hussein. With hindsight she probably wished she had said them. Unfortunately, she – and through her President Bush – failed to convince Saddam Hussein that the United States would resist the occupation of Kuwait by force. As a result, her gaffe constitutes a serious diplomatic blunder.

Yet April Glaspie was merely the sharp end of an entire diplomatic machine which had been malfunctioning for some time. She is no more to blame for what happened than a host of Middle East experts in the American administration, who failed to alert George Bush to the perils he faced in dealing with Saddam Hussein. For some weeks before the Kuwait crisis reached fever pitch in July 1990, American satellites had been reporting big Iraqi troop dispositions on the Kuwaiti border. Western diplomats in Baghdad had watched daily as convoys of heavy armour travelled south. Was this simply a bluff or did Saddam Hussein mean to take Kuwait by force? America's leading Middle East expert concluded, the day before the Iraqis actually crossed into Kuwait, that it was a bluff. The problem was that the Americans had come to regard Saddam as no more than a posturing bully, who liked to rattle his sabre from time to time but would never actually pull it out of its sheath. The Americans were wrong: every stage of Saddam's career had shown him to be an opportunist, who merely waited until the moment was right before striking. He regarded American moderation towards him as a sign of weakness and believed that every American military action since Vietnam had shown that the Americans did not have the stomach for a fight. As he told Ambassador Glaspie during their meeting, 'Yours is a society which cannot accept 10,000 dead in one battle.' At that stage he was right. No modern democratic country can afford to squander the lives of its people in the way that Saddam Hussein could and frequently did. And while Saddam was convinced that this was true – and Glaspie had no brief to tell him otherwise – he knew that he could rely on 'Middle America' to stop President Bush sending American boys to die in the desert. In the final analysis, the United States in the person of Ambassador April Glaspie failed to convince Saddam Hussein that it was prepared to fight to liberate Kuwait. The subsequent costly war could have been avoided, but only if the United States had stopped trying to have the best of both worlds, backing Saddam Hussein against Shi'ite Iran and yet preventing the 'Butcher of Baghdad' from threatening his Arab neighbours and Israel. In the end, George Bush was forced to clamber down from the fence and give his 'pet pooch', who had been frightening the neighbours, a darned good whippin'.

A paid assassin

The assassination of William the Silent, leader of the Dutch Revolt against Spain in the late sixteenth century had at least one unusual feature: the victim paid the assassin to buy the murder weapons. Lest it be thought that the Dutch prince planned his own demise, one should hastily add that William was unaware of Balthazar Gérard's true purpose. Nevertheless, it was by an irony of history – and a blunder – that the great Prince of Orange died a victim of his own generosity.

Many attempts were made by the Catholic emissaries of Philip of Spain and the Inquisition to kill William, not least for the reward of 25,000 écus that had been placed on the rebel prince's head. Yet for a while he seemed to lead a charmed life. In March 1582, a Catholic assassin, Juan Jauréguy, had fired a pistol at William from such close range that he had set the prince's hair and beard alight. The wound in his neck seemed likely to prove fatal but through the astonishing attention of his servants, who held the wound closed with their fingers in relays for seventeen days, William's life was saved. Later in the same year two more Catholics, who had been hired by the Duke of Parma – the Spanish general and William's most formidable enemy – to poison him, were arrested by William's agents. One of the prince's own countrymen, a man named Hanzoon, even made two unsuccessful attempts to blow up William at his palace.

William was eventually assassinated by a young Frenchman named Balthazar Gérard, encouraged – but not paid – by the Duke of Parma. He joined William's service by pretending to be a Calvinist named Francis Guyon, whose father had died fighting against the Catholics. William was taken in by the young man's apparent sincerity and sent him on a diplomatic mission to France. However, Gérard did not leave court and was soon noticed by the prince, who asked him why he had not set out. Gérard, who was far from being a professional assassin, had neither a sword nor a pistol and was uncertain how he was going to kill the prince without a weapon. When William asked him why he had not left for France, Gérard replied that he had no money to buy himself shoes and clothing. The generous prince gave Gérard twelve crowns to buy clothes, whereupon the young man purchased instead two pistols from one of the prince's own guards.

On 10 July 1584, William was attending a private feast at Prinsenhof with his family and friends. As he left the table he paused for a moment to speak to an officer, whereupon Gérard stepped forward and shot him in the chest. He died within minutes. Gérard suffered the martyrdom he had apparently sought. He was executed in public four days later by having his flesh torn from his body with red hot pincers, before being disembowelled and hacked into quarters. It is doubtful if the kind-hearted Prince of Orange would have welcomed such cruelty, even to his murderer.

The assassination sent shock waves around the Protestant lands of Europe. In England a special association was formed by Queen Elizabeth I's courtiers so that in

William the Silent, Prince of Orange, led the Dutch in their War of Independence against Spain. He was assassinated by Balthasar Gérard at Delft, having unwittingly given his assassin the money with which to purchase the murder weapon.

the event of her violent death nobody who might have stood to gain by it – notably Mary, Queen of Scots – would be allowed to succeed to the throne. The royal guard who had sold Gérard the pistols committed suicide. In the Catholic world, however, Gérard achieved great honour as a martyr. King Philip of Spain rewarded Gérard's parents for their son's achievement and the Pope joyfully ordered all the church bells in Rome to be rung.

CHINA – THE PHILISTINE STATE 1966-9

Having failed by the smallest possible margin to return China to the Stone Age, during the Great Leap Forward in 1958 (see p. 124), Mao Zedong and his wife Jiang Qing, had a notion to change the culture of China, a country that had always prided itself on its respect for the past and its reverence for its ancestors, to one where anarchy ruled and Mao Zedong himself presided over a continuing revolution. Such frenzied change took place in the period between 1966 and 1969 that it resembled a raging torrent of water, sweeping away everyone in its path. It was another of Mao Zedong's blunders, which ruined the economy, retarded the education of China's young people and destroyed the nation's cultural heritage. It was the iconoclasm of an ailing giant, of a politician who had lost all contact with his roots and was in the process of metamorphosis from man to living legend. The Cultural Revolution succeeded in ruining the lives of millions of his people. Altogether 729,000 Chinese were 'framed and persecuted' during the upheavals and many of these were 'persecuted to death', which is a euphemism for being beaten, tortured and finally murdered. Thousands more of China's most able and cultured citizens committed suicide to avoid punishment.

Although Mao Zedong had suffered a political defeat in the aftermath of the Great Leap Forward, he was still the favourite of the masses and the founding father of modern China. In addition, Lin Biao, one of Mao's firmest supporters, was now Army Minister, so Mao had no reason to fear any opposition from China's military leaders. For a while after 1960 he was content to bide his time.

Meanwhile, helped by Deng Xiaoping, President Liu Shaoqi was content to run the country in Mao's name, but without ever allowing the great man to influence economic policy. Liu's economic policies began to restore some prosperity to China, though according to his critics the wealth was going to a privileged few. The mass of Chinese peasants, who had hoped for an improvement under the Great Leap Forward, found that they were still no better off. Although Liu never intended a return to capitalism his policies allowed Mao Zedong to accuse him of 'following the Capitalist road'. Liu and his supporters on the right of the party were pragmatic politicians, trying to follow common-sense policies. Increasing production, by whatever means, they claimed, was more important than making sure that everyone was treated exactly the same, because everyone would benefit in the long run as the whole country grew richer. Under Liu industrial and agricultural bonuses and prizes were offered to workers if they could increase output, while those with special skills – administrators, managers, engineers and professional workers – were able to earn more. In the countryside even private farming plots were encouraged and by 1965 a third of all peasant income came through private sales. In country areas there was even a return of the middle and rich peasant classes that had disappeared after the reform of land ownership in 1950. Unfortunately for China, Mao Zedong was not content to remain in the background for long and he began to plot the overthrow of his main enemy, Liu Shaoqi.

Concerned as he was at the reappearance of economic inequalities, Mao was most worried about the minds of the Chinese people. He did not like them having them. He feared that China's schools

Liu Shaoqi and his wife Wang Guangmei photographed in 1949. During the Cultural Revolution in China, Liu Shaoqi and his wife were the two most prominent targets for Mao Zedong's Red Guards. Wang survived her ordeal, but President Liu died from his ill-treatment in prison.

and colleges were producing a new educational élite, which neither understood nor cared for the ideas that had brought about the revolution. This was what had happened in the Soviet Union, Mao believed, where a new class of technocrats – managers, engineers and technicians – had been given the best jobs, the highest pay and the best education. This had encouraged them to think they ruled as a matter of right and they had begun to denigrate their colleagues who worked with their hands. Party officials had turned themselves into a ruling class, demanding instant obedience from the masses. These privileged groups lived in the big cities where they could get better education for their children than those living in the countryside. A new hereditary bourgeoisie had grown up in the Soviet Union and it was beginning to appear in China too, not based on private property as in the past, but on income, status and education. Mao decided that this must stop. China needed a 'cultural revolution' and a change in political direction.

Yet Mao could not rely on the Communist Party to help him as in the past. In fact, he would have to destroy the old party, as it was his old colleagues and allies who were the very people he was going to have to criticize. As he himself said, 'Destroy first, construction will look after itself.' To achieve the destruction of the 'old guard', Mao needed new allies: soldiers, peasants and – above all – the young people of China. Furthermore, speed was essential, for Mao Zedong knew that his health was failing. If he was going to challenge Liu Shaoqi successfully and return China to the right path he would have to act quickly. He was already suffering from Parkinson's Disease and had suffered a mild stroke in 1964. As a display of his fitness to lead a movement based on young people, Mao staged a propaganda coup, swimming 14 kilometres along the Changjiang River. Amidst a blaze of publicity Mao Zedong demonstrated that he had lost none of his strength for the battle ahead.

The 'Great Proletarian Cultural Revolution' was Mao Zedong's attempt to save China from making the mistakes that he believed had ruined Soviet Communism. Mao insisted that Nikita Khrushchev, the Russian leader, had broken away from the Marxist-Leninist principles on which the Russian Revolution had been founded. Khrushchev had allowed capitalism to come back in Russia and had given up the 'class struggle'. This must not happen in China. A completely new revolutionary class must be trained, young people whose minds could be moulded. The older generation of China's leaders must either be re-educated or destroyed.

Beginning in June 1966, the *People's Daily* bombarded the country with a series of powerful editorials based on a single theme: the absolute authority of Chairman Mao must be established and China must undergo a 'cultural revolution'. Mao was helped in this by Lin Biao, who built up a personality cult for Mao among the peasant soldiers. The army published a handbook of 'The Thoughts of Chairman Mao' – known as the Little Red Book – which was aimed at brainwashing the rank and file. This soon became the bible of the Cultural Revolution and a billion copies were printed, some even reaching the West. As the cult of Mao spread the masses were indoctrinated into accepting anything Mao said without question. He made it clear that China's problems could only be solved by a great leader – who else but himself, Mao Zedong, the 'Great Helmsman' and father of the nation? Mao knew this appeal to the masses was dangerously dictatorial, but he felt he had no alternative if he were to save China from following the Soviet road.

The first targets of Mao's attack were the schools and colleges where the minds of China's young people were formed. He knew that he must take command of these young and unformed minds and make them his. He appealed to China's young people, telling them that too much education was exposing them to the dangers of élitism and counter-revolution. 'There is too much studying going on,' he said, 'and this is extremely harmful.' In China's schools teaching came to an abrupt halt, with children forbidden to read their books and simply sitting at their desks listening to loudspeaker broadcasts of the daily newspapers and the thoughts of Chairman Mao. News-sheets showing European leaders reading the works of Chairman Mao were circulated everywhere in an attempt to convince the people that they were not alone in their love of Chairman Mao. Each day the children chanted passages from Mao's 'Thoughts' in unison. In one newspaper story a peasant was praised for sticking 32 portraits of Mao on his bedroom walls so that he could see Chairman Mao's face as soon as he opened his eyes. The peasant was later beaten up when the truth got out that he had only used the portraits as he could not afford any other wallpaper and the pictures were being given away free.

However, Mao was quick to see that the mass of

the people – the middle and older generations – were not responding to his propaganda and so he decided to use 'Red Guards' – schoolchildren and students – as shock troops in the cultural battles ahead. He knew that he could persuade the young people to give him the absolute loyalty denied him by the older generation. As a result, he would use the young to terrify their parents and grandparents. China must undergo a 'Reign of Terror' – the young would be let loose to repair the errors of the old. Children would denounce their parents for 'bourgeois thoughts or actions'. One mother was beaten by Red Guards when her son told them that he had heard her 'complaining about the price of tomatoes'.

Mao specifically targeted teachers, who were greater authority figures than parents for the children. In every school in China teachers were attacked, beaten and even killed. Their authority over the children had to be broken if Mao was to win the battle for the minds of China's young people. Some children even set up prisons inside their schools where they tortured their teachers. Teachers were forced to wear caps and collars bearing slogans such as 'I am a monster'. The teachers were often made to clean out the toilets, and were smeared with black paint by 'monster control' teams of children. Those who had been too strict, too formal or too traditional in their methods were beaten, forced to kneel for hours on end in front of their classes, apologizing for their 'crimes'.

At Beijing University an attack was launched against the university administration. Over sixty professors and senior lecturers, including the chancellor, were beaten and kicked, and dunce caps were forced onto their heads, bearing all kinds of absurd slogans. Ink was poured over their faces to make them black – the colour of evil and of counter-revolution. Each victim, some of them very old men and women, had their arms bent behind them by thugs in a torture known as the 'jet plane'. Teachers who had criticized the work of their students were accused of being decadent and were publicly beaten to death.

But Mao was unleashing a power that he could not control, as he was later to admit. Between eleven and thirteen million Red Guards now swept into Beijing, using the offer of free transport and food. Here they held mass rallies at which they chanted slogans, such as 'The East is Red', from the Little Red Book and elevated Mao to the status of a god. People began to claim that miracles had happened when they thought of Mao's words. The dead came back to life, the blind could see, drowning men were saved. One had only to call on Mao's name for a miracle to occur. A pilot claimed that his aircraft was in flames and crashing towards the ground. As he blacked out he thought of Chairman Mao's words and instantly he was awake again, flying quite normally with no sign of damage to the plane.

At a mass rally in Tiananmen Square, Mao's deputy Lin Biao called on over a million of the Red Guards to charge out and attack the 'four olds': old ideas, old culture, old customs and old habits. This was a signal for a frenzy of destruction beyond anything the Vandals, Huns and Goths achieved in years of ravaging the Roman Empire. All over China Red Guards – like locusts or Luddites – took to the streets in their millions, mindlessly smashing anything which was valued by people older than themselves. Houses were raided, and antiques, paintings, works of calligraphy and fine books were destroyed just because they were fine – and old. Book burnings took place and all China's classics, along with all works of foreign literature, were thrown on the flames. Public libraries were ransacked and any book that did not quote Mao on every page was destroyed. Only Marxist classics and the works of Stalin were allowed to survive. Beijing's bookshops underwent an amazing transformation. Stripped of all their books they were suddenly filled with millions of copies of one book only – 'The Thoughts of Chairman Mao'. It was a browser's nightmare. All records of European classical music were smashed and the goldfish suddenly became an endangered species, hunted down as the supreme manifestation of bourgeois decadence. How many goldfish died in the subsequent holocaust is not recorded.

In a matter of weeks almost all valuable items in private collections were destroyed by the fanatical Red Guards. Chinese writers and artists committed suicide in droves, unable to live in Mao's philistine China or unwilling to survive the cruel beatings and humiliation they suffered at the hands of teenage vandals. The Manchurian novelist Lao She, for example, drowned himself in a pond after being beaten by the Red Guards; the historian Jian Bozan and his wife committed suicide after being tortured by gangs of young thugs, as did the parents of the famous pianist Fou T'Song. At the University of

Shanghai 60 teachers killed themselves in a single day. One English language teacher was arrested for possessing an English typewriter. The Red Guards said it was a radio transmitter and that she was a secret agent of American imperialism. She was tortured and then imprisoned in a cowshed, until she finally killed herself in despair. All Chinese museums, palaces, temples and ancient tombs were raided and wrecked. Statues and pagodas were toppled by the destructive mob. Even the 'Forbidden City' itself would have succumbed had not Prime Minister Zhou Enlai ordered the army to guard it and prevent the Red Guards breaking through.

The Chinese police did nothing to save private property or lives from destruction. They were instructed to stand back and allow the Red Guards to take out their 'class hatred' on their enemies by beating and if necessary killing them. Families of intellectuals were forced to kneel before the Red Guards and kowtow to them, enduring constant beatings from brass buckles and belts but unable to complain. Most of them were subjected to the indignity of having one half of their heads shaved as a sign of their 'crimes'. In fact, a large proportion of the Red Guards were no more committed to Mao than he was to them. Many were just having a wild time, out of control and able to indulge their thuggish energies. The minister for the coal industry, Zhang Linzhi, for example, 'was interrogated 52 times in 33 days and tortured to wring confessions out of him ... besides being beaten and kicked, he was forced to wear cast-iron headgear weighing 30 kilos ... On 21 January Zhang was paraded at the Institute campus and tortured until he died that night'. It was often the criminally minded who made the best Red Guards, and it was notable how many ex-criminals were in the forefront of the movement. Students of a more delicate or tender nature often suffered for their unwillingness to beat and torture their victims.

At the same time Mao's wife, Jiang Qing, had dedicated herself to bringing Maoism to the arts. She wanted to replace traditional Chinese art forms with new revolutionary and politically acceptable forms. Approved plays and ballets were reduced to a mere handful, such as the 'correct' *Red Detachment of Women*, one of only eight plays allowed to be performed on the Chinese stage. Behind the theatre curtains and play sets, and in the changing rooms, a cultural revolution took place that was a microcosm of the greater struggle outside in the streets. One make-up girl was viciously beaten for using too much panstick and charcoal on the villain, thereby making him 'seem unreal'. Dancers were criticized for dancing 'too well', 'too traditionally', 'too individually'. Tutus and traditional costumes were replaced by army fatigues, suitably adjusted for efficiency but not for comfort. The world of Chinese culture became instead the world of Jiang Qing, whose every word was law.

Throughout the big cities, street names were ripped down and replaced by more suitable and revolutionary names. Thus 'The Poplar and Willow Are Green' Street became 'The East is Red' Street. Other less poetic addresses included 'Destroy the Old' Street and 'Revolution' Street. A restaurant known as 'The Fragrance of Sweet Wind' was renamed 'The Whiff of Gunpowder'. In the streets of Beijing traffic was in chaos. As red had become the colour of progress it was viewed as reactionary to have a green light for 'Go'. Thus red became 'Go' and green 'Stop'. Moreover, although Chinese drivers were accustomed to driving on the right, they were henceforth told to drive on the 'revolutionary' left. Then someone mentioned that the British imperialist running-dogs drove on the left and so the argument began again. In the meantime, traffic accidents soared and nobody seemed to care. People were not always safer on foot, however. As people passed by Red Guards would attack them and cut their long hair short, or cut their trouser legs if they were too narrow, or rip their skirts or break the heels off their shoes if they were too high.

In this atmosphere of hysteria Liu Shaoqi, Deng Xiaoping and their supporters were overthrown. Mao had won a complete victory. Liu Shaoqi was the most important victim of the Cultural Revolution. The way in which he was driven from power and persecuted tells us a lot about conditions in China at this time. Even a man as powerful as Liu seemed helpless to stem the tidal wave that Mao had unleashed. Although Liu made a successful self-criticism before the Central Committee of the Party, and was congratulated on it by Mao, it was still not enough to gain his release. Liu trusted Mao to save him but he and his wife, Wang Guangmei, were hated by Mao's wife, Jiang Qing, who was determined to destroy them both. Under a hail of criticism Liu's health began to give way, while his younger children were beaten up at school, his son thrown into jail and his eldest daughter exiled to a

During the Cultural Revolution Maoism was applied to all aspects of Chinese life. The arts, notably the opera and ballet, were reformed by Mao's wife Jing Qing. Here Mao himself is seen with Premier Zhou Enlai (second row, far left) and singers and actors from the Beijing Opera.

distant border region. The Red Guards next turned on his wife, Wang Guangmei, imprisoning her and further ill-treating her children. Only the influence of Premier Zhou Enlai saved her life.

The Red Guards next adopted more direct methods, forcing their way into Liu's house and plastering the walls with posters denouncing him. He was dragged away and forced to recite quotations from Mao's works from memory. When he failed he was beaten. On 13 January, 1967, Mao summoned him to the Great Hall of the People, where he advised Liu to 'read a few books' to improve his understanding of Communism. Newspaper reports accused Liu of being 'China's Khrushchev'.

At 'struggle-and-criticism' sessions, Liu was repeatedly slapped across the face with copies of Mao's Little Red Book. When Liu attempted to defend himself he was told, 'You're not allowed to spread poisonous ideas.' Wang Guangmei was, meanwhile, summoned to Quinghua University where she was denounced, kicked and humiliated in front of 300,000 people. A necklace of ping-pong balls was tied round her neck. At Liu's house, his cook was arrested on a charge of being a secret agent, probably on orders from Jiang Qing. On 5 August

1967, Liu and his wife were finally separated, with Red Guards hanging a cartoon around Liu's neck showing a noose and clenched fists. Liu tried to complain to Mao but received no reply. The end was now in sight. Liu was never to see his wife or his children again. The guard around him was doubled and told not to show any leniency to the old man. He became very weak, could hardly walk or feed himself, and had stomach ailments from the steamed bread and hard rice he was given to eat. He shook all over. Even as they treated him, his doctors abused him. The guards stopped his supply of vitamins and a drug he was taking for diabetes, so that eventually Liu could eat nothing and had to be fed through a tube in the nose. In 1969, President Liu Shaoqi, as much the father of the nation as his one-time comrade, Mao Zedong, died in prison, a martyr to the Cultural Revolution and to Mao's madness.

Meanwhile, the revolution was proving impossible to control. Mao had ordered the Red Guards to travel through the countryside to shake up the existing party administration. But this just encouraged them to behave like a violent mob. It was a terrible time for the Chinese people. As one Red Guard later boasted, 'Because we were afraid that people would hide things, we searched their houses very thoroughly. Some of us would tear down the walls and look behind the plaster while others seized shovels and picks and tore up the cellars looking for hidden items. I even recall seeing two or three people in my group squeezing toothpaste in a quest for hidden jewellery. Our object was to humiliate these people.'

There was no alternative now but to try to stop the revolution by calling in the army. In the big cities workers were setting up their own trade unions and demanding a say in government. The centre of this urban discontent was Shanghai, which had China's largest factories and the most 'politically aware' proletariat. The workers there complained about differences in pay, and the fact that the state-organized trade unions did not represent their interests. Taking their model from the Paris Commune of 1871 they set up their own Commune in 1967, demanding freedom from Beijing's control. At first Mao Zedong gave his blessing to the Shanghai Commune, but he had no intention of allowing it to become a model for other Chinese cities. That way he knew he might lose control of the country. There was still a danger of civil war in some areas where supporters of Liu Shaoqi held out. The time had come to reconcile the differences within the party and restore government by the Communist Party. With the moderate voice of Premier Zhou Enlai now calling for a halt to violence, the Chinese Army began to break up the Red Guard units and restore some kind of order.

By the beginning of 1968 the education system in China was completely stagnant. Those teachers who had survived the attacks of the Red Guards were forbidden to do any teaching. In any case, there were no textbooks as they had all been destroyed as 'bourgeois poison'. Children sat in classes day after day chanting the Thoughts of Chairman Mao or performing 'loyalty dances'. In the universities things were no better. It was finally decided simply to graduate all the students without any exams just to move them off the campuses. These new 'graduates' were then distributed around the country doing useful jobs like working down the mines where, because of the lack of ponies or machines, everything had to be done manually. Both men and women had to crawl down the pit and pull the coal baskets out by hand. Barefoot doctors – whose only qualifications were that they had bare feet and were not doctors – were sent into the countryside to replace the professional medical men who had been 'persecuted' or were being re-educated.

Mao feared that party officials, especially the young who had not lived through the revolutionary times of the 1930s and 1940s, were becoming 'rulers at faraway desks' and 'lofty gentlemen', and were forgetting their proletarian and peasant origins. Only by returning to the land could they rediscover their revolutionary spirit. Thus the 'Cadre Schools of 7 May' were set up. By 1970 it was claimed that 95 per cent of party officials had been 'restored to health' in this way. But the fate of senior managers was very hard. They had to learn to value the work of their lowest and most menial staff. Stripped of their own office jobs, they were given brooms or buckets and told to get on with it. One senior educational administrator was taught to value the job of his cleaners: 'One of the men here was the deputy chairman of East Beijing. There, of course, every child knew him. So it was a particular ordeal for him to go back to his own section of the city, where he had been one of the top leaders, and come in all dusty and sweaty after a long march, to empty the toilets there.' It was an example of social engineering gone mad. All the top people had to change places with all the people at the bottom. Managers had to sweep the floor, technical engineers had to stir the paint, specialist cancer surgeons had to empty the bedpans. Who cared if the patient died as long as the 'operation' was politically correct. Urban workers in their millions were ordered into he countryside to learn the ways of the peasant. As Mao said, even though the peasant's feet were covered in horse-manure, it did not mean that he did not know how to look after horses. On the other hand, neither did it mean that he knew how to repair a tractor. The process was all one way. The peasants learned nothing, except perhaps what they already knew, that city folk were good for nothing but eating the food of country folk. The city folk, meanwhile, learned that it got cold at night in the countryside sleeping on straw, and that mucking out cattle played havoc with the finger nails.

The 'Great Proletarian Cultural Revolution' lasted, perhaps, for a decade, although in its last few years it lost its early momentum and became linked with the slow decline of Mao Zedong and the increasingly malign influence of his wife, Jiang Qing and the 'Gang of Four'. Mao died in 1976 but – fortunately for China – he was not succeeded by any of the leading figures from the Cultural Revolution. Eventually, the succession fell to one of history's great survivors – Deng Xiaoping – who is still the *de facto* ruler of China today. The martyrdom of

President Liu Shaoqi was recognized for the 'frame-up' that it was when his name was rehabilitated in 1980 and his elderly and heroic wife, Wang Guangmei, was released from prison in 1978.

THE ROAD TO MOROCCO

During the early years of the present century Imperial Germany tried to expand her colonial interests in Morocco. By doing so she intended to appease the pressures from her own people for colonial success while at the same time restricting French influence in the Sultan of Morocco's lands. Instead, German diplomats, prompted into action by Kaiser Wilhelm II, achieved results that ran almost exactly counter to their intentions. They forced Britain to stand beside France on two occasions, thereby making the tentative Anglo-French Entente of 1904 into something far more concrete than either power had ever expected. Thus, Germany unwittingly strengthened, rather than weakened, the alliance against her. The much-publicized *Panther* incident of 1911, beloved of textbook writers ever since that time, was far from being an example of the strength of German policy towards France. Instead, it was a semi-farcical affair, that revealed German policy as bankrupt of ideas and dependent on the whims and fancies of the Kaiser. The celebrated '*Panther*'s Leap' was no more terrifying to Germany's enemies than a stuffed toy thrown by a petulant child.

In 1905 the North African state of Morocco was of prime interest to three European states – Britain, France and Spain. As owner of Gibraltar which, with the Moroccan port of Tangier, guarded the western entrance to the Mediterranean, Britain took a strategic and economic interest in Morocco, though not a territorial one. Britain was content to allow France and Spain to divide the Sultan's lands between them as 'spheres of influence'. In case any one power should try to exert a claim to the entire country, all the European powers – including Germany – would have the right to be consulted. Otherwise, Germany had not previously shown any interest in Morocco. France, however, had hopes of

acquiring control over the whole of Morocco and, although British trade with the Sultan was twice as great as that of France, Britain was willing to let the French have their way in return for France withdrawing any claim to Britain's 'sphere of influence' in Egypt. This agreement removed the last stumbling block to a Franco-British Entente, which was duly signed in 1904. Germany found this new alignment threatening and the Kaiser mockingly named his uncle, Edward VII, 'Edward the Encircler' in view of his anti-German attitudes. German politicians, supporting the Kaiser's view, tried to find a way of breaking the new Entente and decided to humiliate France over the issue of Morocco. They planned to resist French claims to extend their influence in Morocco and to express German support for Moroccan independence.

In Berlin the decision was taken to send the Kaiser on a strategic visit to the North African coast, and on 28 March 1905 Wilhelm II left Cuxhaven on the steamer *Hamburg*. When the news reached Paris of the Kaiser's intended destination the press was furious, calling it an anti-French gesture. Wilhelm, however, had more on his mind than the hostility of French newspapers. His destination – Tangier – was the unofficial headquarters of all the European anarchists who had been driven from their own countries. He feared that his arrival there might be just the opportunity somebody was looking for to kill an important figure and make a name for himself. He told Chancellor von Bülow of his fears but the old man was not for turning. Now that the French press had the news the show must go on. If Wilhelm were to be seen to scuttle away without setting foot in Tangier it would be regarded as a national humiliation for Germany.

On 31 March the *Hamburg* arrived off Tangier. Everyone now waited with bated breath for the

The German gunboat *Panther*, which was sent to rescue endangered German civilians from Agadir in 1911. In fact, only one man was rescued, and he was not in danger. The 'Agadir crisis' was manufactured by Berlin as part of Germany's policy of restricting French influence in Morocco.

Kaiser to assert his country's right to set foot on Moroccan soil. But even the seas were uncooperative. The *Hamburg* was too big to go into the docks and the Kaiser was forced to transfer to a smaller boat. The water was choppy, so the German chargé d'affaires in Tangier, arriving in a Bavarian Lancer's uniform, complete with high boots, spurs and dress sword, had to use a rope to climb up the *Hamburg*'s side to present himself to his monarch, who was already standing in a puddle from the seaspray. Wilhelm was not impressed. He was even less impressed when he arrived on the quayside at Tangier and found not the Sultan waiting to welcome him, but some aged relation sent as a substitute. It was a snub and took much of the fire out of the speech that Wilhelm proceeded to give, promising to support the Sultan's independence against any foreign power. The Sultan – a fat little boy of fourteen named Abdul-Aziz, who only liked playing with one toy, the Maxim gun that the British had given him – had remembered to send the Kaiser a present. It was a white Barbary stallion. Unfortunately, it was scarcely broken in and when the Kaiser mounted the beast it bucked and kicked and nearly threw him off. Things were not going well, Wilhelm thought, although at least he had not been shot yet. The Sultan had thought about that as well. Wilhelm

later learned that the boy had ordered all onlookers to be exterminated by his guards if the Kaiser was shot.

Wilhelm stayed in Tangier for just two hours. When he returned to the *Hamburg* he took out his frustration on von Bülow, complaining that the horse had nearly killed him and that every minute he had expected to be finished off by some hidden assassin. The whole visit was turning into a fiasco. He had hoped to visit Britain's Queen Alexandra aboard the royal yacht at Gibraltar, where he would be able to wear his uniform as an admiral of the Royal Navy. But by the time he reached Gibraltar the royal yacht had gone. To make matters worse, one of the German escort boats rammed a British cruiser. When he later met the British admirals, he told von Bülow, they 'stood stiffly and coldly to receive me without a single word more than was necessary'.

Still, much as Wilhelm may have suffered from his visit, the Germans were delighted at the outcome. The Sultan of Morocco, confident now in the support of Germany, refused to allow France to extend her control over his country. But while the Germans were congratulating themselves at this blow to French pride, they would have been very alarmed if they had known the effect the whole charade was having in London. King Edward VII was furious at the way in which the Kaiser, his nephew, had allowed himself to be used in such a deplorable and operatic way. King Edward's ministers were also concerned in case Germany might be thinking of trying to obtain a naval base on the Moroccan coast that might threaten the sealanes to South Africa. In such a case, Britain would stand behind France, even if it should lead to war.

Unaware of British anger, von Bülow demanded that a European conference should be called to discuss the internationalization of Morocco, in the hope that French influence might be removed from the country altogether. In German eyes, France was far too weak militarily to resist Germany at that stage, particularly as her main ally – Russia – was engaged in a war with Japan in the Far East. So the Germans decided to bully the French into making concessions. A conference began at Algeciras in Spain on 16 January, 1906, but from the outset the Germans found themselves up against a bigger bully than themselves. Algeciras was only a few miles from the British naval base at Gibraltar and the British made a point of anchoring their entire Atlantic and Mediterranean fleets in the harbour, consisting of twenty battleships and dozens of cruisers and lighter craft. The effect was stunning. No two other powers in the world could have matched the naval power present. The Germans were presented with a stark fact: however strong the German army might be, it could not walk on water, so any German acquisition in Morocco would depend on the tolerance of the Royal Navy for its survival. While the conference was in session, the British Commander-in-Chief, Admiral Lord Charles Beresford, took every opportunity to entertain the delegates aboard his flagship, the aptly named *King Edward VII*. As result of the ever-present threat of British naval power the Germans won nothing important from the conference and the First Moroccan Crisis ended in a decisive defeat for German diplomacy. In their attempt to humiliate France, von Bülow and his advisers had achieved exactly the opposite of what they had hoped: the strengthening rather than the weakening of the 'Entente Cordiale'.

The Algeciras Conference of 1906 had endorsed the independence of the Sultan of Morocco's lands and had guaranteed an 'open door' policy for the trade of all nations. Nevertheless, the French still maintained their primary role in the politics of the country, much to the chagrin of successive German chancellors. The Germans particularly feared that the French would attempt to turn their 'sphere of influence' into something more concrete, notably in the north of Morocco. Accordingly, the Germans planned to try to assert their own rights in the south of the country.

In 1911 the French claimed that the lives of European citizens were in danger in the town of Fez, to the east of Rabat, and that they were sending a military column on a mercy mission. The Germans guessed that this was simply a first step in a French take-over of northern Morocco. As they told the French government, 'If you go to Fez, you will not depart. If French troops remain in Fez so that the Sultan rules only with the aid of French bayonets, Germany will regard the Act of Algeciras as no longer in force and will resume complete liberty of action.' The threat contained in the last sentence was a necessary sop to the nationalists in the German Reichstag who thought Germany had already been far too moderate in her dealings with France. Furthermore, because of suspicions about the French mission to Fez, the new German chancellor, Theobald von Bethmann-Hollweg, planned to intervene in southern Morocco, using the argument that German nationals were in danger there. Admittedly there were at that time no German citizens in the area and nor were there any German soldiers in Morocco, but both could soon be arranged. A warship would be sent south to the port of Agadir and there 'rescue' the endangered German civilians from the very clutches of the wild Moroccan tribesmen. Even if Germany could not secure the whole of southern Morocco, she would certainly be able to force France to compensate her with part of the French Congo.

The Germans felt more comfortable in opposing France this time than they had in 1905. For a start, the pro-French King Edward VII of England was dead and his son, George V – a young cousin of Kaiser Wilhelm II – was regarded as more easy to intimidate. To test the water 'Willy' had asked 'Georgie' how he felt about France's policy in Morocco. King George had replied that he felt the Algeciras Convention was no longer in force and the French were doing no more than Britain was doing in Egypt. As far as Britain was concerned, France had a free hand. This was not very reassuring for Germany, who now knew that she could expect no help from Britain. Moreover, sending a warship

A German cartoon showing the Kaiser's mailed fist being used to end the 'Agadir crisis' of 1911. The Kaiser's policy was misconceived and only served to bring Britain and France closer together in their resistance to what they saw as German aggression.

to Agadir might be seen as an act of war by France and possibly even Britain. It was a very risky business, but the Germans felt that they would lose too much face if they did not react to France's actions in northern Morocco. As a result, in June 1911, the order was sent out to the gunboat *Panther* to steam to Agadir and there rescue the endangered German civilians.

As a symbol of German power the *Panther* was very poor. Built at the turn of the century, she was 'short, fat and lightly armed'. Her crew numbered 130 men, but of these a proportion comprised the brass band, and up until that moment the *Panther*

had been more accustomed to impressing African natives with the smoke from her funnels, the popping-noises of her old 4-inch guns and the rumbustiousness of her musicians. The *Panther* had done her job well, but one suspects that whoever had named her must have had his tongue firmly in his cheek. Nevertheless, she was all that Germany had available at short notice and she would have to do. In any case, on such a mercy mission she would seem more appropriate than British *Conquerors*, *Thunderers*, *Invincibles* and *Dreadnoughts*.

On the first day of July 1911, the *Panther* sailed into the magnificently scenic bay at Agadir, presumably expecting to see the beaches heaving with suffering humanity like a scene from Géricault's 'Raft of the Medusa'. Instead, there was just a native village in the distance and empty beaches of golden sand. There was no sign of any Europeans, suffering or otherwise. The problem was that the 'Endangered German' as he was later to be laughingly dubbed, had not arrived yet. He had been told to get there before the boat arrived but he had been held up. Was he dodging bullets and ducking spears? Far from it. Herr Wilburg, as the German was known when not being splashed across the newspapers of every European capital, was a representative of a Hamburg business firm then visiting Morocco. Three days before he had been at Mogador, 75 miles north of Agadir, when he received the message to get to the port without delay to be 'rescued'. He faced quite a journey, in appalling heat. On the way he noticed to his surprise that even the goats had climbed into the trees to get some shade. Only he and his horse were braving the heat on the open road. When Wilburg reached Agadir he saw the grey-hulled gunboat anchored in the bay, but he was so exhausted that he could do nothing other than find somewhere to sleep. Tomorrow was soon enough to be rescued.

The next morning Wilburg awoke to find that a second warship, the *Berlin*, had entered the bay and anchored alongside the *Panther*. He walked along the beach waving to the ships but nobody took any notice of him. For a rescue party they certainly lacked a sense of urgency. Wilburg shouted, jumped up and down and waved again. The officers of the watch on the *Berlin* reported his antics as those of one of the natives. An hour passed and Wilbur stood gazing in frustration at the distant ships, with his hands on his hips. That was the giveaway; no native had ever been known to stand in that pose. The word passed around both German ships – it must be the 'Endangered German'. Soon boats were rowing towards the shore and Wilburg was 'rescued' from his plight by the Kaiser's Imperial Navy.

The *Panther* had 'leapt' and throughout Europe newspapers led with the story of the sensational rescue of German civilians from the jaws of death. German ambassadors reported that German firms near Agadir had called on the Imperial Navy to rescue them from the barbarous attentions of the local Moroccans. This had required the government to send a gunboat. Inside Germany extreme nationalists were demanding the immediate seizure

of southern Morocco, or else substantial compensation from France.

On 4 July, the British Foreign Secretary, Sir Edward Grey, called the German ambassador, Count Metternich, to the Foreign Office in London. Grey wanted to know whether German troops would be landed in Morocco. Metternich did not know, for the simple fact that nobody had told him. In Berlin they scarcely knew what to do next. Grey reminded Metternich of Britain's treaty obligations to France – a veiled warning that the Royal Navy could intervene if it chose at any stage to snuff out the German expedition. In fact, the British position was the same as it had been in 1905. Britain was absolutely committed to resisting any German attempt to establish a naval base in Morocco that might interfere with the sea-lanes to South Africa. On the other hand, the Germans were quite aware that they could not possibly support a base at Agadir, 1500 miles from the homeland. Such a base would be a source of weakness rather than strength. Their argument was with France not with Britain.

France had rather more to worry about than Britain. German aggression in Morocco was aimed directly at her and if the '*Panther*'s Leap' should be a prelude to war, the fighting would take place in Europe not in Africa. It was certain that the British Navy could cope with the German Navy, but that would be of little comfort to the French if their homeland was overrun by the enormously powerful German Army. As a result, the French were much concerned with avoiding war at all costs, even if this meant that they were forced to make territorial concessions to the Germans in the Congo.

However, in Britain, events were taking a very different turn. Far from seeking to avoid war, as were the French, the Chancellor of the Exchequer, the previously pacifist David Lloyd George, was making a speech at the Mansion House in which he warned Germany that Britain would be prepared for war in the event of any German aggression in Morocco. This came as a shock as much to Lloyd George's colleagues in Britain as to the Germans, who had previously regarded him as one of the British politicians most friendly to Germany. The German press exploded with anger at this evidence of Britain's interference in matters that did not concern her. They accused the British of wanting a share in any partition of Morocco.

When Count Metternich met Grey on 24 July, it was to inform him that the *Panther* had been sent only to protect German interests and to rescue German farmers who had been attacked by native Moroccans. Grey pointed out that to his knowledge no such attack had taken place before the *Panther* arrived and that the only person rescued was a businessman from Hamburg. Metternich agreed that the attack was news to him as well. Grey then pointed out that there were no Germans in the region where the attack was said to have taken place. Metternich replied that he could not comment. The meeting ended and the embarrassed Metternich withdrew.

Yet with all this talk of war, the British were not taking the matter seriously enough in the eyes of Winston Churchill, the First Lord of the Admiralty. The First Sea Lord, Sir Arthur Wilson, had been so unimpressed by the German threat that he had even gone away for the weekend to shoot grouse. Churchill was profoundly shocked. At any moment hordes of Huns might descend on the Admiralty building in Whitehall or raid the naval magazines. Churchill had every intention of making a drama out of a crisis. He questioned the Chief Commissioner of Police about the responsibility for guarding naval magazines and learned that this task was carried out by a few lowly constables. But what, Churchill asked him, would be the result if twenty determined and well-armed Germans in fast motor cars should arrive outside the magazines? The Commissioner raised his eyebrows. Churchill seized the phone and rang the Admiralty. There he spoke to the admiral in charge of naval magazines. Churchill demanded marines – hundreds of them – to take over responsibility for guarding the nation's reserves of shot and shell. The admiral told him to mind his own business. Churchill next rang the War Office and demanded squads of soldiers to be rushed to the magazines. This time he got his way. The nation could sleep soundly once again.

With pandemonium at the British Admiralty, the Germans took fright. Aware that the British were prepared to use force if necessary to stop any German naval activity on the west coast of Africa, the Kaiser and his ministers looked for a way out of their difficulties. Only by a conciliatory approach to France could the Germans be certain that Britain would not come to the aid of her ally. Initially Germany had made huge demands of the French, insisting on large sections of the French Congo to placate the nationalists within the Reichstag. Most Germans, however, were not really interested in the steamy, plague-ridden rainforest of tropical Africa and were certainly not willing to risk a war to get it. So by early October the French and German governments reached agreement on Morocco, granting France a *de facto* protectorate over the whole country. In return, France agreed to compensate Germany with 100,000 square miles of territory in the Congo, which was added to the German colony of Cameroons. The outcome was a triumph for France and a terrible humiliation for Germany. In the words of Sir Edward Grey, it was 'almost a fiasco for Germany; out of this mountain of a German-made crisis came a mouse of colonial territory in Africa'. The ex-chancellor von Bülow commented that the whole episode was 'deplorable . . . a fiasco . . . like a damp squib, it startled, then amused, and ended by making us look ridiculous'.

The Germans had blundered once again over Morocco. Every attempt they made to drive a wedge between Britain and France as allies only seemed to bring the two countries closer together. The Kaiser's admiration and envy of the Royal Navy was at the root of the problem for Germany. However strong his army might be, he was destined to be pre-eminent only on a European platform and subservient – always – on the world stage where he craved to be the prima donna.

CHAPTER FOUR: SOCIAL AND ECONOMIC BLUNDERS

Pretty bubbles in the air

Abraham Lincoln once said, 'You can't fool all the people all the time.' But had he been living a century earlier, in the England of 1720, he might have had his doubts. For there was something in the air, something that drove people, many of them previously cautious and sober citizens, to act like mad march hares.

In the sixteenth century the gold and silver mines of Mexico and Peru had provided Spain with fabulous wealth. And nowhere was this wealth more coveted than in England. During the next century numerous attempts were made by the English to break into the South American market, but all without success. Eventually victory in the War of the Spanish Succession in 1713 brought Britain the Asiento contract, allowing one British ship a year to trade with Mexico, Peru or Chile. This paltry concession was further limited by the fact that the owners of the ship had to pay the king of Spain a quarter of all profits. Even so, on the basis of this meanest of grants, the newly created British South Sea Company generated boundless public confidence. For some reason the great British public ignored the fact that it was easier to get gold out of a lump of lead than from the Spanish king, and imagined that the South Sea Company was on the brink of a major entrepreneurial coup.

While the new king – George I – was recommending to Parliament the usefulness of paying off the national debt, he invited the two main financial institutions of the time – the Bank of England and the South Sea Company – to make suggestions on how to do it. The South Sea Company came up with the best idea: they would raise £2 million by public subscription and use the money to fund the debt. Even though the Company had few contacts in the South Seas and gained little by trading there, its name conjured images of boundless wealth in the minds of an acquisitive public, willing to risk everything on any speculative venture.

On 2 February 1720 the House of Commons accepted the plan and from that moment the Company's stock rose at an astonishing rate, tripling in value in a single day. Only the Whig politician Robert Walpole kept any sense of balance during this crazily speculative period, warning the people of the dangers of stockjobbing, but nobody listened. They were ready to risk their homes and livelihoods in a vain pursuit of imaginary riches. Even in the House of Commons, members who had previously listened intently to Walpole's words, fled the chamber as soon as it was known that he was going to speak on the South Sea question.

In order to boost the value of the South Sea Company, its directors spread rumours of favourable, though imaginary, treaties between England and Spain. The word was put out that the Spaniards – until then unwilling to give the English the mouldy rind off their cheese – were suddenly overcome by such magnanimity that they were willing to hand over the Potosi silver mine in Peru for England's sole use, so that silver would become as plentiful as iron. And the Spaniards in Mexico were, apparently, so enamoured of the idea of English cotton and woollen goods that they were ready to empty their goldmines to obtain them. The result was that the Company's shares rose to unimaginable heights, and it seemed as if every Londoner had turned speculator. So crowded were the streets around the exchange that no carriages could pass and even the highest in the land had to go on foot. The directors continued to spread rumours to boost their stock, claiming that the Spaniards were ready to exchange parts of South America for Gibraltar, and that the Asiento contract was to be revoked, allowing the Company to send whole fleets of merchantmen to the South Seas.

While the rogues who acted as directors for the South Sea Company were gulling most of the population of London, many other entrepreneurs – some legitimate merchants, others the merest tricksters – began to emerge from the woodwork. Dozens of new joint-stock companies, known as 'bubbles', were quoted on the exchange. The word 'bubble' was entirely appropriate for these highly speculative ventures, few of which lasted as long as a week and most of which had a far briefer career. The Prince of Wales became governor of one such 'bubble', made a profit

A satirical representation of the South Sea Bubble of 1720 showing how public hysteria affected men and women alike. Greed prompted people to invest all their savings in highly speculative and unreliable schemes for making money, known as 'bubbles'.

of £40,000, and then damned the wretched investors, who lost their all. Members of the nobility were prominent in many of the worst 'bubbles', of which more than a hundred were afloat at any one time. One company, which raised an immense capital, stated its purpose to be the making of deal boards from sawdust, another was to perfect a 'perpetual-motion-wheel', and a third – surely the most ridiculous of all – was 'a company for carrying on an undertaking of great advantage but nobody to know what it is'. The last mentioned apparently raised thousands of pounds for its governor, who – having opened an office in Cornhill in the morning, which was beset by crowds of willing investors – fled the country the same evening, as soon as he had the money in his hand. Dean Swift was quick to condemn the folly of his fellow men and pilloried them in verse:

> Subscribers here by thousands float
> And jostle one another down,
> Each paddling in his leaky boat,
> And here they fish for gold and drown.

The highest in the land, of both sexes, indulged themselves in these financial speculations. The men visited their brokers in taverns and coffee houses, while the ladies met theirs in milliners' and haberdashers'. It was fashionable, but it was the purest fantasy.

However, on 11 June the king declared that the 'bubbles' were public nuisances and illegal activities for buying and selling shares. Company directors were henceforth prosecuted and fined. The biggest fish, however, had already swum away with their profits, leaving only the minnows to face the consequences. Despite the king's intervention, many 'bubbles' continued to float upwards and many foolish investors tried to finance them, one for instance offering the improbable purpose of extracting silver from lead. Another bizarre 'bubble' was Puckle's Machine Company for 'discharging round and square cannon balls and bullets and making a total revolution in the art of war'.

Meanwhile, the stock of the South Sea Company was still rising. During May it virtually doubled to a point where most investors, not completely blinded by their own greed, could see that it was past any realistic level and was bound to fall at any time. As a result, many big investors took their profits and sold up. On 3 June so many sellers turned up at the exchange and so few buyers that the stock went into a spiralling decline. The directors were forced to step in to prevent collapse by buying much of the stock offered for sale. Confidence was restored – at least for a while. By August, the stock of the South Sea Company stood at ten times what it had when the speculation began in February, but the 'bubble' was 'quivering and shaking'. At this stage news began to spread that Sir John Blunt, the governor of the Company, and many of his directors had sold out. This was the beginning of the end. As the stock fell, many ordinary people faced ruin. The Company directors were attacked in the streets and the government feared that the collapse of the Company would lead to rioting throughout London. King George I cut short his stay in Hanover and in the late autumn hurried back to England and summoned Parliament to deal with the crisis. Throughout the country public meetings were held at which shareholders voiced their anger at the Company directors. Petitions flooded into London from all parts demanding justice from the villainy of the South Sea Company. Five of the directors were arrested, but the treasurer, Mr Knight, packed up his books and made his escape to Calais. The king thereupon sent out orders to his ambassadors to demand the return of the treasurer from whichever country he should try to enter.

The Chancellor of the Exchequer, Mr Aislabie, who had spoken on behalf of the Company during the parliamentary debates of February 1720, was forced to resign on suspicion of financial irregularity. Furthermore, he was then expelled from the House of Commons and imprisoned in the Tower of London, lest he should join Mr Knight in flight. While poor Aislabie was being taken to the Tower he was hooted and jeered by a large, unruly mob on Tower Hill. Unable to vent their feelings on the fallen politician, they lit a bonfire and burned him in effigy. Robert Walpole, standing head and shoulders above other politicians during the crisis, insisted that the restoration of public credit was the first concern of the government. As a result of his efforts creditors regained at least a third of all their losses, but this was hardly enough to save many thousands of people from the consequences of their greed and gullibility.

Tulipmania

A love of flowers is one thing, but the obsession with tulips that overtook Holland in the early seventeenth century threatened to sweep away the social and economic system on which the Dutch state was built. Mass hysteria replaced rational thinking and families made and lost fortunes in a single day – often as the result of a single tulip bulb.

The word 'tulip' comes from a Turkish word signifying a turban, and the first tulips reached Europe from Constantinople in the sixteenth century. They were especially highly regarded for their shape and colour, and became favourites in Germany and Holland. Indeed, in the latter country, it was deemed a sign of poor breeding for a wealthy man not to have a collection of tulip bulbs. However, in the upwardly mobile society of seventeenth-century Holland, the middle classes and those aspiring to become so refused to leave the tulips to the very rich. By 1634 all kinds of people – including merchants and even modest shopkeepers – were trying to gain social status by possessing tulips. It was soon common for the lower orders to be giving a half of all they had in the world to acquire a single root and join the exclusive 'club'.

Tulipmania, from being a harmless obsession, became a serious threat. Tulips were by now a more secure measure of wealth than silver or gold and people felt insecure unless they had invested everything in tulip bulbs. Throughout the country normal economic and industrial activity came to a halt as thousands embarked on a career in the tulip trade. In 1635 one man was known to have invested a fortune of 100,000 florins in purchasing just 40 roots. To give an idea of what that meant, one could buy a pig for 30 florins or an ox for 100 florins. Particularly rare tulips were given the names of Dutch admirals: the *Admiral Liefkin* was worth 4400 florins, the *Admiral Van der Eyck* a mere 1260. Tulips changed hands for fantastic prices, as well as in exchange for rich farming land, houses and thoroughbred horses.

In one extraordinary incident a rich merchant – and notable collector of tulips – received news from a sailor that his cargo of Levantine goods had arrived at the docks. The merchant welcomed the sailor into his counting-house, where there were piles of goods of all kinds, and rewarded him for his good news with a large red herring for his breakfast. The sailor thanked the merchant and, seeing what he assumed to be a discarded onion lying on the counter, took it and set off to eat his breakfast in the fresh air. Unfortunately, of course, the onion was not an onion at all but a fantastically valuable *Semper Augustus* tulip bulb worth 3000 florins. The merchant at once noticed that his prize was missing and instigated a frantic search, but to no avail. Then he remembered the sailor and assumed that he must have stolen the bulb. The merchant set up a hue and cry but it was all too late. By the time they found the sailor, seated on a pile of ropes down by the quayside, he had eaten the herring and the 'onion'. In spite of his protestations of innocence the sailor was charged with stealing the tulip and was thrown into gaol.

During 1636 regular tulip sales were held at the Stock Exchange in Amsterdam, as well as at centres in Rotterdam, Harlem, Leyden, Alkmar, Hoorn and many other towns. Speculators gambled on the value of tulips, causing prices to fluctuate. Now greed overcame the snobbery that had previously gone with the possession of tulips. No longer valued for what they were, or for the prestige they bestowed on their owners, tulips were seen as merely the way to a quick fortune. Skilful manipulators of the market grew rich at the expense of the naive investors who believed that tulips would be in demand for ever in Holland. It was noticed that even the poorer classes were spending their all in the mad jostle to grow rich. Money that was needed for rent or food or clothing was risked without a second thought. Many people even sold their houses to gain enough money to buy and sell tulips.

As prices peaked the professional speculators, only too aware that the hysteria could not last for ever, decided to offload their tulips on the market and the prices began to fall, never to recover. Ruin was the fate of many Dutch people who had overextended themselves. With the collapse of the tulip market came a wave of social unrest. Those who had lost heavily demanded that the government should do something about it. But the government was as helpless to solve the problem as the victims of the speculation. They tried to declare null and void contracts made during the height of the mania, but this only resulted in a rash of breach of contract cases the length and breadth of the country. In the end it was clear that blame could not be attributed to individuals. Mass hysteria and greed had fuelled the crisis and people had gained or lost according to their skill or their luck. But the cost to the country was far greater than to any individual. During the period of madness, from 1634 to 1636 the trade of the country had dwindled, farming and industry had declined and foreigners – notably the English – had seized foreign markets while the Dutch were preoccupied. It was many years before the Dutch state recovered these losses.

Blowing in the wind

After the death of Stalin in 1953, it was some time before an obvious successor emerged from the Soviet hierarchy. The leading candidate was Nikita Khrushchev, who felt that he could secure the support of his colleagues best by reducing the gap in agricultural production between the Soviet Union and her Cold War rival, the United States. In order to achieve this, Khrushchev was forced to introduce radical new policies and to open up new areas to cultivation. The result was the fiasco of Khrushchev's 'Virgin Lands' policy.

So heavy had been Stalin's concentration on industrial growth in the Soviet Union that the agricultural sector had become seriously under-funded. Previously self-sufficient peasants, who had grown their own grain, made their own bread, produced their own dairy produce and slaughtered their own cattle for meat, now had to buy their food from the towns and cities, just like urban dwellers. The absurd situation had now been reached where the towns were feeding the countryside. This could only be reversed by a massive improvement in agricultural production: output of grain would have to be doubled, meat tripled and dairy produce increased by four or five times. An additional advantage was that these levels of production would enable the Soviet Union once again to become an exporter of food and not an importer. Khrushchev therefore proposed to open up millions of acres of 'virgin' and fallow land in Kazakhstan, north and east of the Aral Sea.

The 'Virgin Lands' policy followed the failure of the 1953 harvest and was originally only intended as a stop-gap measure, to boost production while traditional areas were redeveloped with new fertilizers and the latest technical equipment. The aim was that the virgin lands would produce 20 million tons of grain by 1955. At the beginning of 1954 an army of 300,000 volunteers travelled by special trains to northern Kazakhstan and southern Siberia. Here hundreds of tented towns grew up to house the migrant workers. In addition, 50,000 tractors and more than 6000 trucks and other vehicles were made available. It was an impressive start, comparable in many ways with China's 'Great Leap Forward' (see p. 124) but not saddled with Mao's absurd economic theories. Unfortunately, the 1955 harvest – of which so much had been expected – proved to be a poor one across the Soviet Union. The spring wheat sown in the virgin lands died in its entirety and food became so short there that thousands of volunteers deserted their settlements and headed back home. Khrushchev found himself the centre of vicious criticism from rivals such as Malenkov and Kaganovich. As they pointed out, if all the money wasted on the new lands had instead been used in the old lands, the harvest might have been saved.

However, Khrushchev held on to his seat on the Central Committee and continued to press forward with, and even expand, the 'Virgin Lands' policy. The decisive year would prove to be 1956 when, more by luck than skill, the harvest was abundant. The production of the old lands was poor because of a drought, but in the virgin lands it was a huge success, unprecedented in Soviet history. Khrushchev toured Kazakhstan like a victorious general, travelling in motorcades and cheered by thousands of workers. The 1955 target of 20 million tons of grain had been more than

Soviet leader Nikita Khrushchev photographed in Washington in 1959. After the death of Josef Stalin in 1953, Khrushchev was one of a number of Politburo members vying to succeed him. Khrushchev's policy of opening up the 'Virgin Lands' of Kazakhstan to agricultural production helped him to the top. Yet his agricultural reforms achieved only short-term success and in the long term were disastrous failures.

tripled. However, through poor planning and inadequate distribution much of this went to waste. So much effort had gone into growing the crops that nobody had given sufficient thought to the need for harvesters or storage barns. There were too few lorries and freight cars to shift the grain from the fields to the urban centres. It was the old story – Soviet incompetence wasting the nation's resources. Nevertheless, enough of the harvest was saved to give the appearance that Khrushchev's gamble had worked.

Spurred on by this apparent success, Khrushchev turned his attention to meat and dairy production. In May 1957, he set the nation the target of overtaking the United States' output of these products within three or four years. It was the same kind of insanity that was driving the Chinese to produce 'back-yard' steel and it ended in the same sort of chaos. The worst example occurred in the agricultural *oblast* of Riazan – an *oblast* was an administrative district within a Soviet republic – resulting in the notorious 'Riazan Fiasco'.

The leader of the Riazan *oblast*, A. N. Larionov, was an ambitious politician who was prepared to promise anything to please his superiors. When he heard that Khrushchev was demanding a tremendous increase in food production Larionov promised to increase Riazan's sale of meat to the government from 48,000 tons in 1958 to an incredible 150,000 tons in 1959. On hearing of this Khrushchev apparently promised Larionov a very senior post if he succeeded. But what Larionov was promising was impossible, as any reasonable person must have realized. Yet

Khrushchev – to encourage the spirit of competition among the *oblasts* – allowed Larionov's promise to get nationwide circulation by printing it in *Pravda*. Larionov was in danger of being 'hoist by his own petard'. It was not feasible to increase the number of livestock so quickly, or to fatten up existing cattle – nature could not be rushed. So, in spite of the fact that the entire *oblast* was awarded the Order of Lenin and Khrushchev personally visited the area to present the award, it seemed certain that Larionov must fail.

Larionov, however, was not prepared to go down without a fight and he now began doing things which were anathema to any farming community. He began slaughtering not just the animals earmarked for meat, but all the dairy herds and the breeding stock. In addition, he ordered all privately owned animals to be surrendered for slaughter. And when this still was not enough, he sent his officials to buy cattle from neighbouring *oblasts*. In order to finance the purchase of extra cattle, Larionov used his entire budget quota for machinery and for all other uses. No workers got paid, no bills from creditors were honoured and all kinds of illegal funds were 'created' and thrown into the 'battle for beef'. Neighbouring *oblasts*, meanwhile, were growing wary of Larionov's raids and his men were soon being accused of 'rustling'. A veritable range war broke out, with police road blocks being set up to stop the Riazan gang of 'procurement agents' from smuggling cattle at night. There were even 'Western-style' gunfights as the Riazan rustlers rode the range.

In a last desperate effort to reach his quota, Larionov persuaded the local Party committee to agree to levy local taxes in kind rather than cash, and payment was only accepted in meat. Not only farmers, but schools, hospitals and even the local police department were required to pay their local rates with meat. When a black market for meat grew up, Larionov's men bought the meat there at high prices only to have to sell it to the government for a minute proportion of what they had just paid. It was economic madness, but Larionov was winning his personal battle. Even though the local shops were empty of meat, milk and butter and the sight of a live cow was rare indeed, he reached the 150,000 tons he had promised. Unfortunately, he 'never knew when to quit'. Having won his first gamble, Larionov promptly promised to do even better next year. This was impossible and everybody knew it. Riazan was ruined and had become an agricultural desert, barren of cattle. Larionov was made a Hero of Socialist Labour and received the Order of Lenin, but when the truth dawned on him that production in 1960 was not going to exceed even 30,000 tons he went into his office and shot himself. Although Riazan was an extreme example of what happened throughout the Soviet Union, its experience was shared to a lesser degree by thousands of *oblasts*. The result of Khrushchev's ill-advised policy on meat was that production fell by 200,000 tons in 1960 and, far from overtaking the United States, the Soviet Union fell far behind what it had been producing under Stalin.

If Khrushchev felt that things could not possibly get worse, he was wrong. The initial success of the 'Virgin Lands' policy was giving way to a period of problems. A lack of common sense had gone into the planting of the new lands. Such areas might do well initially, but once the nutritive substances already present in the soil were exhausted the land would need time to recover, by being left fallow. The new lands had been a short-term expedient only and could not possibly sustain the growth-rate of their first great harvest. When, in 1959, it was decided that the new lands would have to become a vital part of wheat growing in the Soviet Union for years to come, trouble was certain. In fact, in the entire period from 1956 to 1965, the new lands exceeded their quota only once, and the average cost of virgin land wheat was three times higher than wheat grown in traditional areas, like the Ukraine. The main problem was that weather conditions in Kazakhstan were just not reliable, being suitable for wheat growing only twice in every five years. All this information had been available to Khrushchev's agricultural and economic advisers, but why had nobody told him – or convinced him to listen?

But the final straw – if one can be excused the pun – was that the new lands were seriously prone to soil erosion. The steppe lands of Kazakhstan were not protected by forest zones: without tree roots to bind the soil or trees to act as a barrier against the strong winds it was absolute folly to dig up millions of acres for an agricultural experiment, however vital. Politics, however, took little account of local soil conditions or topography and where a politician's ambitions were involved – as we have seen with Larionov and even more with Khrushchev himself – the carping of experts was insignificant. The outcome was that in addition to ploughing fertile soil, the pioneers in 1954 also dug in saline areas and on large areas of light sandy loam, which was quickly blown away by the wind.

By 1960 hundreds of thousands of acres in the new lands had been destroyed by wind erosion. Yet the Russians have always regarded their country in the same light as the Chinese have their people – as limitless and therefore expendable. What were millions of acres when there was so much more? The wind conclusively demonstrated the fallacy of this argument in 1962 and 1963, when millions of tons of topsoil were whisked away from the new lands by 95-mile-an-hour winds, eventually piling up in the foothills of a distant mountain range. For weeks at a time it was as if night had swallowed day. Huge dust storms covered the sun, irrigation canals were silted up and many towns were choked with soil to a depth of six feet. Miles of bedrock appeared where once wheat had grown. It was a catastrophe – 'natural' yet man-made – of staggering proportions. It has been estimated that it will take two centuries to restore to some parts of the new lands the arable layer which, through human stupidity, they had lost to the wind.

Khrushchev's 'Virgin Lands' policy ranks with Mao Zedong's 'Great Leap Forward' as a classic error of Communist economic planning. Its effects at a human level were far less than those suffered in China, but as an ecological catastrophe it ranks high in the list of historical blunders.

Heads we win

Poll taxes have an unfortunate record in Britain. They smack less of firm government than of political chicanery, of the 'heads we win, tails you lose' sort. Six hundred years divide the poll tax of Richard II from that of Margaret Thatcher. Much may have changed in that time but not the reaction of the people in response to what they saw as an unjust law. If the first poll tax gave rise to the Peasants' Revolt of 1381, the next one led to scenes of unprecedented civil unrest in the late 1980s and the fall of the 'Iron Lady'.

The medieval Englishman, whether yeoman or peasant, was no more avid a taxpayer than his twentieth-century equivalent. He was particularly suspicious of anything that suggested novelty and he feared, above all, that the government might be trying to put one over him. Thus, when the poll tax of 1377 was introduced by the advisers of the child king, Richard II, it was met with hostility and apprehension. Yet it was a good idea at the time, for there was a great need to raise revenue to combat French raids on the south coast of England. The traditional revenue from tenths and fifteenths was inadequate to cope with the emergency and this 'tallage of groats', which raised some £22,000, seemed to fit the bill. However, the war in France was proving enormously expensive and after John of Gaunt's failed operation against St Malo the government needed even more money. As a result, the king's advisers imposed a second poll tax in 1379, based on a graduated scale of assessment. It would be nice to think that the system was graduated in the interests of greater fairness, but it was not. The aim was simply to raise more money by assessing the wealthy at a more realistic level. Significantly, virtually nobody was asked to pay less than they had in the first levy two years before. But even this levy proved inadequate and the following year, at the parliament of Northampton, the king's advisers called for a tallage of three groats, to pay the English troops in France before they deserted *en masse*. On 7 December 1380, the third poll tax was levied.

The royal tax collectors set about the unenviable task of collecting the third levy in just four years. At first they met little resistance and if their returns had been accepted by the king's ministers all might have passed off peacefully. However, the king's council was convinced that there had been widespread tax evasion and ordered the collectors to compel full payment of the levy. This resulted in the appointment of bodies of commissioners who reassessed payments for the counties of Essex, Kent, Norfolk, Suffolk and Hertfordshire. Those who had already paid found the collectors at their door once again and it was in these counties that tax risings began.

The Peasant's Revolt of 1381, though a widespread demonstration of popular discontent, is best known for the actions of the Kent and Essex peasants led by such men as Wat Tyler, Jack Straw and the priest John Ball. They had many grievances to air, but the poll tax came to stand as a symbol of them all. If a spark was needed to inflame the smouldering discontent of the poorer classes it came from three small, marshland villages in Essex. There the failure of Chief Justice Bealknap to quell the first resistance to the tax collectors was decisive. From these three villages the peasants moved into the countryside, hunting down the royal officials they felt were oppressing them. The news passed from village to village and soon the whole country was alive with rebellion. Now the targets for rebel anger passed from local officials to members of the court, like John of Gaunt, Archbishop Sudbury and Treasurer Hales. Only by going to London could the peasants bring these men to book for their

The Poll Tax of 1381 precipitated the Peasants' Revolt. Here Wat Tyler, the peasants' leader, is killed by the Mayor of London during his parley with the boy-king Richard II.

bad advice to the young king. What followed in London was very bloody. Of the king's ministers, Sudbury and Hales both died, but the king emerged unharmed, having taken fierce reprisals against the followers of Wat Tyler. The poll tax, too, was a victim of the conflagration. It was replaced by a fairer and more reliable system. Not for six hundred years did a British government attempt to reintroduce such an invidious system of taxation, but when they did – in 1989 – the reaction of the British people was the same. This time it was not the head of Treasurer Hales they sought but that of the 'iron lady', Margaret Thatcher.

The poll tax devised by the Conservative government of Margaret Thatcher, no doubt learning from the fate of Treasurer Hales and Archbishop Sudbury in Richard II's reign, was released to the public in disguise. It was *not* a poll tax, it was the 'community charge'. Thus the advocates of open government were presenting their flagship to the country disguised as a pleasure steamer. The problem was that everyone kept forgetting to maintain the pretence. On her last day as Prime Minister Mrs Thatcher almost let the cat out of the bag when she unintentionally referred to the 'poll . . . er, the community charge'.

Margaret Thatcher had been the midwife at the birth of the poll tax idea when, as Shadow Environment Secretary, she had included the abolition of domestic rates in the 1974 Conservative election manifesto. Five years later abolition of the rates was still in the manifesto. The Conservative Party's objection to domestic rates was well established by this stage as a result of a general feeling that a lot of people were getting away with not paying for local services. In 1985 Margaret Thatcher picked up the idea for a poll tax from a pamphlet issued by the right-wing Adam Smith Institute, arguing that 'Domestic rates should be replaced with a simple per capita tax on all adults over the age of eighteen. Such a uniform charge reflects the fact that individuals' consumption of local services is roughly equal.' The then Environment Minister Kenneth Baker took up the torch in 1986 in his Green Paper, *Paying for Local Government*. In spite of strong opposition from the Treasury, Margaret Thatcher now forced through the idea of a poll tax. Her Chancellor of the Exchequer, Nigel Lawson, bitterly opposed her, claiming that the tax would be so unpopular and so difficult to enforce that it would be politically disastrous to introduce it. But by this stage the lady was not for turning. With the support of the hard-line Thatcherite Nicholas Ridley, now at the Department of the Environment, Mrs Thatcher was determined to introduce the new tax in the wake of the 1987 election victory. The poll tax was first introduced in Scotland in 1989–90 and then in England and Wales in the following year.

From the start it was obvious that Nigel Lawson's reservations had been justified. The tax was enormously unpopular and was resisted even by people who had previously been willing to pay rates. The flat-rate system, which was applied regardless of income or level of wealth, was perceived as deeply unfair and far worse than the much derided local rates. The poll tax brought people out into the streets in protest and Thatcher, the 'three-times winner' Prime Minister, found herself the

Plus ça change plus c'est la même chose. Poll tax riots in London in 1990. Fortunately no one was killed on this occasion, but the fall of Margaret Thatcher as prime minister and Conservative leader was a direct consequence of the unpopularity of the new tax.

focus of ferocious opposition. Her dominant position within the Conservative Party was so eroded by her adherence to the unpopular tax that she found herself challenged for the leadership by one of her ex-ministers, Michael Heseltine. Although Heseltine was not strong enough to defeat her on the first vote, she was so wounded in the contest that she was forced to stand down in favour of John Major, who emerged victorious from the second ballot. Ironically, the task of replacing the unpopular poll tax fell to Michael Heseltine, at the Department of the Environment.

Although the poll tax of the 1980s produced no Wat Tyler or John Ball, and its defeat did not require a 'peasants' revolt', it was many of Mrs Thatcher's own supporters – Kentish men and Essex men – who stood to lose most from the fixed-rate system. And it was these people who were forced to take action against the hubris of the Prime Minister.

The pound in your pocket

Was there actually a time when people trusted politicians? It seems doubtful. Yet until relatively recently the vast majority of people were only able to read the words of those who governed them in the newspapers or, very occasionally, to hear them spoken at public meetings or on the hustings. But the advent of television has brought both the image and the words of politicians into the houses of most ordinary people. Thus they can hear their leaders speaking to them directly and are able to make up their own minds. The scandals of the Macmillan government in the early 1960s coincided with the birth of television satire, with the result that the words and actions of politicians came under greater scrutiny than ever before. Even so, a scandal like War Minister Jack Profumo's liaison with call-girl Christine Keeler still seemed excitingly 'distant' for most people. Such things happened to Hollywood film-stars rather than to people whose actions affected the great British public.

However, the economic problems of the second Wilson administration of 1966 marked an important stage in the demystification of ministers and politicians. Even at the time most economists believed that devaluation of the pound was unavoidable. British exports were uncompetitive abroad and this was contributing to high unemployment in manufacturing industry. Yet, in spite of the obvious connection between the level of unemployment and the overvalued pound, Harold Wilson stood firm against devaluation. His thinking was more emotional than economic. He realized that the value of the pound, particularly against the dollar, was a symbol of national pride to most Britons. To reduce the exchange rate was tantamount to devaluing a national institution, like selling off Nelson's Column or mortgaging the Crown Jewels. Yet by not acting sooner, Wilson and the Chancellor of the Exchequer, James Callaghan, cost the country billions of pounds at the hands of speculators. When devaluation eventually came, a year later, it was regarded as a bitter defeat by Wilson himself, and he seemed willing to do anything to conceal this from the British people.

On 18 November 1967, the pound's value against the dollar was reduced from $2.80 to $2.40. The press expected the Prime Minister to announce the news with a due regard for the sombre nature of the crisis and his own bitterness at having finally to give way on an issue that had apparently meant so much to him. But the press was disappointed; Wilson came out whistling as if he had just lost sixpence and found a shilling. Even his Labour colleagues could not understand what was happening. Wilson told one of them, 'Don't you see, devaluation has made me the most powerful Prime Minister since Walpole.' It was a puzzling reaction to what had been a personal defeat. In fact, as a few journalists were quick to remind him, had he devalued the previous year he would have saved the country a hatful of money.

The Prime Minister decided to speak to the nation to explain why devaluation had been necessary. On the afternoon of Sunday 19 November, Wilson appeared on television in what later became notorious as a public relations disaster. He himself commented that he wished the nation had had their sets switched off. Barbara Castle observed, 'too complacent by half'. With the whole nation feeling as if the Union Jack had just been lowered over Gibraltar or the Isle of Wight, they expected to see a mournful Prime Minister sharing their grief at the damage to the national currency. Instead, Wilson seemed 'to exult in the situation'. One might have been excused for

The devaluation of the pound by Harold Wilson's Labour government in 1967 was mishandled by the prime minister. Wilson's public statement that 'the pound in your pocket has not been devalued' earned him the opprobrium of political commentators.

thinking that he had just succeeded in forcing through a vital but unpopular decision against united cabinet opposition. In fact, it was the cabinet who had forced Wilson to climb down.

To the general public there was one phrase from Wilson's speech that rang hollow, so hollow, in fact, that it has become a stick to beat not only Harold Wilson's memory but the veracity of politicians ever since. Wilson was eager to simplify difficult concepts and ensure that the viewers did not think that every pound of their savings had at a stroke been reduced to just seventeen shillings. No doubt he remembered that after the devaluation of 1949, investors had besieged banks claiming that they had been robbed. He explained, 'Devaluation does *not* mean that the value of the pound in the hands of the British consumer, the British housewife at her shopping, is cut correspondingly. It does not mean that the pound in the pocket is worth fourteen per cent less to us now than it was.' Wilson never actually said, 'The pound in your pocket has not been devalued', but it was how the press reported his words and it is what he meant. He had argued for months that devaluation mattered very much to the ordinary people. Now he seemed to be saying the exact opposite. It was not so much a U-turn as a headstand.

In the days that followed the bitter 'joke' grew. Wilson was now ridiculed both in the House of Commons and the country as a 'slippery' politician. As Denis Healey warned him shortly afterwards, he had lost the trust of the country. His reputation never entirely recovered and it is doubtful if the profession of politics was ever viewed in the same way by ordinary people. If the Prime Minister could be so 'economical with the truth' on television – and on a *Sunday* afternoon – how much lying must go on in the House of Commons with nobody to see? In 1967 we did not have an answer. In 1994, with a televised parliament, we do. But are we happier for it?

THE ROAD TO THE ISLES

The adventures of a ship's surgeon, one Lionel Wafer, were to have an important effect on Scottish history in the last years of the seventeenth century. Wafer's account of his time with the Cuna natives of South America came into the hands of a London entrepreneur of Scottish origins, William Paterson, who had been one of the men responsible for the creation of the Bank of England. Paterson was a highly imaginative company promoter and it was his vision of a European settlement in the land of the Cuna – Panama – that led to the disastrous 'Darien Scheme'.

Paterson first tried to interest London investors in his scheme, but when this plan failed he took it to Scotland, where the idea was adopted. Although England and Scotland were countries united by the same king, there had been no political union and the merchants of London regarded those of Edinburgh as upstart rivals. There was no chance that English money would now be made available to back Paterson's Scottish company. Aware of the hostility of the English to their plans, the directors of the Scottish company decided to poach Lionel Wafer from under the eyes of the 'Sassenachs'. Wafer, who was living in Wapping at the time, was invited to Edinburgh in the hope that he could give the Scots as much information as possible about his time in Panama. It was very much a 'cloak-and-dagger' operation, for the Scots knew that if word got out, Wafer would be spirited away by their commercial rivals in London. Travelling as 'Mr Brown', Wafer set off for Edinburgh. He never reached the city, for he was whisked away by Paterson's agents to a secret house, twelve miles from the Scottish capital. Here he was kept a virtual prisoner while company men cross-examined him about his experiences in Panama. Wafer had been promised an enormous reward for his information and was presumably little put out by the antics of his super-sensitive hosts. He gave his inquisitors everything they wanted, even map references and compass bearings for finding a huge forest of dyewood that he claimed to have seen. Satisfied that they had learned everything they could from him, the Scots then told him he could go, refusing to pay him anything, even his return fare to London. They said that they were abandoning the entire scheme as the English had 'wind of it' and might blockade the Panama coast against them. It was a lie, just one of many lies the Scottish directors told Wafer. The surgeon did not know how lucky he was not to be offered a post in the forthcoming expedition. He may have been embittered by the treatment he had received in Edinburgh, but some two years later, when he read of the catastrophe that struck the Scottish settlers, he must have reflected on his good fortune in only being cheated by the Scots.

On 26 February 1696, the Company of Scotland appealed to the people of Edinburgh for funds of £400,000 to finance its ambitious plans. The response was enormous. Many Scots were pleased that the project would be an entirely Scottish one, with no English money involved. As one director wrote, the Scots 'came in shoals from every corner of the kingdom, rich, poor, blind, lame, to lodge their subscriptions in the company's house'. In a matter of days more than half the floating capital of the whole country was pledged in support of the company. Many poor folk were undoubtedly gambling with everything they had, or ever hoped to have.

The first practical step was to acquire ships for the expedition to Panama. Here again the English proved obstructive. The Parliament in London had closed all shipbuilding yards to Scottish customers and the directors were forced to seek ships abroad. Four vessels were ordered from Swedish yards, with a further two coming from Holland. One of the Dutch ships was to be the flagship, named the *Rising Sun*, and decked out in the proud emblems of the company. While the ships were being prepared, medical and food supplies sufficient for 1500 men for a two-year period were assembled. A Spanish-speaking interpreter was sought in London along with the best maps available of the Antilles. In the event a Jew who claimed to speak six languages fluently was brought north, along with a selection of buccaneer charts of the Caribbean.

Unfortunately, Paterson found himself up against the parochialism of the Scots, who were convinced that no self-respecting South American heathen would want to buy anything other than the best Scottish heavy serge cloth, wigs, buckle shoes, as well as 380 Bibles, 51 New Testaments and 2808 Catechisms. Either they had forgotten, or Wafer had wisely failed to inform them, that the Cuna people of Panama had neither money nor much in the way of valuables with which to buy the Scottish wares. Coloured beads should have been taken to attract the Cuna youngfolk, for did the Scots really believe that naked Indians would relish heavy serge 'part black, part blue' in the heat of the tropics?

Once started, preparations for the expedition generated a momentum of their own. By March 1698, men were being recruited to go with the first fleet to sail. This first fleet would make landfall and choose the site of the first settlement. Once good relations had been established with the local inhabitants a second fleet would leave Scotland with further supplies and a second wave of settlers. The backbone of the first fleet was to be a company of three hundred young Scots from leading families, which would form the basis for the future success of the enterprise. Young men arrived at company headquarters in Edinburgh, some even carrying their birth certificates to prove their right to accompany Scotland's first colonial endeavour. Jostling them in the crowded Edinburgh streets were 60 Scots veterans, who would provide the nucleus for the colony's military needs, as well as numerous Gaelic-speaking Highlanders, who would provide the cannon fodder. In the end the first fleet took some volunteers, including three pastors, a few women and William Paterson himself, along with his wife and young daughter.

The fleet was commanded by James Pennycook, an experienced mariner who had been one of the first Scots to interview Lionel Wafer in London. Unwisely, as it turned out, the company had not seen fit to give Pennycook sole command of the expedition, for he was to share his authority with a board of ten so-called 'councillors'. There was ample evidence of the dangers of divided command, even within recent memory: during Cromwell's colonial enterprise, the 'Western Design', Admiral Penn, General Venables and their three fellow commissioners had been quite unable to agree on anything. (See *The Guinness Book of More Military Blunders*, pp. 30–7). But the Scots were convinced that ten minds were better than one, and joint decisions generally safer than sole ones. They were wrong. The Spanish empire in South America had been created by the conquistadores – a strain of strong individualists, who brooked no opposition, and hanged fellow administrators from trees. Councils came later when Pizarro, Cortez and Alvarado had done their work and been 'pensioned off' by the 'second fleet' of bureaucrats. If the Darien Scheme was going to work it needed the same kind of ruthless efficiency that the Spaniards and the English had shown in the previous century.

On 14 July 1698, Commodore Pennycook took the first fleet out into the North Sea and northwards round the Orkneys before setting course for the Caribbean. In true Scots fashion the weather turned foul and the ships were scattered before they had left Scottish waters. It was an inauspicious start and Paterson later instructed the directors in Edinburgh to sail the second fleet from the west coast to avoid the dreadful voyage round the north of Scotland. Eventually, in better conditions, the fleet reached Madeira, where Pennycook opened the secret orders for the enterprise and learned for the first time that his destination was to be the Gulf of Darien, on the coast of Panama, where Lionel Wafer had told the directors of the company he had seen the great dyewood forest.

After a voyage of over a hundred days the Scots reached Darien, and anchored in what Pennycook and Paterson described as a magnificent natural harbour. But their anchorage at the inaptly named 'Golden Harbour' merely confirmed the old adage that 'all that glisters is not gold'. After three months at sea they were dazzled by the azure waters and the bright sun, and the lush green vegetation in the shimmering heat. It was a magical sight to Scots landsmen more accustomed to grey mists and driving rain. The truth was, however, that Golden Harbour, which one settler claimed was capable of containing 'the thousand best ships in the world',

was liable to such heavy tides that it was frequently impossible to even enter without risk of capsizing.

For the moment, the shoreline of golden sand and luxuriant undergrowth seemed to be what they had come to find, a land that would make all of them rich. As one wrote, 'The soil is rich, the air is good and temperate, the water is sweet, and everything contributes to make it healthful and convenient'. Most settlers thought that just over the 'next hill' would be the gold mines that the Spaniards guarded so greedily. So pleased were the Scots with their 'promised land' that they named it Caledonia and its first settlement became 'New Edinburgh'. While the settlers took in the sights and sounds of their Caribbean tour, the more practical of their number began the search for Lionel Wafer's dyewood forest, which was the first target of the expedition. Search parties hunted high and low but the forest failed to materialize. Already there was evidence that the paradise would instead be poisonous to settlers from northern climes. The strength-sapping heat, the humidity and the insects were at first matters of interest and enjoyment, but later became matters of concern and then despair.

The local people, the Cuna, had welcomed the Scots with open arms, paddling out to their ships even before they had anchored. For the dour men of the north, Darien seemed a veritable Eden, with its half-naked beauties, and men wearing lip plates and brilliant body paint. Soon they were enjoying all the pleasures of the simple life. But their enchantment lasted only as long as the Cuna's stock of food.

It did not take long for the Scots to realize that the Cuna had little to offer apart from their own simple and charming selves. There were no gold mines, no dyewood forests and precious little else once the initial feasting had abated. Even the soil was poor, and far from finding evidence of well-cultivated areas, the Scots found patches of sun-baked earth. Not surprisingly the Cuna were only too happy to affix their marks to the company documents acquiring the land around New Edinburgh. In return the Cuna chiefs were given a brace of pistols, a Scottish sword and little Scots flags for the native children to wave.

The next major worry was the weather. The fine conditions that had welcomed them on their arrival had given way to daily thunderstorms, which sapped the endurance of many of the ordinary folk. Their clothes turned mouldy and rotted, their food supplies spoiled and their mood varied from listless

A map of Panama in the seventeenth century. Scottish attempts to establish a colony at Darien foundered as a result of mismanagement at home and opposition from Spain and England in the Caribbean.

boredom to occasional bouts of fury at the dashing of their hopes. Next came disease, in the shape of a fever that sapped their strength even more, while a 'bloody flux' carried off many of the weaker members. Discipline began to break down in the small settlement: thefts and drunkenness became almost routine, and the small jail competed with the growing cemetery for inmates. As enthusiasm for the new country waned, fewer and fewer of the settlers worked in the fields. Many simply sat slumped all day, wishing they had never left their homes in Scotland.

What was lacking was leadership. Of the ten councillors, few had any idea on how to run the new colony, and those that tried came up against the numbing indecision of the majority. Paterson, who might have led the way, fell victim to the strain of seeing his dreams of a great trading empire fade before his eyes. Following the death of his wife he succumbed to a nervous breakdown. When the time came to report back to Edinburgh none of the councillors had the moral courage to tell the truth. Instead they wrote that, 'the wealth, fruitfulness, health, and good situation of the Country proves for the better, much above our greatest expectation'. However, the colony had already failed. The company's plan had laid down that soon after the

settlement had been established it should have reached subsistence level by trading with the local people as well as by growing simple root crops. The truth was that the Cuna people had nothing to offer by way of trade and the land was hopelessly inadequate to support a large population dependent on its products.

To make matters worse, the Scots colony was surrounded by successful Spanish settlements that regarded the Scots as dangerous interlopers. It was only a matter of time before they roused themselves to snuff out the Scottish outpost. What the Spaniards did not know was that the Scots hardly needed to be driven out; they were rotting away, their buildings filled with trade goods such as wigs, stockings and heavy serge cloth that were growing mouldy in the humid atmosphere. At a time when the Scots might have hoped for support from English colonists in Jamaica, they learned to their horror that King William III – their king, even though he was a Dutchman – had forbidden all Englishman to give any help to the Scots. And there was more English perfidy: English ships would not even take despatches back to Scotland. In the end, a passing French ship offered to act as postman for the colonists. Even this turned out badly when the French 'loon' set sail on Christmas Eve in the teeth of a gale and with half his crew drunk. The Scots had to rescue the French crew, at the cost to themselves of a valuable cockboat. while the French ship was smashed on the rocks and wrecked. The Scots despatches were lost and had to be rewritten. It was a dismal start to Christmas Day for Commodore Pennycook, who was nearly drowned in the process of rescuing the French.

Eventually, the colony's accountant, Alexander Hamilton, reached Edinburgh with the despatches after a journey of three months. During this period the fortunes of Caledonia reached rock bottom. Unfortunately, 3000 miles away in Scotland, Hamilton was telling a very different tale, and earning himself a fat purse into the bargain. Instructed by the colony's councillors to 'talk up' the success of the enterprise, he was convincing the company that the second fleet should be hastily prepared to bring fresh supplies and new colonists.

In Caledonia the New Year brought the worst possible news: a Spanish force was setting out to attack them. One of the Scottish vessels had foundered off the coast and its crew had been captured by the Spaniards and treated as pirates. This was not a very reassuring situation for the Scottish settlers. Few of them were soldiers, and most were respectable farmers or tradesmen, as far from being pirates as anyone could imagine. The Spaniards, however, fell victim to their own exaggerations, convincing themselves that the Scots had landed 4000 well-armed and well-trained professionals. As a result the local Spanish commanders panicked, each colony passing the responsibility for driving away the Scots to the next one. The commander in Panama claimed – unconvincingly – that he was afraid to attack Caledonia in case he left his own city open to a Scottish counterstroke from the Pacific.

Even so, Caledonia was doomed. The refusal of the English, notably the strong colony on Jamaica, to render any help at all was the final straw. Already a third of the original settlers had died from disease or malnutrition, and the survivors were reduced to eating mouldy, worm-infested bread. The beef, which had been pickled in Edinburgh, had turned black in the heat and gave off a rank odour. Scurvy was widespread and only the brandy ration gave any relief to the suffering Scots. The council was all in favour of an immediate evacuation, and though Paterson pressed them to stay, re-embarkation began in June 1699. Yet at the very moment that the survivors of the first fleet were preparing to leave

Caledonia, the second fleet – inspired by the words of Alexander Hamilton and still believing that the Darien Scheme was a masterplan – was getting ready to sail from Scotland. It was to be one of history's cruellest ironies and one of Scotland's biggest blunders.

The settlers of the first fleet boarded their four remaining vessels, *St Andrew*, *Unicorn*, *Caledonia* and *Endeavour*, and prepared to sail back to Scotland via New York. At least that was the general plan. But the ships were unseaworthy, the *Endeavour* little more than a floating hulk, which after twelve days at sea turned turtle, though all her passengers were rescued by the *Caledonia*. Saved from drowning, the survivors from the *Endeavour* found themselves aboard a charnel-house of a ship, with fever raging. Before the *Caledonia* reached New York half of its complement died and were thrown overboard to poison the sharks. Meanwhile, the *Unicorn*, bearing William Paterson, was having problems of its own. Crowded with 250 colonists, but short of experienced seaman, the ship was at the mercy of wind and tide. A storm ripped off her foremast, leaving her almost incapable of raising sail in the heavy seas. Only a sustained effort at pumping by every man aboard kept her afloat until she reached Cuba. There the Scots landed the supposedly multi-lingual interpreter, whom Paterson had met in London. However, he apparently did not even know the Spanish for 'friend' and the Spaniards opened fire on him and on a Scottish landing party trying to find fresh water. The *Unicorn* was forced to head out to sea, minus their interpreter. It was his lucky day. He spent the next few months in a Spanish jail, while the passengers on the *Unicorn* endured a nightmare journey north to New York, during which 150 of them died of fever and neglect. Paterson suffered so severely that, on arrival at New York, he was said to have lost his mind and to be as simple as a child.

Perhaps the wisest decision was that taken by Commodore Pennycook in the *St Andrew*. In a drunken haze Pennycook defied storm and tempest and headed for Jamaica. Although he died in the attempt, along with 140 of his passengers, the ship now little more than a hulk, reached the island. The English, however, refused to allow any of its survivors to come ashore. Starving and dying of fever, men slipped overboard each night and swam ashore, selling themselves as virtual slaves to the colonial planters. It was a poor return for these Scottish volunteers who had dreamed of the boundless wealth of Panama. Of the original 1200 men who had sailed with Pennycook the previous year, only 300 returned to Scotland in the *Caledonia*, along with William Paterson.

At this stage there occurred a blunder fraught with the direst of consequences. Before the second fleet had left Scottish waters, rumours arrived in Edinburgh from English sources that the Scots settlers had abandoned the colony of Caledonia and had sailed for home. The rumours were true, but the company directors – in the comfort of their offices in Edinburgh – suspected that it was an English plot to stop them sending out the second fleet with its reinforcements. So, without bothering to investigate the truth of the rumours, these well-fed and well-wined gentlemen consigned 1300 new colonists, aboard four more Scottish vessels, to a wretched fate.

The preparation of the second fleet owed more to Lewis Carroll than to Lionel Wafer, with the Scots directors living in a 'wonderland' of their own creation. Recruits were encouraged to join by being shown maps which contained such misleading trigger points as 'Place where upon digging for stones to make an oven, a considerable mixture of gold was found in them.'

On 18 August 1699, the second fleet sailed for South America but it was at once driven back by contrary winds and forced to shelter from the storm. Anchored off the Isle of Bute it was comfortably within range of the shore and the company directors could have recalled it whenever they chose to send a boat out with new orders. But they did not do so. As the days passed rumours from Panama became doubts, and doubts became uncertainties. The weather-vane was turning, but still the directors remained unconvinced. Soon, it seemed, everyone in Edinburgh knew that the colony of Caledonia had failed and had been abandoned by its settlers. Still the directors dithered. Then, on 22 September, irrefutable evidence reached them that the rumours had been accurate; the colony had been abandoned. At last they sent a message by boat, recalling the fleet. But it was too late. After having been pressed to the Scottish coast for some four weeks, the winds dropped, the weather became fair and the second fleet sailed. Just 24 hours later the directors' boat set out to stop them. The second fleet was embarked on a voyage to nowhere.

The Reverend Francis Borland sailed with the second fleet and recorded the feelings of the whole party when they arrived in Panama and found there not the 'golden' welcome they had expected but 'a vast, howling wilderness'. The settlement was ruined and overgrown with weeds, and the only sign of human presence was the overfilled cemetery. This was a far cry from the 'stately parks', 'fertile soil' and 'salubrious climate' that Hamilton had described to the company directors in Edinburgh. How far these men had been deceived can be seen by some of the curious appointments made in the second fleet, such as an expert coin-minter, a distiller complete with all his equipment, a group of young scholars from Edinburgh University along with their tutor, and a man with a scheme for teaching English to the Cuna people. It all smacked of a cultural exchange rather than a struggle for survival in the face of hostile nature.

Shocked by what they found in Panama many of the new colonists demanded that the ships should return straight away to Scotland. But the leaders of the expedition decided to land and assess the situation. That was their mistake. Surrounded by all the signs of failure, the new colonists became an undisciplined rabble, drinking heavily and stealing food and liquor from the company stores. Desertion was rife, and mutiny never far from the surface. Within days of their arrival the leaders had to hang one of the colonists for 'sedition'. Soon all the problems encountered by the first colonists – malnutrition, heat exhaustion and general apathy – struck at the new arrivals. There was no digging for gold, not even for food, only for burial. Aboard the ships corpses were not sent ashore to the cemetery, but simply tipped overboard to pollute the 'golden harbour'. Leadership was minimal – one councillor even secretly booked passage back to Scotland aboard a passing English vessel.

And at last the Spaniards were stirring themselves. Delighted at the news that the first colonists had abandoned Caledonia, they were shocked when the new and even stronger second fleet arrived. They had no option now but to drive the Scots out by force. In spite of the heroic leadership of Colonel Alexander Campbell, who inflicted heavy losses on the Spanish troops, the Spaniards surrounded the Scots settlement and forced the beleaguered settlers to surrender on 31 March 1700. The Spaniards gave the Scots two weeks to evacuate the colony and return to their ships. It was the end of the Scottish scheme to colonize Panama. Even now fate was not kind to the Scots, for the wind was too slight to fill their sails and their ships too unseaworthy to leave the 'golden harbour' unaided. They suffered the final indignity of being towed out by Spanish rowing-boats.

Aboard the *Rising Sun*, the great ship which had been built for the Scots in Amsterdam and had come to symbolize the entire endeavour, the sick and starving were crammed together, according to one description, like 'hogs in a sty or sheep in a fold' so that 'their breath and noisome smells infected and poisoned one another'. As the colonists fell sick and died, they were consigned to the deep without ceremony, often as many as eight men each morning. Two of the Scottish ships were wrecked on the South American coast, with the loss of most of their crew, but it was the appalling suffering aboard the *Rising Sun* that cast a pall over the final stages of the Darien Scheme. When a hurricane finally struck the flagship and her consort, the *Duke of Hamilton*, off the Carolina coast, sinking them both with the loss of all hands, it was as if fate had tired of tormenting the Scots and had swept them from the board in a single act of kindness.

Of the 1300 members of the second expedition to Panama only a handful ever returned to Scotland. One of them was the injured Alexander Campbell who had bested the Spaniards in open battle but had been wounded in his moment of triumph. He returned home as the single hero of a tragic episode. The Reverend Borland, whether through divine intervention or just good luck, decided to leave the *Rising Sun* at Jamaica and travelled safely to Boston aboard an English ship, before returning to Scotland, thus missing the hurricane and almost certain death.

The demise of the colony at Darien marked the end of the Company of Scotland, which collapsed under the weight of a vitriolic press and popular outcry. In London the Scottish scheme was denounced so ferociously that the pamphlet of one English writer was burned by the public hangman in Edinburgh. Yet the Scottish shareholders who had so unwisely invested everything they had in the scheme were not ruined. As if feeling a pang of conscience, when the Act of Union of 1707 united England and Scotland, the English government paid the Scots a sum of £400,000, part of which was distributed as compensation to the shareholders in the Company of Scotland. William Paterson, who had been the moving spirit in the scheme all along, finally recovered his health and tried to revive the company by planting a new colony in South America with English help. But the Scots were too canny to be bitten by the same bug twice. They paid Paterson the princely sum of £100 and told him to be gone. He returned to London, lost much of his money, and finished his days as a tutor of mathematics.

IN A NUTSHELL

If conquering Africa in the name of cooking fats has a curious ring to it today, back in 1946 – in an era of food rationing – the hearts of millions of housewives in Britain warmed to the news that an army of brave but ordinary British men and women – the Groundnut Army – was battling against the worst that the Dark Continent could throw at them. Alas, the scheme was less Stanley meets Livingstone than Stan Laurel meets Oliver Hardy. When the Groundnut Army arrived, the 'Dark Continent' would never know what had hit it.

Yet the idea of growing groundnuts in Africa began as a perfectly sound one. It originated amongst the experienced businessmen of no less a company than Unilever, which at that time dealt in millions of tons of fats and oils every year. They already produced brand-leading margarines, like Stork and Blue Band. Their hard-headed – one might almost suggest fat-headed – businessmen would not have seen the funny side of the groundnut scheme. They knew that under rationing Britain's housewives were going short of fats and if they could develop new production sites – and, in the process, contribute to the development of a primitive part of Africa – then everyone would benefit. So when Frank Samuel, head of the United Africa company – a

Food Minister John Strachey (right), accompanied by A. V. Alexander, leaving a cabinet meeting at 10 Downing Street in 1947. Strachey was the man most responsible for the ill-fated Groundnut Scheme.

subsidiary of Unilever – was looking for an area for groundnut expansion he was attracted to the idea of developing 20,000 acres of scrubland in Tanganyika. Samuel decided to tour Tanganyika where, according to United Nations statistics, just three per cent of the country was under cultivation. He believed he had found the answer to the prayers of British housewives – an area ripe for development of groundnuts, sometimes known as monkey nuts or more popularly peanuts. For Samuel, the groundnuts were nature's answer to a fat shortage, producing, when the nut is crushed, 40 per cent oil for margarine, with the remainder providing a source of cattle feed and thereby a source of butter. It seemed too good to be true. It was. Samuel's report was highly optimistic and, unfortunately, very misleading. What was possible on the highly mechanized farms of the developed world was quite impossible in Africa.

Nevertheless, in April 1946, the British Government, eager to solve the fat shortage, authorized a special mission to visit Tanganyika, led by John Wakefield. Wakefield was a visionary who saw in the groundnut scheme a chance to bring to a benighted part of Africa all the advantages of prosperity and civilization. To a socialist government in the new spirit of the post-Hitler world, such visions were convincing. Their new Minister of Food – ex-Marxist product of Eton and Oxford, John Strachey – welcomed Wakefield's positive report on what he had found in Tanganyika. During a journey from Euston to Colwyn Bay – a spiritual train ride to Damascus – Strachey was won over to the groundnut scheme by the time he had reached Crewe. At a capital cost of £25 million, three and a quarter million acres of Tanganyika scrubland would be brought under cultivation. Fleets of bulldozers and tractors would pit themselves against aeons of darkness and ignorance and bring out of Africa food for a hungry world.

Unfortunately, the Wakefield Report was a deeply flawed document. In its scope it was magnificent – it inspired upwards of 100,000 men to volunteer for service in the Groundnut Army – but in its realism it was almost wholly deficient. It spoke of agricultural problems – of how to grow groundnuts – but completely overlooked the greatest challenge facing the whole scheme: how to clear thousands of acres of African scrubland. It seemed to take for granted than mechanical means would be used, but gave no thought to where the machines were to be found,

or how they were to be transported to a Tanganyika almost completely devoid of adequate road or rail transport, and in Dar-es-Salaam equipped with a port facility more suited to slave dhows than modern freighters. In a sense, Wakefield is not entirely to blame for this glaring weakness in his report. Nobody had thought fit to equip his mission with an engineer. Had this been done, the right questions would have been asked – above all, how to service and repair tractors in the middle of the African bush. Wakefield, had he but known it, was asking for an instantaneous African industrial revolution. What had taken Britain and Europe centuries he was asking the Tanganyikans to achieve almost overnight. Without a vast incursion of skilled British labour, the local natives would have to learn to build workshops, operate tools, service and repair advanced agricultural machinery and ultimately drive the tractors themselves. Critics have accused Wakefield's Report of being little less than a Five-Year-Plan on the Russian model. Nevertheless, the British Government was swept along by Wakefield's vision and decided to go ahead with the groundnut scheme. Recruitment of men to get the scheme up and running now began and British 'muddling through' became the order of the day.

To clear the ground at the first selected site – the ominously named Kongwa, which means 'to be deceived' in the local tongue – dozens of ex-soldiers answered the call. These men had made roads and airfields in all the war zones of Europe, Africa and the Far East and had thought nothing of driving tractors under heavy enemy fire. They echoed Churchill's words, 'Give us the tools and we'll finish the job.' But where were the tools? And, particularly, where were the heavy tractors suitable for clearing the African bush? The fact was that Britain in 1946 simply did not have heavy-duty tractors. British land clearance had long since ceased to offer such a challenge to its farmers. Eyes now turned as by long habit to gaze across the Atlantic in the hope that – as usual – the New World would solve the problems of the Old. But not this time. Lend-Lease was over and American tractor makers had full books from their own farmers. And then – two pieces of luck. Canada came up with some heavy tractors, while in the Philippines it was found that hundreds of old American bulldozers had been left behind for disposal and were available at a bargain price.

The next problem was how to get all the heavy

agricultural equipment to the groundnut site. For the first time consideration was given to transport or the lack of it. It was now discovered that in the Central province of Tanganyika – where Kongwa was located – the only railway transport was provided by a wood-burning engine running on a single track. Even worse, at Dar-es-Salaam the port facilities were quite unable to deal with the expected influx of heavy machinery and supplies. Undaunted, the British 'muddled on'. As Dar-es-Salaam had no deep-water berths to allow the freighters to come into the docks, the heavy equipment had to be lifted from the ships' holds on board a lighter, brought alongside the quay and then lifted ashore. Once piled up on the quayside it took weeks to move it inland. As a result, the quayside was soon piled high with every kind of stores, unloaded in no kind of order. The chaos was incredible. From every part of the English-speaking world supplies poured in to the small East African port – 'anything from electric bulbs to worn-out lathes, from second-hand military trousers to first-rate generators'. Army Surplus departments were having a field-day. Buyers from the Groundnut Army went on a spending spree, hunting down many excellent – and some dubious – bargains in war-disposal goods from Egypt.

Meanwhile, Africa demonstrated that she was not going to succumb to the Groundnut Army without a struggle. The solitary railway line from Kongwa to Dar-es-Salaam was suddenly washed away when the Kinyasungwe River burst its banks. And when the advance guard of the army finally set out from the coast they encountered another hitch – their African workers immediately went on strike for more pay, leaving them with just one African cook to accompany them to Kongwa. Nevertheless, although being 'bitten almost to pieces by mosquitoes', the intrepid pioneers arrived at Sagara, where they decided to build their first camp, fourteen miles from the proposed groundnut site at Kongwa. Waiting for them was George Nestlé, a great white hunter, complete with python-skin belt and an enormous paunch surrounding a pair of very brief shorts. Nestlé's hospitality was as overwhelming as his belly and came as a welcome relief to men emerging from a Britain still subject to rationing: forty fried eggs with ham, washed down by Bristol Cream sherry. While the British pioneers wolfed down their feast, they were introduced to the local African chieftain, complete with 6 wives and 42

children. Replete, two of the pioneers climbed a nearby hill to survey the 'Promised Land', but were driven off by the locals, a tribe of chattering baboons.

As the pioneers settled in at Sagara, it was decided to do something that one might have thought should have been done rather earlier: test the soil to see if it was suitable for growing groundnuts. Using a tea-strainer as part of a soil-testing kit worthy of Heath Robinson, the decision was reached that the soil would do. It was 'all systems go'. Unfortunately, the pioneers missed one important fact that was to bedevil the entire project. The soil at Kongwa was rich in clay and this would make harvesting the nuts almost impossible. A second error was made at this stage. The proposed camp at Sagara had ample water, but as the camp grew it would impinge on local native land. Thus it was decided to move to a new site – minus water and still seven miles from the groundnut area.

Meanwhile, the exodus of equipment from the coast began. Lacking a Moses to part the waters for them, these latter-day children of Israel found the Dark Continent far from amenable. With the single-track railway a victim of flooding, the intrepid pioneers had to force their way along one, inadequate, road. The crocodile-infested waters of the Ruvu River could only be crossed by ferry and as if privy to the continent's conspiracy to frustrate the invaders, the ferry sank at the sight of the heavy tractors and bulldozers it was expected to carry. With the crocodiles eventually behind them, the pioneers now found elephants chasing their jeeps, lions leaping from trees onto the backs of their lorries and tribes of gibbering baboons contesting every inch of the way. With grim determination, they forced their way through to Kongwa. Meanwhile, Tanganyika's white population viewed the newcomers as a not unmixed blessing. The general view among the expatriate British planters was that the whole scheme was a socialist conspiracy to 'upset their quiet corner and put up the price of gin'.

Up at Kongwa, the pioneers were setting about clearing the bush. This was easier said than done, as they had come completely unprepared for the task ahead. The Wakefield Report had spoken of clearing 150,000 acres in twelve months. But had anyone in London bothered to read accounts of what the Tanganyika bush was really like? One expert report spoke of thickets of scrub impenetrable to anything except a rhinoceros or a snake. Only the strongest bulldozers could do the job. But none could be transported, even on the hastily built branch railway to Kongwa, because their blades were too wide for the railway cuttings. The result was that as the trains advanced, teams of Africans had to move up to widen the cuttings once the bulldozer blades got stuck. The tractors, meanwhile, were driven by road to Kongwa. In his report Wakefield had demanded that 200 tractors would be needed at Kongwa by February 1947. In fact, none had arrived by then. The icy conditions in Britain that winter meant that ships were frozen up in their harbours. It was not until April 1947 that the first 16 tractors arrived. It did not take long to realize that under their new coats of paint most of the American tractors were very much second-hand.

The man charged with heading the clearing operation was straight out of Evelyn Waugh's *Black Mischief*. 'Wog' Richards was a legend in his own lifetime, who had once been elected headman of a wild and remote village in Persia. At Kongwa, he frequently rode out into the bush in his tractor and single-handed took on the worst the Dark Continent could fling at him. Once he was attacked and driven off by wild bees, while on another occasion he was forced to hide under his tractor by an enraged elephant. Richards found that by equipping his tractors with bulldozer blades the bush could be 'bashed' rather than cleared. Another major problem was the massive baobab – 'upside down' – trees, some of which were over twenty feet in diameter. It was not just their size that posed a problem. The hollow trunks of the trees were often used by the Africans to bury their dead, particularly those who had died from infectious diseases. In one case a tractor assaulted a baobab only to find that it was occupied by two natives. It appeared that the tree was being used as a tribal jail. Far more serious was the case of the skull of the 'Unknown One'. When one tractor uprooted a baobab tree and caused a skull to topple from its perch in the tree's aerial roots the locals were incensed: the Groundnut Army had insulted the spirits of their tribal ancestors. The local manager was able to quieten the natives only by allowing the skull to occupy a place of honour in his unit headquarters to 'let it whisper wisdom in our ears'.

Angry natives were not the worst of the problems facing the land clearance workers. Everyone was agreed that the greatest peril came from the local bees which, in 1914, had driven a British invasion force back into the sea at Tanga (see *The Guinness Book of Military Blunders*, pp. 4–6). Now the descendants of those bees were ready to take on a new British army, even though this one had come to grow groundnuts rather than drive the Germans out of East Africa. The bees had built many nests in the hollowed-out trunks of the baobabs, and it was impossible for the tractor drivers to check every tree to make certain that they were not disturbing the winged occupants. The result was a series of unpleasant encounters, some swollen drivers and a surveyor on the danger list for a fortnight. The tractor drivers were pestered less by four-footed animals, although on one occasion a group of vehicles were forced to joust for half an hour with four rhinoceros, before putting them to flight.

As the ground clearance continued the decision was taken to employ African workers, both in driving the tractors and in the vehicle repair shops. The process, while laudable, was not free from complications. The eagerness of the local drivers resulted in the wrecking of many of the tractors, while in the repair shops it was decided by the Colonial Office in London that the African workers should be organized into trade unions. It was good socialist practice in 1947 that trade unions, where they existed, should develop on the right lines. As a result, two trade unionists were sent from Britain to help organize the groundnut workers. Their success was immediate and dramatic. Within days of the arrival of the trade unionists, the workers at Kongwa had come out on strike in sympathy with the dock-workers at Dar-es-Salaam. In addition, the groundnut workers were demanding more pay and better food. Having set fire to some of the camp buildings they armed themselves and formed a roadblock to prevent the Europeans reaching the coast. They had reckoned without one of the most formidable and voluble of the Scots workers who, finding the road blocked by the strikers, leapt from his jeep and bellowed abuse at the Africans in Gaelic. Shocked by this strange and barbaric verbal assault the natives immediately surrendered their weapons and fled.

Some consequences of the European presence in Tanganyika were far more difficult to solve. The increased wages of the tribesmen who worked at Kongwa caused price inflation in that part of the country and villagers soon found they were unable to afford milk and eggs. Malnutrition became prevalent as a result and many babies died. Without realizing it, the Groundnut Army had instigated a

The difficulties faced by men and machines in attempting to tame the dry and tangled wastes of Tanganyika to make them suitable for growing groundnuts are graphically depicted in this photograph. Bulldozers are trying to level the ground and clear it of light scrub and bamboo. The Groundnut Scheme foundered as a result of official underestimation of the problems of ground clearance.

process of de-tribalization. Local men looked to the Europeans for the basic needs of themselves and their families, and the authority of local chiefs began to decline. In addition, many local women began to offer themselves as prostitutes, while professional streetwalkers moved up to Kongwa from the coast and began to surround the camp.

By the summer of 1947 it was apparent that the scheme was not fulfilling the high objectives it had set for itself. The sheer difficulty of farming in Africa had been overlooked in the rush to achieve Wakefield's vision of progress. As the Groundnut Army knew, on their success depended 'whether the harassed housewives of Britain get more margarine, cooking-fats and soap, in the reasonably near future'. Yet nearly two thirds of all the tractors that had reached Kongwa were already out of action, beaten by a combination of over-eager and incompetent African drivers and a pitiless terrain, more like concrete than soil by mid-summer. Then someone thought of tanks. Could surplus World War II

tanks be adapted for land clearance? It was worth a try. After all, tanks had been adapted to clear the *bocage* in Normandy just three years before. And so the 'Shervick' was born – half Sherman tank and half Vickers tractor. But it was a false dawn. After a promising start, the Shervicks broke down one by one and were left to rust.

The error, made in the earliest days of the scheme, of moving from near the water supplies at Sagara to the waterless base at Kongwa was beginning to present severe problems for the ever-growing European encampment. Daily supplies of 5000 gallons of water had to be brought in by tankers and kept in a cement water-hole nearby. It proved difficult to convince everyone that this water was for drinking only. Frequently locals had to be fished out from what they took to be Kongwa's first swimming pool. Local water, obtained from boreholes, tasted strongly of Epsom Salts and had that product's same laxative qualities. It seems incredible that more use was not made of boreholes, although the groundnut workers could hardly have been impressed when one learned civil servant informed them that Athens had been dependent on boreholes for all its water since the fifth century BC.

By the autumn of 1947 Kongwa gave the impression of being a British town transported to Africa, complete with prefab houses built from local brick and British women – wives of some of the officials and female secretaries who were equipped with *pangas* (heavy knives) for their own protection against 'the wolves who try to scale the wall'. In several other respects the conditions were not all that the ladies might have wished: the rainy season brought out a plague of scorpions, some six inches long, and new arrivals needed to be reminded to shake out their shoes every morning.

When the rain fell in torrents another problem was discovered at Kongwa: the stores and workshops had been sited in an old lake-bed. As soon as the rain fell the tents and shanty buildings were simply swept away by flash floods. Taming Africa was harder than it seemed.

In February 1948, the groundnut scheme became the official responsibility of the newly formed Overseas Food Corporation, and the Kongwa site came under the direct control of Major-General Desmond Harrison, CB, DSO, MICE. The problem was that Harrison was already a sick man and quite unsuited to the demanding task of making a success of something that was so obviously doomed to failure. To make matters worse, the general felt that only an approach based on military precision and discipline could succeed. This might have been possible in wartime, but many of the workers at Kongwa had been attracted there by the challenge of Wakefield's vision and the opportunity to use their own individual – often eccentric – skills to turn that part of Africa into a garden of Eden. Harrison had no time for such nonsense. Outside his tent a polished wooden board was hung bearing his name, his decorations and his title 'Resident Member'. In future, everyone had to enter his tent after waiting in a specially constructed ante-room. It was as little like the free and easy regime that had existed when the first pioneers met George Nestlé the previous year as anyone could imagine. But would it work? The answer, unfortunately, was a conclusive 'no'. Africa refused to yield to military discipline. Original targets of 150,000 acres of groundnuts sank with alarming regularity, first to 70,000 and then below 50,000. Nor was the yield per acre the same as

Wakefield had predicted. It slowly began to dawn on the Groundnut Army that not only had they lost all the early battles but they were in danger of losing the whole war.

Meanwhile, the vast influx of European workers and their families, with the consequent rise in wages and prices for the local Africans, was having serious social implications, far beyond the vision of the pioneers of turning the Dark Continent into a 'green and pleasant land'. Crime rates were soaring around Kongwa, with drunkenness and prostitution rife. The traditional life of the African was being transformed. Skilled black workers from Nigeria had been brought in to Kongwa, who resolutely refused to mix with the local Africans. One university-educated Nigerian was given control of the Kongwa airstrip. When a visiting VIP from a neighbouring African country arrived he was met by the Nigerian as he alighted from his plane. 'Jambo,' said the VIP in friendly greeting, to which the Kongwa air chief replied, in perfect English, 'Sir, I neither speak nor understand that language, but allow me to take the opportunity of according to you a most cordial welcome to Kongwa.' In African eyes Kongwa was a glitzy boom town like Johannesburg had been. But when a glamorous new European shop was opened there Africans were denied admittance. The groundnut scheme was now threatened by a groundswell of racial antagonism, with all opinion turned against it. Even the local ex-pats hoped to see it fail so that their quiet corner of Africa could return to what it once had been.

Whether or not General Harrison was aware of these undercurrents we cannot tell, for his job was already being made impossible by the sheer unsuitability of the soil at Kongwa. It was so abrasive that it wore away all the best ploughs, root-cutters, tractor blades and other metal implements that were used to try to dig out the groundnuts. After the rainy season the hot African sun simply baked the soil into hard bricks, useful for building purposes but quite resistant to farming methods. The only solution was to confine all operations to the period before or during the rainy season – a desperate remedy that was bound to halve production at a stroke. Faced with such problems Harrison turned in on himself, became more aloof and concerned himself increasingly with paperwork, of which there was plenty. In one fifteen-day period no fewer than 104 letters arrived from Britain for his attention. The man, who had been called 'Bonaparte' on his arrival was now increasingly referred to as the 'Myth'. And as Harrison sank deeper into depression, aggravated by anaemia, so the groundnut scheme became more 'myth' than reality. Late in 1948 Harrison was ordered home on sick leave. At Christmas the Groundnut Army put on a production of *Cinderella* under the African stars. One character held up a single groundnut while singing:

> I came out to grow the groundnuts,
> Nearly eighteen months ago;
> But with all this blinkin Admin -
> This is all I've got to show.

There was more truth in this ditty than in all the reports that flooded back to London. The plan had failed, weighed down by unnecessary administration and technically ill-equipped to tame the unforgiving African soil.

As if to demonstrate its victory, in 1949 Africa inflicted drought on Kongwa. Virtually no groundnuts could be harvested from the baked earth. In the local villages hunger became a problem. The Groundnut Army had consumed more food than it had produced and in drawing the Africans from their normal farming to help in the groundnut fields the Europeans had reduced the local food supplies.

In London members of the Overseas Food Corporation refused to face facts and still spoke vaguely of groundnuts growing in 'a really large acreage running into millions'. But it was all an illusion. The politicians and civil servants were deceiving themselves just as readily as they were their listeners. They said what they themselves wanted to hear and became victims of their own rhetoric. Yet it was no one man's fault. They were all simply in too deep. From the moment that soil samples at Kongwa were not subjected to proper chemical analysis for clay content the scheme was doomed. It was Britain 'muddling through' but instead ending up in a muddle. At a cost of £25 million 2000 tons of groundnuts were harvested. They did not solve Britain's fat shortage. The scheme did not transform the economy of East Africa or improve the lives of the Africans. It was a well-meaning gesture, but as someone once said, 'the road to hell is paved with good intentions'. One of the last acts of a fading Labour Government was to put the groundnut scheme quietly out of its misery in January 1951.

A LEAP IN THE DARK

During 1957 China's leader, Mao Zedong, began to formulate an entirely new economic policy for his country, to be known as the 'Great Leap Forward'. Rejecting traditional approaches to economic planning, he decided to industrialize China in one enormous leap, by harnessing the one natural resource which China had beyond any other country in the world – its huge population. Rejecting Malthusian fears of food shortages, he abandoned any attempts to control population growth and decided that the more Chinese there were in the world, the greater would be China's strength, both politically and economically. Military threats of nuclear war by the United States would mean nothing to China. Even if hundreds of millions of Chinese died in an unimaginably vast holocaust, there would still be so many left that they were bound to emerge victorious. But what China needed most was industrial growth, at superhuman speed, so that the capitalist countries like Britain and the United States could be caught up and passed in a matter of a few years. No matter that China's technology was primitive, she would make up for what she lacked in knowledge with the sheer size of the effort. Great irrigation projects would be built by 'millions of people with teaspoons'. Mao knew little about economics but he knew a lot about poetry. In poems men were allowed limitless visions – it was called poetic licence. But it was a curious basis for an economic policy.

Mao viewed the Chinese people as little more than ants in a nest. In April 1958 he referred to the then 600 million Chinese as 'first of all poor, and secondly blank . . . a clear sheet of paper has no blotches and so the newest and most beautiful words can be written on it, the newest and most beautiful pictures can be painted on it'. Mao was prepared to squander lives to make economic progress and the human cost of this 'hit and miss' method would be incalculable. But by 1958 Mao felt so confident in his ability to manipulate a quarter of all humanity that he fell victim to hubris.

Even before embarking on his industrial insanity, Mao had revealed that in agricultural affairs he was just as misguided. Part of the reforms of the first Five-Year Plan involved combating what Mao poetically called 'The Four Pests', namely flies, mosquitoes, rats and sparrows. Few would have disagreed that these four creatures were enemies of the farmer, but a little bit of extra thought might have suggested that they all had a part to play in the ecosystem, particularly the sparrows. But, as usual, Mao insisted that the Chinese learn things the hard way. Millions of Chinese spent their time banging household objects, ranging from musical cymbals to saucepans, to drive the birds out of the trees until

they died from exhaustion. It was only after the mass slaughter of the sparrows revealed that the birds had played a vital part in controlling the insect population, that the killing was stopped and bedbugs promoted to replace sparrows as one of the four pests.

But Mao's errors in agriculture shrank into insignificance when compared with the insanity of the backyard steelworks plan, which must rank as one of the most foolish decisions taken by a national leader in all recorded history. Certainly its consequence – at least 30 million deaths – places it in the first division of historical blunders. In order to make China a modern industrialized power, during the autumn of 1958 Mao ordered a drive to double, treble and then quadruple China's steel production in successive years. One hundred million peasants were taken away from their farms to work on building 600,000 backyard steel furnaces. Every commune and every labour unit was given a quota that it must meet or exceed. However, nobody gave any thought to where the raw material – especially

Mao Zedong visiting a cooperative farm in Honan Province, during the 'Great Leap Forward'.
The smiling faces are misleading. Nobody dared to tell Mao the truth that thousands of Chinese
were dying from starvation as a direct result of his mistaken policies.

iron ore and coal – would come from to fire the furnaces and make the steel. As a result the entire country was subjected to a hunt for scrap metal.

What followed was a script penned by an idiot and acted out by madmen. China's peasants sacrificed everything in their hunt to appease Mao's appetite for metal. First to go were the cooking pots and pans that every Chinese needed to cook their daily meals. All private cooking was now forbidden, said Mao, as everyone would henceforth eat at the communal canteen. Next went the peasants' iron bedsteads and their irreplaceable agricultural tools: picks, shovels, rakes, hoes, pitchforks, axes and water-buckets. After the farm tools had been swallowed by the furnaces, with scarcely a burp, off came the galvanized iron roofs from the farm buildings, and with them nails, bolts, locks and so forth. Then, down came the barbed wire fences and off went the animals. Then into the furnaces went the main course – tractors and agricultural vehicles – anything that would boost production. No matter that these were the very things that the steel would be needed to make. Everything must go if Mao's fantastic production figures were to be met. And as the furnaces yawned, the call went out for more wood to feed the flames and charcoal to fuel the smelting pots. So the hunt shifted to the fields. Throughout China, hillsides were stripped of trees, whole orchards were ripped up, trees that had provided shade or stopped erosion were hacked down and rushed back to keep the furnaces working. Today China still bears the scars of this wanton massacre, with land washed away by floods and topsoil whipped off by the eroding wind. The 'steel rush' eventually extended to schools. Every child, however small, was involved in steelmaking, scratching around in search of every nail or other metal object that could be found on the ground. The school walls were draped with banners proclaiming 'Everybody, make steel'. In the kitchens, huge vats of molten metal sat on the cookers, where once food had been cooked. Lessons were suspended while the teachers devoted their energies to making steel or instructing their students how to do so. Even hospital staff, nurses and doctors, had to suspend operations so that they could feed the furnaces situated in the hospital grounds. Millions of city workers were forced out into the hills to pan for iron ore. Undaunted by the bitter cold, students, women and local government workers worked ankle-deep in the rivers, washing for the iron-bearing sand that

had been carried down from the nearby mountains. What was found was a pitiful trickle in return for the labour of millions of man hours.

But even these acts of insanity were to be surpassed when it came to bringing in the harvest, on which the lives of all Chinese people had depended throughout their history. So many workers had been moved from the farms and into steel production that grain was left rotting in the field. Local party officials told the peasants that this did not matter as Chairman Mao had assured them that this year's harvest was going to be a record, indeed twice as high as ever before. And while the peasants cringed around the filthy, flaming monsters that had consumed the tools they needed to bring in the harvest and plant next year's, Mao Zedong was receiving the first shocking news that the backyard steelworks were producing steel of such poor quality that it could only be used for scrap. Just one per cent of all the steel produced was usable, the other 99 per cent would have to be mixed with iron ore and fed into the furnaces of China's few conventional steelmills. The new steel was aptly named 'cattle turds' by the people. The steel programme was an economic miracle – an industrial revolution in reverse – tools and machines turned into scrap in one easy process. It would have been the stuff of high comedy but for the tragedy that was descending on China with all the velocity of an avalanche.

As famine began to close in on China Mao, who had a poetic phrase for every situation, let it be known that, 'Capable women can make a meal without food.' It was not very reassuring for China's 600 million people that their leader's grasp on reality had become so tenuous.

The year 1958 also saw the completion of the commune system by which the entire rural population of the country was concentrated into 26,000 units, each supposedly self-supporting. The political heads of these communes were the last people to admit that Mao's policies were a disaster and so each commune began claiming that its production of grain would be larger than that of its neighbours, in fact easily the largest harvest in history. At first the peasants were enthusiastic and sang these words:

> We work at such white heat,
> If we bump the sky it will break,
> If we kick the earth it will crack,
> If the sky falls, our commune will mend it,
> If the earth splits, our commune will patch it.

But as the peasants began to starve their leaders ran

A back-yard steel furnace in Szechuan Province, China, during the Great Leap Forward. Six hundred thousand such furnaces were built, but they produced poor quality steel that had to be scrapped. In the pursuit of rapid industrialization China suffered economic catastrophe.

a campaign of 'deceiving themselves while deceiving others'. It was less a matter of lying than a political act of faith. Everywhere that Mao travelled he met commune leaders boasting of enormous food surpluses. Mao seemed to be swept away in the euphoria, telling peasants to eat as much as they liked – even five meals a day. It was madness, but nobody dared to admit it. The emperor was stark naked, but not even the tiniest Chinese boy dared to tell him. Where honest men tried to tell the truth they were beaten up by their neighbours, who refused to see their own communes shamed when they heard that the rest of the country was doing so well. It was a vicious circle. Party officials moved supplies of grain from place to place so that there was always a good supply for Mao to see wherever he stopped.

At last Mao was being criticized in the highest levels of the party. His oldest friend and colleague, Defence Minister Marshal Peng Duhai became his harshest critic. Peng had made his own visits to the communes and he had not found everything well. When he visited his native village he had come upon a large pile of ripe crops lying on the ground apparently abandoned. After a lengthy search, an old peasant was located who explained that all the able-bodied people were too busy launching a 'steel sputnik' (i.e. attempting to set a record in steel production). Peng asked him, 'Hasn't any one of you given a thought to what you will eat next year if you don't bring in the crops? You're never going to be able to eat steel.' The old peasant nodded vigorously in agreement, but added pointedly, 'True enough. Who would disagree with that? But who can stand up against the wind?' Mao was that wind and Peng was soon to feel its strength. At a meeting of the Communist Party leadership at Lushan, Mao admitted that he had made some mistakes – 'I understand nothing about industrial planning', he confessed – but what he was best at doing was staying in power. By the close of the Lushan meeting Peng and the men who thought like him had been silenced, Peng losing his party rank and being placed under house arrest in a distant province.

Elsewhere, peasants were still playing Mao's game, returning from the fields singing of the fantastic harvest. In a massive propaganda effort pictures were displayed of children staggering under the weight of a single tomato, of a cucumber half as long as a truck and of pigs too enormous to fit into trucks (in the last-mentioned case the paint had not even covered all of the pig's papier-mâché skin). The final madness was achieved when the *People's Daily* reported that the harvest of 1958 had exceeded even that of the United States. The paper ran a discussion piece on how to cope with surplus food. The truth was very different. Between 1959 and 1961 China endured one of the worst famines in her history. And what made this worse was that it was self-imposed, or at least imposed on 600 million people by one man – Mao Zedong. In one commune where the harvest had been good, 35 per cent of the peasants still died because all the men had been forced to work on producing steel while the grain withered in the fields. In many areas the horror of cannibalism returned, as several times before in this century. Wind-dried meat was found, on investigation, to be not rabbit as claimed but human. Peasants were beginning to eat their own babies or else to sell them as meat.

To compound the suffering of the Chinese people all manner of natural disasters – typhoons, floods, drought and disease – struck China in the aftermath of the 'Great Leap Forward'. It is estimated that thirty million Chinese died of starvation and disease during the period from 1958 to 1960. Yet by the beginning of 1961 China had begun to emerge from the darkness. Mao had voluntarily surrendered his position as China's head of state to his rival Liu Shaoqi, and under the wiser economic policies of Liu and his protégé, Deng Xiaoping, the worst excesses of the 'Great Leap' were undone. The mass production of steel was stopped and impossible industrial targets were moderated. Grain was imported from Canada and the United States to feed the peasants and there were signs of an improved future for China's hard-pressed millions. But Mao had retained the chairmanship of the party and with his wife, Jiang Qing, he was already planning a new attack on what he saw as the 'rightist tendencies' of Liu Shaoqi and Deng Xiaoping (see p. 84).

SPEAKEASIES AND BLIND PIGS

When Groucho Marx jokingly said that he had been teetotal until Prohibition was brought in, he was summing up what many Americans felt about the campaign to beat the 'demon drink' during the 1920s. What started off as a crusade to improve society by outlawing an undeniable social ill, soon became a challenge to civil liberties. Many Americans resented the tyranny of the anti-drink laws, which hit the moderate social drinker as hard as it did the alcoholic. As a result, what should have been 'the era of clear thinking and clean living' as the anti-Saloon League loudly trumpeted, instead became the most alcoholic period in American history. Not only that, but the 1920s witnessed the rise of organized crime in American cities and an outburst of gangland violence on a scale never before seen. Once booze was banned it became the property of the outlaw and in the rise of Al Capone, America was to see the greatest and most feared criminal in its history.

Temperance Unions and Anti-Saloon Leagues had been a part of American history for more than a century before the Eighteenth Amendment to the constitution in the shape of the Volstead Act became law in 1920, enforcing Prohibition on the American people. From its earliest years, in the heady period after its victory over the despotism of George III, the young United States of America had been known as the 'alcoholic republic' as a result of its heavy consumption of spirituous liquors. New England Puritans looked scornfully on the beer-swilling German and Irish immigrants, believing that the 'demon drink' was at the root of most of the social ills of an industrialized society. Blue-stockings in Boston or Philadelphia pointed out that alcoholism was at the root of unemployment and wife-beating. For prohibitionists, the control of liquor would solve a thousand wrongs: increase industrial output, raise the moral climate of the country, protect the family and reduce crime. It was asking a lot.

Yet the passage of the Volstead Act on 17 January

1920 was by no means the first step in prohibition; 24 states already had anti-drink laws and many other states had 'dry' counties. But the act now gave Federal backing to what had previously been an essentially local movement. 'The noble experiment' as Herbert Hoover called it, could now call on the US government to support its formidable team of do-gooders, which included Wayne Wheeler of the Anti-Saloon League, Bishop James Channon Jnr, Clarence True Wilson of the Methodist Board of Temperance and Andrew Volstead from Minnesota. In addition, the formidable Carry Nation travelled through Kansas from bar to bar like a solitary horseperson of the Apocalypse, carrying an axe beneath her coat with which to smash open the beer kegs or vats of illegal liquor. To help the crusade its moral guardians felt the need to purify the Good Book itself, removing all biblical references to wine and thereby spoiling one of Jesus's miracles: changing water into a cake of raisins did not have quite the same ring.

On 17 January, 1920, the Anti-Saloon League announced 'It is here at last – dry America's first birthday. At one minute past twelve tomorrow morning a new nation will be born. Tonight John Barleycorn makes his last will and testament. Now for an era of clear thinking and clean living. The Anti-Saloon League wishes every man and woman and child a Happy Dry Year.' Billy Sunday, an evangelist, saw a solution to America's farm surplus. The children of drunkards 'will consume this surplus in the form of flapjacks for breakfast'. But were the American people ready for such a radical change? The answer was not long in coming: millions of people who had never thought seriously about how much they drank now reacted as if their right to breathe was being questioned. Like Groucho Marx many previously sober Americans turned into 'rebellious tipplers, home-brewers and hipflask-swiggers'.

John F. Kramer, the head of the Prohibition Commission, began the new era with a prophecy: 'The law will be obeyed in cities, large and small, and in villages, and where it is not obeyed it will be enforced. The law says that liquor to be used as a beverage must not be manufactured. We shall see that it is not manufactured. Nor sold, nor given away, nor hauled in anything on the surface of the earth or under the earth or in the air.' Kramer must have been high on something when he said this: presumably rhetoric rather than the last few fingers

of whisky in the last bottle in Washington. As prophecies go it must rank as one of history's worst.

Within hours of the Volstead Act coming into force, a rather naive British journalist telegraphed his editor that the banishment of alcohol had simply had the effect of sending Americans rushing into candy stores and ice-cream parlours. New – and rather weird – ice-cream concoctions were appearing on the market. Milk-shakes, sundaes, flips and colas were apparently selling in unprecedented numbers. But was the British reporter right? Were the hardened American drinkers turning to soft drinks and ices? Pigs might fly. At least 'blind pigs' would, taking off as never before.

Had our reporter looked more closely into the amazing phenomenon he was describing he might have been less sanguine about the eventual success of the 'noble experiment'. For many of the ice-cream parlours were merely fronts for 'speakeasies' or illegal drinking houses. Elsewhere 'blind pigs' – buildings with blank facades – were opening. Most of them were entered through a basement door, complete with peephole. New York boasted at least 30,000 speakeasies, while every major city had hundreds of such illegal bars, shut down and padlocked by Federal agents, but still operating behind closed doors. Everywhere the race was on to beat the system. Ordinary citizens took up home distilling, following magazine and newspaper articles on how to set up their own stills. Ironically, the Prohibition Commission was undermined by official information leaflets from the US Department of Agriculture, which gave away historical recipes on how to manufacture alcoholic liquors from pumpkins, parsnips and walnut-tree chips. Specialist shops provided kits for would-be moonshiners. In American homes the bathrooms took on a special significance, not as part of the social cleansing then under way, but as the domestic centres of illicit gin-making.

Enforcing the anti-drink laws proved to be enormously expensive and ultimately futile. At the height of Prohibition, the Treasury Department was employing more than 3,000 agents at a cost of two and a half billion dollars a year to close down an industry which at the time of the Volstead Act produced an annual income of only two billion dollars. But after 1920 everyone lost their sense of proportion. Temperance men and tipplers alike behaved as if they were drunk. The law-enforcers simply refused to believe what was happening and remained convinced that Prohibition was working. Commissioner Roy Haynes even claimed that now the Volstead Act was in force only fifteen per cent of previous drinkers were still drinking and that everyone had 'quietly acquiesced' in the new law. Haynes was in cloud-cuckoo-land. As a result of his moral crusade there had been an explosion of immorality on a scale beyond the wildest excesses of ancient Rome. In the first year of Prohibition, Americans consumed 200 million gallons of hard liquor, 684 million gallons of malt liquor and 118 million gallons of wine. All previous records had been broken and illegal bootlegging was worth over four billion dollars a year, double the pre-Prohibition level for all liquor sales. Booze was not just big business, it was by far America's biggest industry.

As the Treasury Department called in reinforcements from the Coast Guard and from the Customs and Excise and Immigration services, the bootleggers, rumrunners and moonshiners found ever more outlandish ways of circumventing the law and its enforcement officers. Convoys of trucks loaded with whisky filled the back roads leading from the Canadian border to Vermont, New York, Minnesota and Washington. Up from Mexico came a similar traffic in tequila and mescal. On the coasts of the United States, notably along 'Rum Row' in Florida, smugglers came in from the West Indies and South America. It is thought that 2000 cases of illegal liquor were landed every day in Long Island Sound alone. The total for all the coves and inlets on a twelve-thousand mile coast defies the imagination.

Within weeks of the Volstead Act becoming law millions of Americans were hunting for alcohol in the most unlikely places. Hundreds of perfectly legal products, ranging from anti-freeze to perfume, contained enough to satisfy the tastes of a thirsty population. During the thirteen 'dry' years of Prohibition, illicit distilling posed the greatest single threat to both the law and the nation's health. Ingenuity was one thing, toxicity quite another. As a result of distilling alcohol from paint and anti-freeze, 34 people died in New York during a four-day period in 1928. Unscrupulous distillers used alcohol from hair tonic, cosmetics and even, in one case, 'Parisienne Solution for Perspiring feet, 90 per cent Alcohol'. The distilled liquor circulated under the names of 'Kentucky Tavern', 'Pebble Ford', 'Coffin Varnish' or 'Rot Gut'. Rich and poor alike fell victim to vile concoctions of corn mash or potato whisky. When one cautious drinker had his bootlegged liquor tested by a chemist he received the alarming and baffling answer, 'Dear sir, your horse has diabetes.' In fact, the medical profession was not slow to exploit its unique position. Home-distillers, armed with prescriptions from their doctors, found chemists willing to supply them with the alcohol they needed. Some doctors speeded matters up by selling their prescription books outright to the highest bidder. As 'drink fever' mounted, speakeasies were set up near schools and colleges, and young people served 'near-beer' so virulent that it caused nausea and often death. Some unscrupulous dealers even used a compound of sulphuric acid, while one sample of bootlegged liquor ate the enamel off the sink in which it was being tested.

Hand-in-hand with the illegal distilling and distribution of liquor went a rise in gangs of criminals who fought for control of this lucrative new business. In cities throughout the north, whole neighbourhoods – notably the South Side and the ominously-named Great Dismal Swamp in Chicago – abandoned their usual jobs to take up distilling. It was out with the sewing machines and in with the vats or three-spout copper stills. Thousands of impoverished workers slaved around the clock producing hundreds of gallons of alcohol every day, sweetened a little by juniper drops or grape juice. A boom in corn sugar during the 1920s corresponded with the new demand from home-brewers and the Chicago mobsters. In 1930, in Chicago alone, mobsters were pulling in a weekly income of three and a half million dollars from speakeasies.

The authorities thereby faced a war on two fronts. Along America's coastline the fight against the smugglers continued, while in every northern city there was the squalid battle against the illegal distillers and their minders. Violence was an ever-present fact of life for Federal prohibition agents, some of whom – like Izzy Einstein and Moe Smith – became public celebrities through the ingenuity of the methods they used to combat the bootleggers. The enormously fat Izzy once staked out an infamous speakeasy for so long, waiting for an illegal shipment of liquor to arrive, that he almost succumbed to hypothermia. Finding his partner more dead than alive, Moe dragged him into the speakeasy, hammered on the bar and shouted, 'Give this man a drink! He's just been bitten by a frost.' When the startled barman complied, Izzy and Moe promptly

Izzy Einstein and Moe Smith, the two most successful federal enforcement agents, whose task
was to crack down on illegal liquor sales in the United States during the Prohibition era.

arrested him and closed down his business. But Izzy and Moe were no comedians; in just five years they made 4000 arrests and seized five million bottles of illegal liquor. Even so, it has been estimated that for every still the authorities closed, another ten remained in operation and it was true, as one cynic pointed out, that any American who wanted a drink during Prohibition could find one within a minute of stepping off a train in any US city. By 1927, in Chicago, drunken driving cases had risen by 476 per cent against their pre-Prohibition figure, and deaths from alcoholism by 600 per cent. No fewer than 35,000 American citizens died from poison liquor during the thirteen 'dry' years.

What had started as a moral crusade soon began to flounder as more and more of the forces of 'law and order' found themselves on the wrong side of the law themselves. Ten per cent of all Federal agents had to be dismissed for corruption, while throughout the country local juries failed to convict popular bootleggers. Mayors, police chiefs and even district attorneys patronized speakeasies and were in the pay of the criminal gangs that ran them. In Kansas the chief of police was himself convicted of violating the Volstead Act, while judges and local politicians were so deeply involved in the profitable business of circumventing the Prohibition laws that it was often pointless for the police to try to prosecute bootleggers. In Chicago, Mayor William Hale Thompson – popularly known as 'Big Bill the Builder' – admitted that he was 'as wet as the middle of the Atlantic Ocean' – and that was probably true of most of the city's police force. In an attempt to turn back this tide of corruption, political leaders in Philadelphia appointed an ex-Marine Corps general, Smedley D. Butler, to be Director of Public Safety. 'Treat 'em Rough' Butler was famous for the skill and efficiency with which in 1917 he had quelled a revolt in Haiti by massacring hundreds of unarmed villagers. It had won him the Medal of Honor and what had worked in Haiti – known as his 'slash-and-burn' campaign – might just work in the City of Brotherly Love. It did not. Within twelve months Smedley Butler was out of a job, blaming politicians, police and judges for thwarting him.

While the Prohibition lobby looked for ways to strengthen the laws against alcohol, men like Mayor Thompson of Chicago claimed that the law enforcers were threatening the constitutional rights of ordinary citizens by their destructive searches of homes, garages, offices and warehouses, often car-ried out just on a tip-off and without valid search warrants. During the 1920s police shot dead more than 2000 bootleggers, losing 500 men of their own in the process. It was a bitter period of unprecedented violence. In their struggle against the evils of drink Federal agents stretched the law to breaking point, making the cure far worse than the complaint. As the Chicago Tribune wrote: 'This paper is against Prohibition because of the methods of enforcement.' Appalling miscarriages of justice occurred. In 1929 a housewife in Aurora was shot dead and her husband clubbed to the ground by a Federal agent who thought he smelled alcohol. A mother of ten children in Michigan was given life imprisonment for concealing a bottle of gin. In 1928 an innocent insurance agent was ripped to pieces by dumdum bullets fired by a Federal agent during an abortive raid on an illegal still in Chicago. The general feeling of disgust with Prohibition is shown in this popular chant of the early 1930s:

> Prohibition is an awful flop,
> It can't stop what it's meant to stop.
> It's filled our land with vice and crime,
> It's left a trail of graft and slime,
> It don't prohibit worth a dime. . . .

The truth was, of course, that with the Volstead Act the United States government had scored one of history's great own goals. What had started as an operation to clean up a whole society, had in fact opened it up to an invasion of criminal 'bacteria' from which it has probably never recovered. Prohibition had been aimed at reducing the influence of the German-American brewers and the Irish-American saloon and bar owners throughout America. Instead, it had replaced a legitimate liquor industry with a two billion-dollar windfall for the underworld, dominated by second-generation Italian and Irish immigrants. Crime became the fastest-growing industry in the world. Syndicates that had concentrated on drugs, prostitution and gambling, found that they could make far more money organizing the production and distribution of illegal liquor. Pre-eminent among the new super-gangs was the Torrio-Capone gang of Chicago, which specialized in exploiting the business opportunities provided by the Volstead Act.

For more than a decade Johnny Torrio, Al Capone and Irish gangsters like the O'Banions turned the streets of Chicago into a bloodbath. Bombings, shootings and all kinds of mayhem made

Barrels of wine are poured into the sewers by a U.S. marshal. In spite of such propaganda pictures, alcohol consumption during the thirteen 'dry' years of Prohibition reached record levels.

the city the crime capital of the world. Al Capone, who listed his profession as 'second-hand furniture dealer', controlled the supply of illicit liquor to thousands of Chicago hotels, brothels and speak-easies. When other gangs challenged his domination he 'rubbed them out'. After an unsuccessful attempt by the O'Banions to kill Capone and wipe out his headquarters, the 'furniture dealer' staged the most famous retaliation in the history of crime – the St Valentine's Day Massacre in 1929, when seven members of the O'Banion gang were machine-gunned to death in a garage of the SMC Cartage Company. It was a decisive event; Capone had won the 'beer war' in Chicago, leaving himself and Torrio undisputed heads of the city's under-world. Yet as Capone pointed out, he was only responding to a social need. Without the Volstead Act Americans would never have heard of Al Capone. 'If people didn't want beer and wouldn't drink it,' he once said, 'a fellow would be crazy for going round trying to sell it . . . I've always regarded it as a public benefaction if people were given decent liquor.'

Al Capone as a public benefactor? This was too much for American public opinion to stomach, and in 1931, a distinguished panel headed by the Harvard professor Zechariah Chafee and Attorney General George Wickersham, warned President Hoover that he had unleashed a 'mad dog' on his country-men which was doing more harm than good. Nobody could reasonably pretend that Al Capone was less of a threat to America than a social drink in a bar with one's friends. The whole thing had got out of proportion. The Volstead Act had missed its mark, making criminals out of ordinary folk and encouraging the upholders of the law – policemen and Federal agents – to behave like criminals them-selves. It had to end. Even so, Hoover stubbornly clung to the moral crusade and decided to run on that platform in the 1932 presidential election.

But by 1932 there was no doubting the mood of the country. While Herbert Hoover campaigned on Prohibition – 'a great social and economic experiment, noble in motive and far-reaching in purpose' – his democratic opponent Franklin D. Roosevelt promised the repeal of the Volstead Act and offered 'a New Deal and a pot of beer for everyone'. It was a winning slogan for Roosevelt and, a week after his inauguration as president, he had killed Prohibition once and for all. The only tears shed were by Capone and his hoodlums, crying into their now thoroughly legal beer.

CHAPTER FIVE: RELIGIOUS BLUNDERS

Peter the Hermit and the Peasants' Crusade

The crusaders who responded to Pope Urban's great rally at Clermont in France, in 1095, made their way to the Holy Land under a variety of leaders. Prominent among the purely spiritual leaders was the man known as 'Peter the Hermit', or 'Little Peter', who was apparently an oldish man, short and swarthy, born somewhere near Amiens in France, who travelled everywhere on the back of a donkey. He ate neither bread nor meat, only fish, and went barefoot and in rags. In spite of his lowly appearance, Peter was a man who could inspire others with a few words. A few years earlier he had tried to make a pilgrimage to Jerusalem, but had been mistreated by the Turks and was burning to take his revenge.

In April 1095, a great shower of meteorites had been seen in the heavens which was felt to presage a great movement of peoples. As a result, following Pope Urban's speech at Clermont, Peter sent 'disciples' – including Walter the Penniless – into the areas of France that he could not personally visit and soon had a mighty following, mostly of peasants but also including some knights. Thousands of ordinary people, believing that the Second Coming was imminent and with it the Day of Judgment, hoped to expiate their sins by going on crusade to Jerusalem. Simple peasant folk thought that a man like Peter was going to lead them out of the misery of their everyday life to a land of 'milk and honey', like Moses in the Bible. They knew that the journey would be hard, and many would fall on the way, but at journey's end they would find salvation. It was an age of visionaries and of great faith, and Peter was believed to be a man divinely inspired.

Throughout the year 1096, thousands of pilgrims were moving across Europe towards the east, some heading towards Italy to take ship to the Holy Land, others moving down through the Balkans towards Constantinople, capital of the Byzantine Empire and gateway to the east. The problem was that the main crusade – to be known as the Knight's Crusade – was taking shape much more slowly in France. Until this military crusade was able to reach the Holy Land the well-intentioned peasants, like the thousands who followed Peter, would be helpless against the full strength of the Turks. The Byzantine emperor in Constantinople, Alexius Comnenus, had asked for military support from the west, but he had not bargained on getting huge numbers of peasants instead of soldiers, nor was he willing or able to accommodate such a mass of people.

Undeterred, Peter moved into Germany and arrived at Cologne on 12 April 1096

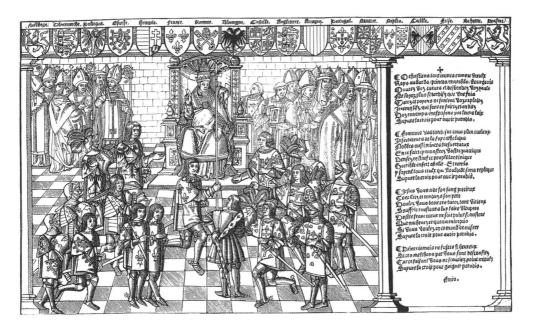

Pope Urban II presides over the Council of Clermont (1095), which launched the First Crusade. While the princes and knights of Western Europe made their preparations, many thousands of ordinary people followed the preacher Peter the Hermit and set out on a separate 'Peasants' Crusade'. This was an ill-organized affair that ended in disaster.

with 15,000 pilgrims. After addressing a great meeting of the pilgrims, he toured the area around the city preaching to the Germans. But his deputy, Walter the Penniless, was impatient to begin. Setting out towards Hungary with a large following, Walter had reached the Hungarian border by 8 May and there he asked for food and help from King Coloman of Hungary. Coloman sent what food he could spare and the crusaders marched on towards Belgrade. Here the harvest had not yet been brought in and, with food in short supply, Walter's followers began ravaging the countryside. Some of the French pilgrims began looting Hungarian shops and houses, whereupon the Hungarians captured the perpetrators, stripped them naked and sent them back to Walter as a warning. Fighting now broke out between the crusaders and the Hungarians, with Walter's followers shaming the cross they wore on their clothes by killing their fellow Christians.

Peter left Cologne on 20 April with the main body of crusaders, numbering some 20,000 men, women and children. Peter's followers moved up the Rhine in the footsteps of Walter's pilgrims and soon reached the Hungarian border, where they were far from welcome. When they reached Semlin trouble broke out: a dispute over the sale of a pair of shoes resulted in rioting which led to a pitched battle between the pilgrims and the Hungarians, in which the town was besieged and captured by Peter's men. It is said that 4000 Hungarians were killed in the fighting and the whole town thoroughly looted. It was a disgraceful event that reflected badly on the motives and discipline of the pilgrims, who behaved more like an invading army.

From now on, Peter's pilgrims were a ravening mob, looting and burning towns and massacring the Christian civilians. It was an unholy distortion of a crusade, made more so by the flagrant attacks on Jewish communities that took place. Before leaving Hungary, Peter's men captured the capital of Belgrade and burned it to the ground after a thorough pillage. Throughout these sorry episodes Peter proved quite incapable of disciplining his followers and was content to plod on to Jerusalem on the back of his donkey, oblivious to the destruction all around him.

When Peter reached Sofia, he met ambassadors from the Emperor Alexius, who were instructed to move the pilgrims quickly to Constantinople so that they would not do too much damage in Byzantine territory. At least the crusaders found that food was made available. On 1 August 1096, they reached Constantinople, where Peter was given an audience with the emperor. Alexius was not impressed. The crusaders, in his opinion, were just a rabble of peasants and would soon be wiped out once they encountered the Turks. Nevertheless, so undisciplined were these westerners that he decided to shift them across to Asia as quickly as possible. In the few days that they spent in Constantinople, the French and German peasants committed endless thefts and assaults, breaking into the magnificent palaces and even stripping the lead from church roofs. They were a poor advertisement for western Christianity.

While at Constantinople Walter the Penniless and Peter were reunited and on 6 August 1096, the whole body of crusaders was shipped across the Bosphorus. Free from the policing activities of the Byzantines, Peter's men fell back into their old ways, pillaging houses and churches and behaving in an undisciplined manner. This was especially dangerous as they were moving into territory controlled by the Turks. Alexius had warned Peter that if he marched on without waiting for the main body of crusaders from France, which would contain many knights of renown, he would risk disaster, but Peter's men were too foolhardy to listen. Their ragbag of an army stumbled towards oblivion like a host of drunken men, massacring the Christian Greeks and stealing their herds. Peter could see that his followers were completely out of control and decided to return to Constantinople, to await the arrival of the Knights' Crusade led by the Pope's representative, the Bishop of Le Puy.

The Turks, meanwhile, had prepared an ambush for the pilgrims. Not possessing the military intelligence of real crusaders, the riffraff that had left France under Peter headed blindly into the trap. The French knight Geoffrey Burel, who had more or less ousted Peter from his command of the crusade, ordered the pilgrims to advance to confront a Turkish army which was said to be approaching. On 21 October, at dawn, the crusaders – to the number of perhaps 20,000 – met the Turks, but not in the way they imagined. Passing through a defile, they were attacked from both sides by the waiting Turks and massacred almost to a man. In the nearby Christian camp, the priests, along with the old men, the women and children were taken unawares by the Turks and slaughtered. For miles the bodies of the pilgrims lay unburied, to be picked clean by the buzzards. Amongst the dead was Walter the Penniless, who had paid for his indiscipline with his life. The news that reached Peter the Hermit and the Emperor Alexius at Constantinople came as no surprise. The Peasants' Crusade had been a horrible mistake, costing thousands of lives and showing the Christian world that faith alone would not win back the Holy Land from the Muslims.

Pope Innocent III and the Albigensian Crusade

The Fourth Crusade of 1204 marked a vital turning point in the history of the crusading movement. For the first time Christians turned against their co-religionists, the Orthodox Greeks of Byzantium, instead of the Muslims who had captured Jerusalem in 1187. Once this shift in emphasis had occurred it was not a very big step for the papacy — in the person of Pope Innocent III — to preach holy war against Christian 'heretics' in southern France. This new crusade of 1209 was against the devout Christians of Languedoc, who were known as Cathars – or Albigensians, on account of their strength around the city of Albi.

During the twelfth century Christian missionary activity had not been a simple one-way process, west to east. Missionaries from eastern Europe and even the Near East – like the Bogomils and Paulicians – travelled into western Europe, teaching a different brand of Christianity. They made many converts in the area of southern France known as Languedoc. Soon a Church developed there to rival the established Catholic one, attracting many new converts. It is sometimes erroneously believed that the courtly culture – the Troubadour culture – of southern France was in some way linked to the development of Catharism, but the two developments were independent of each other. Nevertheless, the late twelfth and early thirteenth centuries marked a great age for the culture of the region.

The new Christians called themselves the *Cathari*, or 'pure ones', and what we know of them comes only from the denunciations by their enemies, for all their works were destroyed in the bitter aftermath of the Crusade of 1209. Their teaching most resembled that of the Gnostics, a heretical movement in the early Christian Church, whose works had been similarly suppressed in the first and second centuries. Catharism was basically a dualist heresy, believing that there were two principles at work in the world, one good and one evil. The Cathars held that the world had been made by an evil one, who was not divine himself, but who was in constant struggle against God. Jesus had been sent by God to redeem mankind, but he was not the son of God, only an angelic figure who never actually took human form. As a result, his death had not been a real one and his resurrection was consequently similarly unreal. His importance lay in his divinely inspired teaching rather than in his death and resurrection, which meant that the Cathars rejected the orthodox doctrine of the Incarnation.

The Cathars were divided into two bodies: the 'perfect', who formed an élite and were devoted to the highest moral standards, and the 'believers', who were not expected to attain the same high standards and were often accused of sexual licentiousness (including polygamy) by the Catholics. The 'perfect' Cathars led such holy lives that the common people were greatly impressed by them, particularly as so few Catholic priests were able to match their dedication to poverty and learning. As these men rejected all earthly things, including food, as evil, some of them insisted on fasting to death.

The main objection to the Cathars in the mind of Pope Innocent III, however, was that they rejected orthodox Catholic views on the Cross and the Holy Sepulchre, which were fundamental to the medieval crusading movement. The Cathars regarded pilgrimages to holy places and veneration of holy relics as pointless, whereas they were the very foundation of medieval Catholicism. In the eyes of the Cathars concepts like the Holy Land, the Holy City or the Holy Cross were wrong, as each of the things so sanctified was earthly and therefore, in their view, inherently evil. Furthermore, Cathars were pacifist by nature and the idea of a Holy War was anathema to them. They liked disputing with the Catholics in open debate, but their tolerance allowed them to engage in such activities as academic exercises rather than with a view to converting their opponent. To them, the idea of taking up the sword against anyone – even an enemy of Christianity – was fundamentally wrong.

The Cathars were not isolated heretics or mavericks, but an organized Church that offered a real alternative to the Catholic Church. They had their own bishops and dioceses, and their religion was one that was as easily assimilated by the rich as by the poor. In fact, Catharism made notable progress among some of the greatest families of Languedoc, who would eventually fight for it against the crusaders in 1209.

Pope Innocent III was unwilling to allow the Cathars to make further progress in southern France. Initially, he sent Cistercian monks to preach against Catharism. But the Cistercians were very much establishment figures, rich and unacceptable to the poor peasants, who mistrusted their worldliness and preferred the simplicity and sincerity of the Cathars. Working on the principle that those you cannot beat you must imitate, Innocent next turned his attention to providing a Cathar-like alternative in the shape of the Dominicans, an order of monks founded by a Spanish

The Albigensian Crusade was directed against the Cathars, a heretical Christian sect based mainly in Languedoc in southern France. It was marked by a bitterness and fanaticism exceeding that displayed in crusades against the Muslims.

priest named Domingo de Guzman, later to become St Dominic. These poor priests tried to follow the lifestyle of Christ himself, adopting poverty as a rule rather than paying lip-service to it like so many of the Catholic priests of the time. As far as Innocent was concerned the Dominicans were the perfect weapon to use against the Cathars. Yet, the people of Languedoc, while respecting the Dominicans, still stayed loyal to the Cathars. Few people converted from Catharism and the heresy continued to spread.

At the end of his tether, Innocent now resolved to defeat the Cathars by the sword. On 17 November 1207, he called on King Philip Augustus of France to take up the cross and fight the heretics in Languedoc. Philip, threatened by enemies in both England and Germany, was unwilling to do so and begged to be relieved of the burden of crusading. He was also concerned by the fact that the Pope was calling on Christians to fight other Christians in the name of their faith. Although the Cathars were regarded as 'heretics', Philip knew them to be gentle, peaceful and true Christians. Innocent III was unleashing holy war inside Christendom for the first time and thereby establishing a precedent that would lead to religious wars well into the seventeenth century. It was a momentous decision and one with the most serious consequences for European history. Innocent III's hatred of the Cathars knew no bounds: he accused them of being irredeemably evil and even decried their simple and holy lives as being 'Satanic traps' to catch the unwary Christian. His abuse of the Cathars reflected his deep psychological unease, a paranoia which could only be cured by the extermination of the entire Cathar sect. It was a display of intolerance without parallel in European medieval history and one that paved the way for the later excesses of the Inquisition.

Although King Philip Augustus was unwilling to lead a crusade against the Cathars, there were many French noblemen who were prepared to do the job for him. Foremost among these was Earl Simon de Montfort – whose son, as Earl of Leicester was to lead a rebellion in England against King Henry III. Simon had quit the Fourth Crusade in 1204 because of his disgust at Christians killing other Christians. Yet he would have no qualms about killing Cathar heretics. Pope Innocent first directed the two great lords of Languedoc, Count Raymond of Toulouse and Count Raymond-Roger of Béziers, to root out the heresy in their lands. Although neither man was a Cathar, both sympathized with the sect and were unwilling to act against them. In January 1208 an incident occurred which triggered the violence. The Pope's legate in Languedoc, Peter of Castelnau, was murdered by one of Raymond of Toulouse's knights, and instantly became a martyr to the papal cause and an excuse for a crusade against the Cathars, who were accused of being involved in the crime. Innocent declared that the Cathars were a threat to the peace of southern France and that they were 'sharpening their tongues to crush our souls [and] they are also in reality stretching out their hands to kill our bodies: the perverters of our souls have also become the destroyers of our flesh'. This was palpably untrue – the Cathars had never shown violence to anyone. But the truth was no longer important to Innocent, for the greater good he demanded the destruction of the Cathars, to which minor evils, like lying, cheating and killing, were subordinate. Innocent therefore instructed Simon de Montfort to lead his 'Crusade for Peace' to annihilate the Cathars. In order to weaken resistance, Innocent excommunicated Count Raymond, thereby releasing his feudal vassals from their obligations to defend him. Innocent declared that the Cathars now posed a more serious threat to Christianity than the Muslims and must be ruthlessly suppressed.

In the absence of King Philip Augustus, the Abbot of Citeaux, Arnauld-Amalric, led the large army of crusaders south in 1209. Count Raymond tried to patch things up with the Pope, but Innocent was unrelenting. The first city to suffer was Béziers, which surrendered to the crusaders to avoid being sacked. But when the soldiers asked the Abbot how they could tell heretics from true Catholics, Arnauld-Amalric replied in words that have become famous: 'Kill them all; God will know his own.' (They were words that have inspired ruthless dictators ever since, even as recently as 1910 when the anti-Semitic Mayor of Vienna, Karl Lüger, campaigned on the motto 'I decide who's a Jew.' Lüger's echo of the Abbot's words inspired one of his listeners – Adolf Hitler – to acts of even greater intolerance.)

Every inhabitant of Béziers was promptly put to the sword. The terror the crusaders inspired went before them, so that town after town surrendered in the hope of mercy, but none received it. At Carcassone Count Raymond-Roger surrendered himself to save his city. He was imprisoned and his fief given to Simon de Montfort, the temporal leader of the Crusade. Simon cut a swathe of killing and burning right across Languedoc, destroying every centre of Cathar worship and killing the heretics by burning them at the stake.

In desperation the people called on Peter of Aragon to come to their aid against the crusaders. In August 1213 Peter crossed the Pyrenees with an army of his vassals and contingents of knights from Toulouse, Foix and Comminges, but he was decisively defeated at the battle of Muret by de Montfort's crusaders. Simon's victory gained him extensive lands at the expense of the defeated lords of Languedoc, including the County of Toulouse. But he did not enjoy them for long. During the siege of Toulouse, Simon was struck and killed by a great boulder from a catapult. Although their greatest enemy had been slain, crushed as if by the hand of God, the Cathars were still relentlessly hunted down. Once the Crusaders had broken the military resistance, the Inquisition was established by Pope Innocent's successor, Gregory IX, in 1233, to stamp out Catharism with a finality that marked the triumph of Christian orthodoxy over heresy. The Cathars finally perished in the holocaust that followed the fall of their isolated fortress of Montségur in the Pyrenees in 1244, after which the pitiful remants of the once great movement fled to Italy.

The Albigensian Crusade unleashed a wave of intolerance within the western Christian Church that has darkened its history ever since. The victory of a repressive Catholic establishment, maintained through the work of the Inquisition, condemned Europe to centuries of religious turmoil, the ripples from which are still apparent even today. Pope Innocent's victory was achieved at a terrible cost to the Troubadour culture that had flourished in Languedoc for more than a hundred years and which was now trodden under the booted heel of the crusading knights and the sandals – softer but just as deadly – of the Dominican monks who efficiently rooted out the final vestiges of the Cathar heresy.

The Children's Crusade

The disillusionment in Western Europe that followed the Fourth Crusade came close to killing the entire crusading movement. In 1204, instead of travelling to the Holy Land to free Jerusalem from the Muslims, the crusaders had – at the instigation of the Venetians, who had extensive trading interests in the eastern Mediterranean – besieged and sacked Constantinople, the great capital of the Byzantine Empire. For many Christians this was the nadir of a movement that had started with such clear and holy aims at Clermont in 1095, when Pope Urban had first called on the Christians of the west to take up the cross in the name of Christ. Ironically, it was to be the 'little children' who showed the crusaders the way back to their duty. But the tragic fate of the Children's Crusade of 1212 showed Christians everywhere that there was as much sin in their own hearts as in the Muslims who held the Holy Land.

The children's movement began suddenly, when Philip Augustus, King of France, who was holding court at Saint Denis, was approached by a shepherd boy named Stephen from the village of Cloyes. The boy – aged no more than twelve years – had with him a letter which, he claimed, had been written by Jesus Christ in person, who had appeared to him in a vision on the hillside where he tended his sheep. Jesus had told the boy to go on crusade and preach his holy word. King Philip, ever the realist, was unimpressed and told the boy to go home and obey his parents. But Stephen spoke as one inspired and refused to be deterred by those who had already failed so many times to free the Holy Land. He preached at the door of the Abbey of Saint Denis with such sincerity that he had soon gathered a following among the young people of the town. He told them that Jesus had said that the seas would open to let them pass through to Jerusalem. So convincing was his message that even the older townspeople were impressed by him.

Like a pied piper, Stephen now set off on his travels around France, preaching everywhere and collecting children as he went. Some of the older and more able of his followers became apostles and travelled far and wide, preaching the crusading message. Stephen ordered everyone to assemble at Vendôme in four week's time. In June 1212 a large assembly of children filled the market place at Vendôme, though whether there were really 30,000 of them as contemporaries wrote, we cannot be certain – perhaps a third of that number would be a safer estimate. In any case, they were a mixed bunch, predominantly peasant in origin, although there were a number of boys of noble birth, who rode fine horses. Although the majority were boys, there were also many girls, some priests and, curiously, a number of prostitutes. As they marched in their separate bands, each group held the Oriflamme, the great national flag of France. So crowded were the streets of Vendôme that the children were forced to camp in the fields nearby. Once everyone was assembled the march south began. Apart from the few aristocratic riders, everyone was on foot. Stephen, however – now treated as a saint, locks of whose hair were regarded as holy relics – insisted on being drawn along on a gaily coloured cart, with a gaudy canopy to shade him from the sun, and surrounded by a group of aristocratic riders. Their intended destination was the great port of Marseilles, where Stephen had told them the miracle of the parting of the seas would take place.

The journey was a hard one, conducted in appalling heat, and many children fell by the wayside, dying of exhaustion or thirst. Nevertheless, the majority who had left Vendôme reached Marseilles safely and all eyes turned towards Stephen and then out to the blue waters of the Mediterranean, waiting for them to part and let the crusade pass on. But the seas did not part. The children felt let down. Some, claiming Stephen had betrayed them, set off to return home, but the majority stayed, hoping as day followed day that the seas might still part. It was at this time that the adult world reimposed itself on the world of the children. Two city merchants, William the Pig and Hugh the Iron − the names may be apocryphal − offered to help the children reach the Holy Land by transporting them free of charge in their ships. Stephen accepted this offer on behalf of his followers and seven vessels were filled with the child crusaders. Tragically, this was the last that anyone heard of these young people for nearly eighteen years.

Meanwhile, the story of Stephen and his vision had spread into the Rhineland region of Germany, inspiring a boy named Nicholas to take up the message and preach it at the Shrine of the Three Kings at Cologne. Nicholas pointed out that adults had so far failed to win back Jerusalem from the Muslims and now it was time for children to do so. He told his listeners of Stephen's claim that the sea would open to let them through. But whereas Stephen's followers had believed that they would retake the Holy Land backed by an army of angels with burning swords, Nicholas's message was less apocalyptic and stressed the need to convert the infidel. Soon the Rhineland was swept by a crusading fervour and, as in France, thousands of children left their homes to go on crusade. The German children assembled at Cologne and marched south to reach the sea on the North Italian coast. So large was the German contingent that it split into two groups, one, led by Nicholas, crossing the Alps from western Switzerland and reaching the sea at Genoa, the second group travelling further east, over the St Gotthard Pass and reaching Ancona. At first the Italians welcomed the extraordinary sight of so many children, travelling without any adults, but soon they began to regard the young crusaders as a nuisance. When the sea failed to part for Nicholas's group, he ordered his followers to move south to Brindisi where a few actually found ships to take them to the Holy Land. But the vast majority could find no way forward and began to stream backwards towards Germany. Few ever reached their homes. The second group of Germans was no more fortunate, the sea at Ancona being no more responsive to visions than it was at Genoa or Marseilles.

And so the story of the Children's Crusade ended in tragedy for the vast majority of the young people. When the miserable survivors of the German crusade reached the Rhineland the following spring, the parents who had willingly let their children set out on the holy mission learned the dreadful fate of their young ones. Unable to take revenge on Nicholas himself, they had his father arrested and hanged in his place. But this was not the end of the story. In the year 1230 a priest arrived in France, having travelled there from the east. He told a strange story. He had been one of the young priests who had travelled with Stephen to Marseilles and had set out in the ships provided by the two dubious merchants of the city. Out in the Mediterranean, the ships had rendezvoused with a Saracen squadron from Africa and had sold the children to Muslim slave traders. The young crusaders had been landed on the Algerian coast, where most of them were sold in a slave market and spent the rest of their lives in captivity. A few others had been taken to Egypt and some even to Baghdad, where Christian slaves fetched a higher price. Perhaps 700 of the children had survived the rigours of their journey and were now slaves in Muslim lands. The priest had been one of the crusaders sold in Egypt, whence he had escaped to bring his dreadful story back to his homeland.

The Flagellants

At the time of the Black Death in Europe, during the 1340s, it is hardly surprising that human beings were driven to some of the strangest and most extreme beliefs in history. With the evidence of death all around them and mortality rates in every town and city reaching nearly 40 per cent, it must have seemed that the end of the world was near. In parts of Germany and Austria the plague seemed to be particularly virulent: a chronicler recorded in 1348 that, 'Men and women, driven to despair, wandered around as if mad . . . cattle were left to stray unattended in the fields for no one had any inclination to concern themselves about the future. The wolves, which came down from the mountains to attack the sheep . . . turned and fled back into the wilderness.' Nobody understood the nature of the disease that was killing them. It was hardly surprising then that people were willing to listen to any explanation, however implausible. One theory was that the plague poison descended from the sky as a ball of fire. One such ball was seen hovering over Vienna and was safely drawn to earth by a local bishop. Where it landed the people raised a stone effigy of the Madonna. Elsewhere, however, the clergy were less successful and huge numbers of priests succumbed to the plague, leaving the Catholic Church in central Europe weak and the people prone to listen to plausible rogues.

The rise of the Flagellants was a symptom of a disease in the body spiritual just as certainly as the black buboes were signs that bubonic plague was present in the physical body. There had been similar reactions to crises earlier in European history, notably in Italy, and self-scourging had often been seen as away of allaying God's anger. Yet if the Black Death was a sign of divine anger then never before had mankind seen God so angry. To placate such divine retribution required penitence of an extreme kind. One story claims that the flagellants – or the 'Brethren of the Cross' as they were sometimes called – originated in Hungary, among a group of 'gigantic women'. Unlikely as this may sound, historians have no better explanation for its inception.

Flagellants travelled in long crocodile-like columns, two abreast, each column consisting of two or three hundred devotees, though at the height of the Black Death groups of more than a thousand were reported. Men and women were segregated, the women being placed towards the rear of the column. At the head marched the

Master of the Flagellants, accompanied by two assistants carrying banners of purple velvet and cloth of gold. They marched in silence, except for very occasional hymn singing, their heads and faces hidden in cowls and their eyes turned down towards the ground. They wore dark, sombre clothes, with red crosses on the front and back on their cowls. As they marched the news travelled quickly ahead, so that crowds of villagers came out to greet them and church bells were set ringing. The Flagellants were not always welcomed by the Church authorities as they frequently brushed aside the local priests and took over the churches for their own activities. Generally, however, they conducted their activities in market places, forming wide circles before stripping to the waist and flinging their clothes into the middle of the circle, where they attracted the attentions of the local sick and afflicted who hoped to gain cures from handling the garments of such holy people. At a signal from the Master the Flagellants flung themselves down, usually with arms outstretched in imitation of the crucified Christ. Some, who had committed particular crimes, reacted in ways appropriate to their sins: adulterers face down in the dirt, perjurers on their sides holding up three fingers. The Master then walked round the circle whipping those who had committed crimes. This was immediately followed by the self-flagellation for which the movement was famous. Each Flagellant carried a heavy scourge or whip, with three or four leather thongs tipped with metal studs or sharp spikes. With these they began furiously to whip their backs and breasts, while three of their number cheered them on with a rhythmic chant. Three times in total each Flagellant threw himself or herself to the ground and three times rose up to continue the

A procession of Flagellants during the 14th century. The Black Death which struck Europe in the 1340s was interpreted as a sign of God's anger, leading many people to seek to placate the Almighty with acts of penance. The Flagellant movement was a spontaneous expression of public hysteria.

beating, until their bodies were purple with blood and bruising. On the edge of the market place the townsfolk urged them on or wailed in horror at the dreadful sight. Soon all the Flagellants were bleeding profusely and collapsing from sheer exhaustion. Chroniclers relate that the Flagellants repeated this process two or three times a day for 33 days – one day for each of Jesus' earthly years of life – but it is difficult to believe that anyone would have survived the shock of this treatment or the inevitable infection that would ensue from the filthy conditions in which the Flagellants lived. It is all the more unlikely given that the Flagellants were forbidden to wash themselves or their clothing, or indeed to change anything they wore.

In its early days the Flagellant movement was sternly disciplined, although as times grew worse in the 1340s standards dropped and more disreputable members joined. Original members had to obtain the permission of their spouses before joining and confessed all the crimes they had committed since the age of seven years. They each had to show that they could afford to pay the four pence daily required to meet the cost of their food. As a result, Flagellants tended to be middle rather than lower class.

In the early days of the Black Death the Flagellants were often welcomed by the inhabitants of the towns they passed through, presumably in the hope that their self-sacrifice might allay God's wrath. However, as it became clear that visits by the 'Brethren' were associated less with clearing the plague from towns that already had it, and more with introducing it to towns that did not, the Flagellants increasingly found their way barred. It soon occurred to people that these 'pilgrims' might be spreading the plague unwittingly as they travelled. These accusations only drove the Flagellants to greater acts of frenzied self-sacrifice. Some of their number began to claim that they were divinely inspired and that they could drive out devils, heal the sick and even raise the dead. A lunatic fringe claimed to have personally eaten and drunk with Christ himself and to have spoken with the Virgin Mary. The blood that these men spilled was soaked up in rags by the poor peasants and regarded as holy relics. But the Flagellants were exceeding their original brief, which was the allay God's wrath, and were beginning to criticize and challenge the established Catholic Church. Other 'heretics' in Europe, like the 'Lollards' and the 'Beghards', began to join the Flagellants in their attacks on the Church. It could not be long before the whole machinery of the Catholic establishment was turned against them.

When the Flagellants told the people of Germany to expect the resurrection of their emperor Frederick II, an ardent opponent of papal supremacy in his country who was going to massacre the clergy and abolish the differences between rich and poor, there was a threat of social upheaval. With their numbers growing all the time – in 1349 5300 Flagellants visited Tournai and at Constance there were even more, some chronicles estimating over 10,000 – they were a clear threat to the social order. They were becoming more violent as well, attacking and murdering priests, and sacking churches. In 1349 a small group of Flagellants visited England and flogged themselves in London. The English folk thought they were mad and treated them with complete indifference. Whipping yourself in public was bad enough, they said, but stripping off in England in September was just plain lunacy. The Flagellants were deported as 'undesirables'.

In October 1349, Pope Clement VI issued a bull against the order, denouncing them as heretics. When Flagellants arrived in Avignon, where the Pope was holding court, Clement ordered them to be flogged. This curiously inappropriate punishment failed to deter them and Clement next threatened them with excommunication. Rulers throughout Europe picked up the Pope's lead, many threatening to kill any Flagellants in their lands. In Breslau, one Flagellant master was burned alive. As a result of such draconian measure, the Flagellant movement collapsed as suddenly as it had risen, vanishing 'like night phantoms or mocking ghosts'.

The Flagellant movement was just one of the many absurd ideas that humans have shared at moments of crisis. So terrible was life during the period of the Black Death that no human action, however absurd, could be seen as damaging in the face of so relentless an opponent. Unfortunately, travelling about in large bodies from one place to another was far more likely to spread the plague than to contain it or persuade God to relent and remove it. Yet it took courage to stand up and try to do something about the crisis, rather than crouch in a corner and wait for death to come. The Flagellants may seem strange to modern readers, yet what will future readers think of those who believe in UFOs or in the idea of a flat earth, or of people who think the world will end in the year 2000 or on St Patrick's Day? Most of the Flagellants were followers rather than leaders and if their actions probably did more harm than good, they were acting within the limitations of their knowledge. They deserve not our ridicule but our pity.

The first blast of the trumpet

Queen Elizabeth I of England was no feminist but she knew that she was born to rule, and if any man cared to dispute it then that was his mistake. She dangled men on the end of her prerogative and that was as far as any of them ever got. So when the Scottish Calvinist, John Knox, then sheltering in Geneva, presumed to let fly a blast from his trumpet against what he called 'the Monstrous Regiment of Women', he was tangling with more than he had bargained for.

John Knox deserves our sympathy. The second half of the sixteenth century was remarkable for its strong women, monstrous or otherwise. Knox's blast was not directed against Elizabeth at all, whom he considered quite an acceptable ruler, for a woman. No, Knox had fired his broadside against three Marys, who had earned his contempt. The Regent of Scotland, Mary of Guise, had maintained a rigid Catholicism in Scotland much to Knox's fury, and her daughter, Mary Stuart, was likely to keep the land of his birth as a 'Papist land' when she took the throne. And, worst of all, Mary Tudor, Queen of England, had driven Knox and his fellow Protestants out of England and forced them to seek sanctuary in Switzerland and Germany. To Knox's way of thinking, there were just too many women in positions of power. And they all seemed hostile to him.

Ironically, it is doubtful if any of the Marys took Knox very seriously. The only

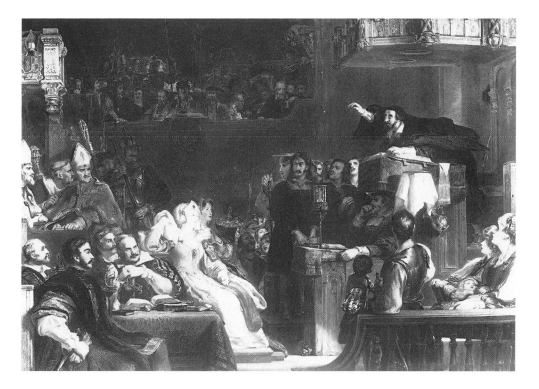

David Wilkie's 19th-century depiction of John Knox preaching before the Lords of the Congregation, c. 1559. Knox's attack on the 'Monstrous Regiment of Women', though not aimed at Elizabeth I, won him the hatred of England's queen.

woman who did, to Knox's dismay, was the one he had most reason to want to impress. On Mary Tudor's death, in 1558, the throne of England had gone to her sister, the Protestant Elizabeth. This was a woman that Knox could admire – as a woman. He regarded her as the best of that sex, which was not saying very much. Nevertheless, she was the ruler of England and he hoped to return from Switzerland and take up a bishopric in England until the time should come for a religious revolution in Scotland. However, Knox was underestimating Elizabeth. Although Knox's pamphlet had not been aimed at her, she had taken it very personally indeed. Knox's chauvinism was apparent and, in spite of his obvious abilities and the fact that his English colleagues like Richard Cox and Edmund Grindal suggested that she appoint him as one of her bishops, nothing would have induced her to allow the man to enter England. Knox's blast had damaged him rather than any of the women against whom he had aimed it.

Knox's friends suggested that he should write personally to Elizabeth, reassuring her that his fierce article had not been intended for her. But the Scots cleric was not good at apologizing. He did his best, telling Elizabeth, 'I cannot deny the writing of a book against the usurped authority and unjust regiment of women; neither yet am I minded to retreat or call back any principal point or proposition of the same till truth and verity do further appear'. This, apparently, was Knox's apology. He could not understand why the queen was annoyed with him. What he had said was common sense, as she must realize. She was only ruling England, he told her, by 'a peculiar dispensation of God's mercy, permitting in her what law and nature denied to all other women'.

So furious was Elizabeth with what the Scotsman wrote that, rather than inviting him to become one of her new bishops, she would have readily hanged him from the gallows at Tyburn if he had chosen to return to England with his fellow Protestants in 1558. As the other learned men came home from Switzerland and Germany on hearing the news of the death of 'Bloody Mary', Elizabeth's leading minister, William Cecil, hastened to warn them not to mention Knox's name when they met the queen. To do so, he told them, would be fatal to their chances of preferment. The fact was that Elizabeth was not content simply to reign, it was her intention to rule England and that involved establishing a religious settlement of the country. She knew that to appoint extremists and bigots like John Knox would ensure a continuing religious strife in her lands. In her appointment of new bishops she was determined that men of moderation and tolerance would be needed. If Knox was prepared to criticize a whole sex as inadequate to rule a kingdom then she had no time for such a man. Chauvinism was expected of a man, but piggery . . . that was too much. The 'monstrous regiment of women' would walk all over John Knox and flatten his trumpet.

Sunspots for the 'Sun King'

Religious strife had come close to destroying the unity of France in the second half of the sixteenth century. The nation owed much to Henry of Navarre, who as Henry IV reunited the country and brought an end to the Wars of Religion with the Edict of Nantes in 1598. Henry's policy granted freedom of religion to all Frenchmen and gave the French Protestants – known as Huguenots – the protection of being a 'state within a state'. However, after Henry's assassination in 1614, his successors viewed the great edict as a barrier to French unity rather than a guarantee of it. In the first half of the seventeenth century, Huguenot numbers shrank and the Protestants came to realize that they could only maintain their status in France as a privileged minority as long as the monarch allowed the edict to stand.

As a young boy, the future Louis XIV had made a solemn oath to eliminate heresy from the land of France and once he was old enough to rule alone he began to unravel the work of his ancestor, Henry IV. In his anti-Protestantism, Louis had enormous popular support, particularly among the lower classes and the poor peasantry who were almost all Catholic. The Huguenots were strongest among the artisan class and were also well represented among the merchant and manufacturing classes, in the armed forces and among the nobility. In fact, it was the wives of prominent Huguenots who were strongest for their faith and who prevented their husbands returning to Catholicism. Several important nobles, including the marshals Turenne and Schomberg, were tempted to abjure their Protestantism but were persuaded otherwise by their wives. The Huguenots were also far better educated than the

Catholics, each of their households possessing a Bible. As such their contribution to French life was inestimable and their persecution was likely to have serious consequences for the well-being of the French nation. Nevertheless, hostility to the Huguenots was strong among the king's ministers and civil servants, and they were widely regarded as a divisive factor within the country.

From the beginning of his majority, between 1660 and 1664, Louis XIV had increased pressure on the Huguenots, closing some of their places of worship, forbidding them to emigrate from France to other Protestant lands and producing a series of catechisms to make their return to Catholicism easier. Yet the Huguenots proved remarkably resistant to such pressure. It was not until 1679 that Louis tightened the screw, planning to bring about an immediate end to the Protestant heresy. In that year conversions from Catholicism to Protestantism were officially prohibited and henceforth only Catholic midwives could attend births. In 1681 the first *dragonnades* were introduced: soldiers, instead of being billeted on tax-evaders, as had happened previously, would be billeted on Protestant households. The soldiers – dragoons – were encouraged by their officers to behave badly and to pressurize the Protestant families with whom they stayed. Next Louis decreed that many professions would in future refuse to admit any Protestants. Louis remembered always to hold out a carrot to potential converts to the 'true' religion. 'Returnees' were granted tax concessions and immunity from the *dragonnades*. Yet this was a mistake that had been made by Catholic persecutors since the sixteenth century and earlier, who seemed less concerned with the quality of the converts rather than their quantity. Thus it was enough for Protestants to say that they were Catholics for them to be counted as true believers. This gave Louis an entirely exaggerated view of how successful his campaign of persecution was proving. Furthermore, to please the king his agents, who reported the progress of the campaign from the regions, often milked the figures to make them more impressive.

By September 1685, Louis XIV had dismantled the Edict of Nantes brick by brick. Its subsequent revocation by the Edict of Fontainebleau on 18 October was merely the rubber-stamping of a process already achieved. As far as Louis and his ministers were concerned, the Protestant religion no longer existed in France and therefore there could be no more Huguenots. Their pastors were ordered to leave the country within two weeks and the property of any Huguenots who had already emigrated was confiscated. It sounded impressive, but it was both a political and religious blunder from which it is doubtful that France ever really recovered.

The consequences of revoking the Edict of Nantes were simply stupendous. In a period of months more than 200,000 of the most educated, active, rich and industrious French citizens left the country and took their skills to France's Protestant neighbours, Holland, Germany and England, where they were welcomed and given good employment. France's economic, social and intellectual life was struck a fatal blow by this great migration of talent and France's neighbours became even more hostile to her as a result of housing so many of her discontented élite. The French Navy lost 9000 sailors and the Army some 600 officers and more than 12,000 of its best soldiers. Significantly, William of Orange had over a thousand French officers

The Edict of Nantes of 1598 brought an end to 40 years of religious war in France. But by 1685, King Louis XIV was no longer willing to tolerate Protestantism within his realm and revoked the Edict. The subsequent emigration of 200,000 people struck a fatal blow at France's economy and industry.

in his army at the battle of the Boyne in 1690, and his army was led by the same Marshal Schomberg whose wife had stiffened his resolve to remain a Protestant. English, Dutch and Brandenburg forces in the wars against Louis XIV in the next thirty years boasted many French officers, some of great talent. In Brandenburg–Prussia the 'Great Elector', Frederick William, welcomed over 20,000 French Huguenots to settle in his lands, who helped establish new industries, such as velvet, lace, silk, soap, paper and glass. The economic and political rise of Prussia owed much to the transfusion of the best blood from France.

On his death bed Louis XIV regretted what he had done in driving the Huguenots out of France. But he had believed it necessary and claimed he had acted in the interests of the vast majority of Frenchmen who wanted to see the religious schism brought to an end. The consequences were disastrous for France yet if the king blundered, he had nineteen million French Catholics as accomplices.

The witch craze

Witchcraft has not always played an important part in European culture. Until about the year 1000, belief in witches was generally dismissed by Christian writers as an illusion rather than a sign of heresy. However, from the eleventh century onwards the subject of witchcraft became a growth industry. Writers, both sacred and profane, filled their works with ever more salacious details of what witches got up to. Yet it was merely the feeding of their own fantasies. As there was no objective evidence against which people could measure their experiences, it was open to every blackguard with a pen and a feeling for words to tell the simple folk that the earth was swarming with demons of both sexes who, like them, were descendants of Adam, but who had been led astray by devils. Soon everyone feared to travel by night in case they saw these insubstantial beings passing through the night sky. Swans reflecting the moonlight as they flew were identified as spirits, and birds and woodland animals provided country folk with many sightings of the devil's brood.

The casting of spells or muttering of curses, aimed at harming people's health or their livestock, was referred to as *maleficium*, and it was this rather than the more dramatic devil-worship that played the most significant part in popular European culture. After 1500 there was a notable increase in accusations of *maleficium* against neighbours or even members of the same family. And witches were not simply old women – or occasionally men – who muttered curses and spells. Writers began to add to their list of activities the killing and eating of babies, their metamorphosis into birds and animals, and the power of flight by broomstick or goat, by which they attended their Devil's Sabbath, a kind of inverted Christian ceremony. They were also thought to have familiars, animals who would do their bidding and would leave a tell-tale sign on the body of the witch, a spot or mark on the skin which witch-finders would point out to justify their accusations. This led to the appalling 'pricking' of witches, whereby the suspected women were stripped naked and then had sharp needles pressed into their bodies to see if they could feel the pain. If they did not scream it was clear that they had the mark of the devil. The demonology contained in the writings of St Augustine served to inspire men to become witchfinders in the sixteenth century and to convince ordinary folk that the world was alive with devils and witches. One priestly writer told the story of a nun who had forgotten to make the sign of the cross before she ate her supper and inadvertently swallowed a demon hidden among her lettuce leaves.

At Como, in Italy, a witchfinder claimed to make 41 discoveries of witches in a single year. In 1484, two formidable German witch-hunters, Heinrich Krämer and Jakob Sprenger, so alarmed Pope Innocent VIII with their tales of witchcraft that he issued a Papal Bull empowering them to pursue witches throughout Germany. It was the start of the great witch-craze in central Europe. Two years after the Bull was published, Krämer and Sprenger published the witch-hunter's encyclopaedia – *Malleus Maleficarum* – containing everything you wanted to know about witches but were afraid to ask. The book was packed with every kind of detail about witchcraft and contained, furthermore, instructions for interrogating suspected witches. As a result of being forced to answer the questions contained in this book thousands of so-called witches, most of them women, would suffer death in the sixteenth century. *Malleus Maleficarum* was nothing more than the mindless ramblings of two rogues who knew they were on to a good thing by playing on people's fears of the unknown. Unfortunately, in the century after it was written it achieved the status of a witchfinder's 'bible'. Its contents were taken as literal truths in the way that people took the gospels to be true. With the book as support, princes and lesser rulers insisted that action should be taken against any witches in their lands.

The first casualty of the witch craze was the law. All cases involving accusations of witchcraft were conducted with rules on evidence, on disinterested juries and on the reliability of witnesses suspended. Uncorroborated testimony from hysterical children was considered enough to secure a conviction and to condemn a person to death by burning. Sometimes there were no witnesses at all and evidence against an accused person was entirely circumstantial. Torture was often used to secure the names of other witches. Thus perfectly innocent people were accused by someone enduring the agonies of the thumbscrews or the strapado. Apparently, experience told the witchfinders that sleep deprivation, though necessarily slow, was the surest way to secure a confession. After many hours of sleeplessness, it was found that the accused woman would usually confess to anything, including attendance at the witches' sabbath, copulation with demons and all kinds of obscenities and absurdities. In this confused state of exhaustion the prisoner became entirely suggestible. Any witnesses to the interrogation would hear the witchfinder prompting her confession and indulging his own fantasies at the same time.

Public hysteria both fed the confessions and fed on them. The lists of names that poured out of the mouths of poor, confused old women seemed to confirm everyone's worst fears that witches and demons were abroad in their thousands. Nobody, not even your neighbours of many years, your own children or your husband or wife were above suspicion. The problem was that some of the old women who were accused were of simple intelligence, senile or psychotic. They sometimes liked to shock their interrogators with their lewd confessions or please them by saying what they wanted to hear. Under torture the 'witches' would admit to using the most ridiculous lists of ingredients in their cauldrons, sufficient to make Shakespeare's Scottish crones seem quite conventional in their tastes. Babes' blood was a staple ingredient and apparently most effective when mixed with vulture fat.

The publication of numerous demonologies provided people with the names of Satan's followers as well as the appropriate language of witchcraft. Both the accused and the accusers were able to use the mythology that had grown up on the subject as if there was real evidence for the existence of the demons. After an outbreak of witch fever in 1610 in the Basque region of Spain, Inquisitor Salazar shrewdly observed that there 'were neither witches nor bewitched until they were talked and written about'. This was the nub of the problem and explains why communities throughout Europe experienced visits from the same devils and demons, and had witches who behaved in exactly the same way regardless of national differences. The publication of the *Malleus Maleficarum* acted as a kind of textbook or consumer's guide for everyone who wished to take part in the great game of 'find the Witch': hunt your neighbours out of doors; torment ugly old women who no longer have a place in society; inform on those who have done you a bad turn; condemn the woman whose husband you covet. It was a game for all the family, and everybody from the youngest child knew how to play and how to win.

Significantly, it was after 1550 that the witch craze really took flight. As such it must be seen as a concomitant of the Counter-Reformation, which was entering its most aggressive phase. Faced with the need to extirpate heresy, in the form of the Lutheran and Calvinist Churches, Catholic princes and archbishops felt that it was not a great step for them to extend their struggle to those other enemies of the true Church – the witches. The Archbishop Elector of Trier, Johann von Schönenberg, was a strong supporter of the Counter-Reformation in Germany. Having first driven the Protestants from his lands, he next turned his attention to the witches. Between 1587 and 1593 he had 368 witches burned, leaving two villages with only one female inhabitant each. One of his judges was thought to be too lenient and so Johann had him tried as a witch, tortured, strangled and burned. In one rural township in Piedmont, so many witches were burned that every single family lost a member. The witch hunters were just as busy in Protestant Switzerland as in Catholic Italy or Germany. In the single canton of Vaud, witches were executed at a rate of 40 a year throughout the sixteenth century. In Obermarchtal, which had a population of only 700, 43 women were burned in just two years. In Germany, a trick was sometimes used to force a suspected witch into confessing her guilt. As she sat in the darkness of her cell, she was visited by the devil himself who promised to save her from death at the stake if she would worship him. The devil, of course, was an impostor – the public hangman dressed up in a bearskin, with horns and a long tail. The Germans found this cruel joke so amusing that they recorded it in poetry and song.

By the 1620s witch-hunting was common even in Calvinist Scotland: nearly three times as many witches were executed there as south of the border. During one witchcraft trial in North Berwick, a woman named Gellie Duncan was put to the – apparently – terrible torture of the *pilliewinkis*. Whatever it was, it persuaded her to admit to joining some 200 witches and warlocks in naked frolics in a kirk on the edge of the town. There they were told by the Devil to assassinate King James I who was, according to the evil spirit, 'the greatest enemy he ever had'. When the king heard this he was privately delighted. He ordered Gellie Duncan to attend him at court and play the same reel that she had played at the witches' frolics in the church.

However, the decline of religious conflict in Europe by 1650 largely put an end to the witch craze. Even so, isolated examples still occurred well into the eighteenth century. The 'swimming test' – the accused woman was immersed in the local river or pond and proclaimed innocent if she sank, and possibly drowned, but guilty if she floated – was still used as a trial of witchcraft. In 1751, in Hertfordshire, Ruth Osborne died – presumably found innocent posthumously – as a result of a 'swimming test'.

A 17th-century engraving showing the famous Witchfinder General, Matthew Hopkins, surrounded by an assortment of witches and their attendant demons.

The most significant feature of the whole subject of witchcraft is the fact that though men could be witches, more than 80 per cent of all people accused were women. This naturally raises an important point about the treatment of women during the period from 1500 to 1650. How was it possible for one half of the population to come under such suspicion and endure such appalling treatment, usually at the hands of the other half? The answer appears to stem from men's fear of women and their need to control them by marriage. Old widows and spinsters – old in those days meaning anyone over 40 – were no longer under the control of a man and therefore were presumably free to indulge their natures, whatever they might be. Since Eve had been the initiator of Original Sin, women were seen as sexually lustful and only able to control their insatiable appetites within marriage. In the eyes of many men, women were the givers of life and might just as easily be the bringers of death. In villages it was usually the old women who acted as midwives, who knew about herbs and natural medicines and were the recipients of the oral tradition of the countryside passed down to them from their mothers. They knew many things of which men had no understanding. In self-defence they might use curses and black magic. On the other hand, these so-called 'wise women' were also defenceless in that no man would defend them if they were accused of witchcraft. It was this vulnerability that made them natural victims. Furthermore, once a woman had lost her looks and was unable to bear any more children, she was regarded as useless to the community and potentially dangerous. Any solitary, eccentric or bad-tempered woman could be a worthwhile target, particularly if she was sharp-tongued and ugly to look at. And sometimes the motives for accusing women of being witches were financial. Widows left with valuable property might be open to accusation by male relatives who coveted their property.

Fundamentally, the most important strand in the witch craze of the sixteenth century was the process of reducing women's rights. Witch-hunting was a clumsy but very real first step in the repression of women from the status they had enjoyed in the Middle Ages. Their marital property rights were already being diminished throughout Europe, their ability to take part in guilds was being restricted, and wage differentials between men and women were increasing sharply. Stereotyping witches as old, husbandless women, was certainly helpful to men in controlling the activities of older and sometimes wealthy women.

DIES IRAE

The power of suggestion has always been strong in Africa, where sympathetic magic has played a vital part in both medical and social aspects of tribal life. When the intention has been to do good it has been welcomed. Even when it has been used to do harm, one suspects, the extent of the damage done has generally been limited to an individual or to a small group. However, in the case of the 'cattle killing' in the eastern part of what is now South Africa in 1856 the power of suggestion assumed such a hold on an entire people that its capacity for harm assumed cataclysmic proportions. In the space of twelve months the population of Xhosaland fell by 80 per cent, mostly through starvation. And unlike similar catastrophes, both human and natural, the Xhosa embraced their fate and even welcomed it. Through a form of mass hysteria the Xhosa convinced themselves of the need to kill all their cattle, destroy all their food and sow no crops for the future. It was mass suicide by starvation. It was also one of history's strangest socio-economic blunders. Yet it all began innocently enough.

In April 1856 two young Xhosa girls were sent to chase birds from cornfields near the River Gxara. The elder girl, Nongqawuse, reported later that while they were drinking at the water's edge two mysterious figures materialized alongside them. They told the girls to take back a message to their kraal that a great resurrection was about to take place, and that the people should kill all their cattle as these would no longer be needed. Once the great day came there would be no shortages of any kind, so they must tell their people that there must be no sowing or cultivation of crops, all stored grain must be thrown away and witchcraft must be ended forever. Once this had been carried out, the strangers told the girls, no further work must be done except to prepare for the new world that was coming. And when all the Xhosa cattle had been killed the new people would come, sweeping all the English and all the unbelievers into the sea. Naturally the girls were frightened, but they duly carried the message back to the kraal where they lived. At first everyone simply laughed, ridiculing them for their naivety. But the girls went back to the river the next day and received the same message. Nongqawuse was told to ask her uncle Mhalakaza, who was something of a seer, to come with her to the river in four days' time.

Four days later Mhalakaza went to the river with his niece, but he could not see the figures the girl assured him were there and could hear their words only when Nongqawuse translated them for him. This is what she claimed they said: 'We are the people who have come to order you to kill your cattle, to consume your corn and not to cultivate any more.' Mhalakaza, very reasonably, asked what his people were to eat if they destroyed their cattle and threw away the grain, and was told that all would be taken care of. Mhalakaza was instructed to take this message to the paramount chief of the Xhosa, Sarili, and to all the other chiefs.

One of the oddest features of the entire story was that Mhalakaza had, shortly before these events, been befriended by the Christian Archdeacon of Grahamstown, Nathaniel James Merriman, a man both eccentric and unconventional. Mhalakaza had been converted to Christianity by Merriman, had taken the European name of Wilhelm Goliat and had built himself a hut in Merriman's back garden. He was something of a dreamer, who had burned with shame when ridiculed by Merriman's wife for his talk of the visions that came to him. He had told her his aim was to become a 'gospel man', but when he found that the avenues to preferment in the Christian world were closed to him, he returned to his kraal, abandoned his European name and became Mhalakaza once again.

Mhalakaza now found his vocation. He had found his own gospel – the message of the new people – and he started to spread it fervently. He began by killing his own cattle, one a day, and soon his neighbours followed suit. There was general excitement at the thought of the new herds of cattle that the strangers had promised would appear on the great day of resurrection. Even the paramount chief Sarili listened to Mhalakaza's words and was prepared to believe that Nongqawuse had really seen the strangers. He was encouraged in this by his own hopes of seeing the British driven away from his lands and of seeing the influence of the white men removed from Xhosa life and society. He particularly objected to European dress, saying that his naked followers, coated in red clay, were clean compared to the white men who wore their clothes until they rotted on their backs. He refused ever to attend a Christian church as he hated the bad odour of 'clothed natives'.

Another curious feature of the Xhosa visions was the fact that during 1855, and well before Nongqawuse's vision, news had reached South Africa of events in the Crimean War. It was heard, for example, that the much-hated Sir George Cathcart – who had slaughtered many Xhosa in earlier frontier wars – had been killed in the fighting by the Russians. The Xhosa hoped against hope that the British would be beaten and that the Russians would come and force them to leave Africa as well. The idea soon took root that Nongqawuse's strangers had been Russians, black men in military coats, for in the minds of the Xhosa the Russians were really the ghosts of past Xhosa warriors and there-fore must be black. All along the coastline of Xhosaland people thronged the clifftops looking out across the sea, waiting for the Russian ships to come to liberate them. But none of this could happen until all the cattle had been slaughtered.

However, the Xhosa were forgetting their own age-old saying: 'The cattle are the race; they being dead the race dies.' The slaughter of their own cattle by the Xhosa was one of history's most enormous 'acts of faith', a ritual suicide to western eyes, a desperate act of self-renewal to the African. By the summer of 1856 the sayings of Mhalakaza were heard throughout the land and thousands of cattle were dying at the hands of their owners. British officials were aghast at these developments, but felt helpless to stop them. Charles Brownlee, brought up among the Xhosa and fluent in their language, was alone in visiting the Xhosa kraals to try to counteract Mhalakaza's influence, but to no avail. As he told his wife, 'There will either be war or you will see men, women and children dying like dogs about your door.'

With Sarili admitting that he believed Mhalakaza's message, the whole Xhosa people became divided between 'believers' and 'unbelievers', with the large majority following the paramount chief. The British representative at Port Elizabeth, John Maclean, failed to comprehend the ritual significance of what the Xhosa were doing and sensed instead a plot against the British authority in South Africa. He responded by sending Sarili a threatening message, warning that if the Xhosa chief did not put a stop to Mhalakaza's mischief than he, John Maclean, would do it for him by force. The British High Commissioner Sir George Grey was also alerted about the supposed plot and he and Maclean prepared to intervene militarily in the strange affair if they felt Britain's interests were being challenged.

Sarili, to prove to the unbelievers that Mhalakaza was telling the truth, now went with the prophet to the Gxara riverbank where the strangers had first appeared to Nongqawuse. There he was shown one of his sons who had died recently, and a long-dead favourite horse, as well as corn and beer that miraculously appeared as presents from the new people. Sarili was impressed and when Mhalakaza told him that all his cattle and goats must immediately die, he readily agreed. Mhalakaza warned everyone present that the Russians would not come until all the cattle had been killed and all the grain

wasted, nor would any of the other predictions come to pass. He then named the places within the Xhosa lands where the Russians would appear and where the dead would return to life. Sarili at once returned to his kraal and began to kill his cattle, as did all the other believers.

Sarili had wanted the story of his meeting with the strangers to be kept secret, but this was too much to expect and soon pilgrims from throughout his land were hurrying towards the River Gxara in the hope of witnessing a miracle. With the hysteria mounting and the cattle killing increasing to a frenzy, Mhalakaza decided that a date should be set for the fulfilment of everyone's expectations. At the end of July 1856 Mhalakaza declared that the resurrection would occur at the time of the full moon. Excitement reached fever pitch as the day of the full moon approached, but in spite of the fact that hundreds of thousands of Xhosa people were willing it, nothing out of the ordinary occurred. The Russians stayed at home.

Sarili began to have doubts. Already the young children were going short of food and soon the famine would be affecting everyone. He decided that Mhalakaza had better produce some of his new people in order to convince the Xhosa that their sacrifice was justified. Mhalakaza now got the 'wind up' and left his own kraal, fearing that Sarili might have him killed. He sent a message to the chief saying that the new people had moved to 'a strong-hold' to await the day of resurrection. Clearly they had not been impressed by the numbers of cattle that had been killed. All cattle must die if the Russians were to come. And Mhalakaza made a fresh prediction: the Russians liked new moons and would appear around 16 August. Visitors to the riverbank found that the now frequent appearance of new people was stage-managed by Mhalakaza and his team of marshals. Nobody was allowed to get close enough to speak to the distant shapes or to hear what they said. They seemed to speak only to Mhalakaza or through him. Sometimes the prophet pointed out to sea and told the pilgrims that there were the heads of Russians 'bobbing about in the water'. At other times ghostly lowing was heard from spectral cattle, or bleating from insubstantial goats.

Hysteria now ruled in the land of the Xhosa. An afternoon mist, one day at the beginning of August, was construed as the beginning of the day of resurrection and everyone fled to their homes and waited for something to happen. The day passed and night fell, and nothing happened. Every sound was interpreted as having a bearing on the coming of the new people. On the great day, Mhalakaza had said, two suns would rise in the heavens and collide, whereupon all the English would march into the sea, which would divide revealing a road down which they would march to the place of creation, known as Uhlanga. There Satan would take his revenge on both the English and on those Xhosa who had disobeyed the call to kill their cattle. Then the world would be plunged into darkness until a new sun would rise and herald the new world. This apocalyptic vision, part Old Testament, part Book of Revelations and part concoction of a scrambled brain, drove the Xhosa into an orgy of cattle killing.

As the resurrection of the Xhosa dead took place, the Xhosa were told by Mhalakaza, there would be a thundering as of every ox-hide shield ever beaten by Bantu warriors, signifying the approach of herd after herd of the fine, new cattle that had been

A Xhosa warrior, fully armed for battle. In the 1850s the Xhosa people suffered not defeat in battle but a self-imposed catastrophe as a result of the visions of a young girl.

promised. New corn would cover the land and every human ill would be put right, the lame would walk, the blind would see, the old would become young, the young become younger, nobody would have to work, everything would always be new. Significant by their absence on the day of resurrection would be the evildoers who had died by snakebite or had been drowned in river or sea. Still, it would be quite a show.

But 16 August passed without anything happening and Mhalakaza pressed for a postponement of the Day of Judgment. The new people would not appear, he warned, unless those cunning Xhosa who had sold their cattle to avoid killing them carried out the decree properly. At one stage, a rumour spread that hordes of well-armed strangers had emerged from the sea and were lining the shores, but they could only be seen by the righteous, and there were not many of those about at the time. Mhalakaza next ordered everyone to thatch their huts securely as there would be a great storm and tempest on the Day of Judgment. Again Sarili was becoming suspicious. He was under intense pressure from his councillors, who were aghast at his willingness to continue slaughtering the nation's cattle. So once more he visited Mhalakaza at the riverbank, in order to speak to the strangers. He was told by Mhalakaza to look at the ground and, under no circumstances, to look up. He would then see the shadows of the new people passing across the ground in front of him. Sarili swallowed all this nonsense and was duly convinced when the shadows passed by him. But reports of this meeting were so embroidered as they spread, that eventually it was claimed Sarili had seen boatloads of new people arrive at the mouth of the river, informing him they had come to establish the freedom of the black people.

Meanwhile, frustrated at his inability to understand the Xhosa mentality, Sir George Grey threatened Sarili with dire consequences if he encouraged his people to kill any more cattle. Grey could see that starvation in the land of the Xhosa was now unavoidable but he could not understand why they were blind to their own danger.

As the year drew to a close the skies over Xhosaland were filled with buzzards, circling and diving at the bovine and human carcasses lying in almost equal numbers in the uncultivated fields. Already upwards of 200,000 cattle had been slaughtered and, in the subsequent famine, at least 100,000

Xhosa had already died of starvation between the Fish and Kei rivers. Sarili, meanwhile, still showed a touching and yet criminal faith in the word of Mhalakaza. Each time Sarili met him, Mhalakaza had a new excuse to explain why nothing had happened at successive new moons. Sarili was so upset that he had tried to kill himself after one failure, and his servants were forced to remove all knives and sharp objects from near him. Mhalakaza, reaching the end of everyone's patience, now spread the word that the new people had abandoned the Xhosa 'in disgust' because they had not killed all their cattle. But so desperate were the Xhosa by this stage that more visions were seen, some so bizarre that they might have stemmed from a canvas of Salvador Dali. The Xhosa claimed to have seen Russian armies marching on the surface of the sea and people sailing in umbrellas, and to have heard thousands of cattle beneath their feet.

On 31 January 1857, a great assembly of more than 5000 Xhosa met near the town of Butterworth. Believers from all across the land attended, and Sarili himself was present. There they received another message from Mhalakaza that they must all go home and kill the milch-cows that had been spared so far to provide milk for the babies and young children. The cows were then to be skinned and the hides used to protect the doors from the furious lightning that would proceed the arrival of the new cattle. This time Mhalakaza added a few new touches. Once the new sun had risen in the sky, the sea would dry up and the sky would descend to just above head height. As a short man, Mhalakaza would at least not be the first to notice if this prediction came true. One has to concede that Mhalakaza had a vivid imagination, and Sarili had a fund of patience beyond human computation.

On 18 February 1857, the Day of Judgment was deemed to have arrived. An English settler, Robert Mullins, was with a group of Xhosa when the great moment came. The sun rose . . . the sun set, as usual . . . Mullins recorded the day's events in his diary with clinical accuracy. In between, nothing much happened, except a lot of waiting and hoping on the part of the Xhosa and the twiddling of thumbs and the sharpening of pencils on the part of Mullins. Mrs Brownlee, a more sensitive witness, noted, 'One of the saddest sights was that of an old woman wizened with age, and doubly wrinkled by starvation, decked out with brass rings jingling on her withered arms and legs. They had kept on their ornaments hoping against hope, till too weak to remove them.' As the sun set there was a silence across the land as of death. No children laughed and played, no cattle lowed, no sheep bleated, and no happy herdsman laughed and joked with his friends at the end of a day's work. As if seeing the light for the first time, Sarili pointed at Nongqawuse and said, 'The reason we are broken today is on account of this girl.' But she was not to blame. Sarili, himself, had succumbed to the fantasies of a charlatan, of Mhalakaza, the dreamer, who wanted to be a 'gospel man'. Was Mhalakaza a madman or just an inadequate human being, unable to cope with his life either among the white men or among his own kind? He was not evil. Perhaps he even believed his own stories. The tragedy was that so did most of the Xhosa people.

British officials who toured round the Xhosaland, trying to distribute food, found heart-breaking sights. In some places the people had climbed into their grain pits to see if they had been miraculously filled in their absence. But, too weak to climb out again, they had died there. Emaciated women with children clinging to their flattened breasts raked the hard ground for roots. Starvation drove others to boil and eat their ox-hide shields or their leather skirts. Those who reached the soup-kitchens provided by the British were no more than walking skeletons and many died of exhaustion only yards from safety. A missionary wrote, 'Famine has effaced all human likeness. Young men of twenty lost their voices and chirruped like birds. Children were wrinkled and withered and grey. Men and women presented the appearance of baboons, and like baboons search under stones for insects to devour.' And as the vultures and wild dogs devoured the dead and half-dead Xhosa, the survivors turned to cannibalism in their last desperate urge to live, killing and eating their own children. Fittingly, Mhalakaza himself died of starvation with his niece Nongqawuse.

To compound their tragedy, when many of the Xhosa who had left their lands in search of food tried to return, they found that in their absence it had been occupied by European settlers. The foolish Sarili, with the remnants of his people, now found himself banished by the British authorities to a poor strip of land across the Kei River. The Day of Judgment had indeed come – and gone – for the Xhosa people.

THE GREAT MUTINY

The Indian Mutiny of 1857 was one of the greatest threats the British Empire faced in the nineteenth century. In its first few weeks there seemed every chance that the British hold on India – the 'jewel in the crown' – would be broken by a general uprising led by the sepoys, the native soldiers of the English East India Company who had previously enabled the small British presence of soldiers and civilians in India to keep a population of 150 million in subjection. The fact that the mutiny was the result of crass policies – notably the annexation programme of Lord Dalhousie – is certain, but that the spark that ignited the revolt was the imposition on Muslim and Hindu troops of new cartridges greased with pork or beef fat seems almost too inane to be believed. It was one of the worst errors in British imperial history and it nearly cost Britain the wealth of India on which much of her greatness as a power depended.

Prior to 1853 the British troops in India – both European and native – had mainly used a smooth-bore musket, easier and quicker to fire than contemporary rifles, but with poor reliability at long range. In their search for a new and improved weapon the British Army carried out tests at Enfield. It was as a result of these that the new Enfield rifle came into general use. Previously it had been necessary to ram the bullet and charge down the long bore of the gun with a ramrod, and this task was facilitated by wrapping the bullet in a piece of cloth lubricated with wax and vegetable oil. But for the new Enfield rifle, the bullet and charge had been combined and to load the gun the end of the cartridge paper was bitten off before pushing it down the barrel. The packet, in which the bullet and charge were wrapped, was heavily greased with tallow which, it was believed was a better lubricant than the vegetable oil. However, it did occur to one or two of the more prescient members of the Bengal Army – and they were few and far between – that this greasing of the cartridge might offend some of the sepoy soldiers. The tallow contained animal fat and, if the fat was from pigs it would seriously offend all Muslims, while if it was beef, it would similarly offend the Hindus. What seemed a minor matter to European soldiers was a potentially explosive one to the sepoys. As a precaution it was suggested that the new cartridges should only be issued to European troops. A batch of the new ammunition was sent to India in 1853 and, through general carelessness, some of it came into the hands of the sepoys, who used it without knowing the insult it represented to their religious beliefs. The lubricant proved very suitable in the Indian climate and, in 1855, further batches were sent from Britain. Manufacture of the cartridges was started at Dum Dum in India, where there was evidence from the beginning that beef and pork fats were employed for cheapness' sake, rather than the sheep and goat fat that the British authorities said was being used. The new cartridges were ready for issue to the sepoys at the beginning of 1857, and large quantities had been shifted to the musketry training centres. The question was how would the native troops react to this potential threat to their beliefs?

Their fears concerning the greased cartridges was only the tip of the iceberg for many sepoys. Their confidence in the British as masters had already been deeply shaken by a series of foolish decisions resulting from a breakdown in respect for the Indian people on the part of many British officials. Gone were the days when young military officers knew their sepoys well and took the trouble to learn their language and understand their customs. Too often the new officers straight out from England were careerists, always looking to their next posting or promotion and willing to devote little time to the men under their command. They regarded the sepoys as inferior and called them 'niggers' or insulted the Muslim soldiers by addressing them as 'pig'. Others were looking for the easy ride provided by appointment to civilian posts in India, which offered the army officer more status and a much higher salary. Soldiering was for the second-rater or the eccentric

gentlemen, who did not mind the heat and stink of India, and the insects and foul diseases. Part of the problem was the increasing influence of the Christian missionaries. These had insisted on putting a stop to liaisons between Europeans and Indian women on moral grounds, neglecting the fact that unmarried men were frequently better off with native 'wives' than with prostitutes from whom they might contract venereal diseases. The young officers had learned more about the native languages and customs from the better 'nautch' girls than from any language course ever devised. But by the late 1830s fraternization with the 'blacks' was increasingly viewed as unacceptable behaviour for both white officers and men.

The greatest fear of native Indians, however, and one reinforced by the greased cartridge issue, was that the British intended to forcibly convert the Indian people – Hindus and Muslims – to Christianity. During the eighteenth century, the British had seemed more comprehensible to the Indians – concerned as they were with gold and power like latter-day conquistadores, but having no wish to interfere with the customs and beliefs of the people. However, the 'Age of Reason' seemed, for the British, to have given way to the 'Age of Ridicule'. By the 1830s and 1840s new recruits to the administrative or military service in India were often smug, convinced that they represented the greatest power for good that history had ever known. They were in the forefront of the spread of Christian civilization to the 'dark places' of the Earth. In truth, the Indians had much to fear from the Christian missionaries, one of whom spoke for many when he said, 'The missionary is truly the regenerator of India. The land is being leavened, and Hinduism is everywhere being undermined. Great will some day, in God's appointed time, be the fall of it. The time appears to have come when earnest consideration should be given to the question whether or not all men should embrace the same system of religion.' The Indians were giving it 'earnest consideration' and they had decided against it. But when rumours began to spread about the use of fat from forbidden animals they felt they needed to resist by force this clear attack on their religion.

Having created a crisis, the British then proceeded to mishandle it. In the early months of 1857 rumours of trouble to come abounded in India but no action was taken to scotch them. One of the most destructive rumours from the point of view of

British prestige was the garbled account of the fighting in the Crimea that was filtering through to the native population. The sepoys learned from professional agitators and rabble-rousers, some working for the native princes, others for the Russians, that the British were not invincible and had been defeated and conquered by the Russians during the Crimean War. Nor was this the only fanciful rumour the Indians fell for – there were also claims that there were only 100,000 Britons in existence, and that it was impossible for any reinforcements to be sent to India to support the troops already there. Other reports said that the new Governor-General, Lord Canning, was coming to India to convert the people to Christianity and that the greased cartridges were but the first step in this process. Some stories were quite fantastic, like the one that claimed that the British had placed mines under all their parade grounds so that when the sepoys stood on parade they would all be blown up in one stroke. More salacious rumours included one that the widows of English soldiers killed in the Crimea were being brought to India where eminent Indian civilians would be forced to marry them. In another one, it was said that ground cow-bones were being added to the bread sold in the bazaars. The stories were seemingly endless and were dismissed by the British as the sheerest nonsense. However, the failure of the British authorities to counteract such negative propaganda undoubtedly contributed to an atmosphere in which mutiny and rebellion could flourish.

In March 1857 there occurred a curious event that has even today not really received an adequate explanation. It was the strange appearance of what in the west would be called a 'chain letter' system, except in this instance it consisted not of a letter but of four or five chapatties, or small pancakes of unleavened bread, which mysteriously appeared in a village with the instructions that more should be baked and delivered to the next village. The British were baffled by what was happening, for these chapatties were moving across the northwestern provinces of India at the rate of a hundred miles a day. Even greater distances were recorded and each night village watchmen were running through the darkness with their turbans stuffed with chapatties. Along with this curious phenomenon a phrase was passing from mouth to mouth: 'Everything has become red.' Magical symbols were found scrawled on walls in many Indian towns, and though nobody

seemed to know what they meant, they were eagerly copied. Fakirs were travelling about the north, gathering crowds and spreading the word that the last days of British rule had come and that 'the Firinghis will soon all be killed'.

Unrest was apparent within the ranks of the Bengal Army, but the British officers – some of whom still had a deep affection for their sepoy troops – felt that a mutiny was out of the question. Nevertheless, they were beginning to receive warnings from loyal sepoys that a general rising in the country was imminent and that they should return home to England to avoid the massacre that was to come. The truth, of course, was that the European troops were massively outnumbered by the sepoys, and were living in a fool's paradise of 150 million potentially hostile natives. Of the Indian Army of 300,000, just 14,000 were European, and although there were an additional 23,000 British troops in the recently conquered Punjab, they had their hands full with a still active and dangerous enemy. In 1857 the Europeans in northern India were merely a tolerated presence. Should the Indians decide to drive them out, their chances of survival were exceedingly poor. As one of the wisest of the British military commanders, Sir Henry Lawrence, observed, 'Until we treat natives, and especially native soldiers, as having much the same feelings, the same ambitions, the same perception of ability and imbecility, as ourselves, we shall never be safe.'

The clearest indication of trouble ahead occurred at Dum Dum in January 1857. Here, a low-caste labourer asked a sepoy for a drink of water from his water bottle. The sepoy – a Brahmin – angrily repulsed the man, who replied by saying 'You will soon lose your caste altogether, for the Europeans are going to make you bite cartridges soaked in cow and pork fat and then where will your caste be?' News of what the man had said soon spread through the camp and the sepoys were frightened and infuriated by what they heard. What was needed was the reassurance of their officers that they would not be asked to use the cartridges. Instead they got the absurd attentions of men like Lieutenant-Colonel Mitchell, commander of the 19th Regiment of Native Infantry, a self-righteous martinet, who was convinced that mutiny was not something that could ever happen while he was in command. Addressing his men, he told them that unless they agreed to use the new cartridges he would take them all to Burma 'where, through hardship, you

The Indian Mutiny of 1857 began at the Meerut military camp in northern India. It was a result of mismanagement by the British authorities who introduced greased cartridges that offended the religious sensibilities of the native soldiers, both Hindu and Muslin.

will all die'. So angry did Mitchell become that his native officers had to ask him to restrain himself or they would not be able to answer for the men's reaction.

In military posts right across northwest India sepoy soldiers were firmly but politely refusing to handle the new cartridges. Their fears were very real but, as yet, their loyalty was still unbroken, and it was a measure of the incompetence of British senior officers that the mutiny took fire with the ferocity that it did. The Military Secretary to the Governor-General, Colonel Richard Birch, concerned more with the loss of British prestige than with the fears of the sepoys, failed to circulate to military depots Lord Canning's decision that the new cartridges could be torn rather than bitten if the men preferred it. The Commander-in-Chief in India, General the Honourable George Anson, a man of sixty years and very little sense, reacted to the crisis with the immortal words, 'I'll never give in to their beastly prejudices.' He decreed that the sepoys must be forced to use the cartridge or be immediately court-

martialled. While Anson enjoyed his luxurious quarters in the cool comfort of Simla in the foothills of the Himalayas, on the burning plains of northern India hundreds of junior British officers were to suffer the consequences of this old man's intransigence. Several voiced their fears in letters to Anson, but they received neither reply nor acknowledgement.

The crisis was eventually brought to a head on 23 April, by the stupidity of Colonel George Carmichael-Smyth, commander of the 3rd Indian Light Cavalry, at Meerut. Having just returned from leave, and with his head filled no doubt with the prejudices of the officer's mess, he was not in a mood to compromise with mutineers. Other British officers had already heard the news that the sepoys had taken a solemn oath – the Muslims on the Koran and the Hindus by the holy waters of the Ganges – not to handle the cartridges. The worst possible course of action would be to provoke a confrontation, but this is what Carmichael-Smyth proceeded to do. All the other regimental commanders at Meerut realized the need for calm, but Carmichael-Smyth ordered a parade of his men, during which they would be required to use the suspect cartridges. His men humbly petitioned him not to have this parade but he was adamant, insisting that not to do so might be construed as cowardice on his part.

On the morning of 24 April, 90 men of the 3rd Light Cavalry assembled on the parade ground, and were ordered to take three cartridges each. All of them, with the exception of five men, refused to do so. The men explained that they were afraid of losing caste or getting a bad name if they took the cartridges. They were then dismissed and Carmichael-Smyth reported their actions to General Hewitt, a man so obese that he could not ride his horse on parade but reviewed his troops from a buggy. Hewitt may have had little military value at this stage, but he had more common sense than Carmichael-Smyth. 'Oh! Why did you have a parade?' was the General's piteous cry. 'If you had only waited another month or so, all would have blown over.'

There was no alternative now but to try the 90 men by court martial and this was duly done. The accused were all found guilty and most were sentenced to hard labour for ten years, with the younger ones getting a lighter sentence of five years. Some members of the tribunal had voted for the death penalty and it was generally felt that some of the men should have been shot as an example to the others.

On 9 May, the entire garrison at Meerut – at least 4000 men, half of them European – paraded for punishment to be carried out. Significantly, though the sepoys were ordered to parade with their ammunition, they were told to leave their guns behind. Only the British troops present were armed. This was a further blunder as it showed even the loyal sepoys that they could not escape from the suspicion that surrounded all native soldiers. The prisoners were then paraded in front of the assembled soldiers and their legs shackled, their gold buttons cut off and their uniforms ripped up the back. Their humiliation was complete. As the parade ended and they were marched away, many of them shouted abuse at Carmichael-Smyth and flung their boots at him. There was an angry buzz of disaffection from the assembled sepoys and as they dismissed it was clear that there would be serious repercussions.

Some of the junior British officers visited the prisoners in the jail and were upset at the severity of their treatment. As Lieutenant Hugh Gough wrote, 'Old soldiers with many medals gained in desperately fought battles for their English masters wept bitterly, lamenting their sad fate and imploring us to save them from their future.' When, on 10 May, Gough tried to tell Carmichael-Smyth of the fact that fires were burning in the native quarters of Meerut, the colonel dismissed his report with contempt. But later it became clear that large parts of the city were on fire and that the native troops were rioting. Apparently, the trouble had started when the prostitutes in the bazaar had taunted the sepoys with their failure to help their imprisoned colleagues. Pricked both by their consciences and the taunts of the women, some of the soldiers gave way to their feelings. Seizing both wine and hashish they worked themselves into a frenzy. The first European casualty – the first of many thousands throughout India in the weeks to come – was a British colonel who rode through the city calling on the sepoys to return to their barracks. A single shot rang out – followed by some twenty more – and the officer fell from his horse. It was as if a dam had given way. During that night over fifty Europeans, men, women and children were hacked to death in an orgy of killing.

To compound their folly, the military commanders at Meerut – fat General Hewitt and his second-in-command, the supine Brigadier Archdale Wilson – allowed the mutinous sepoys to move out of Meerut and head off towards the capital Delhi, 40 miles to the south. Even though there were over 2000 British troops still in the military camp, Hewitt and Wilson ordered no pursuit. It was the arrival of the Meerut mutineers at Delhi – capital of the old Mogul Empire – and their choice of the last Mogul emperor to lead them that gave the mutiny a focus. From this point onwards the rebellion became widespread and Britain's hold on India very tenuous indeed. Her tiny garrisons were besieged all across northern India, notably at Lucknow and Cawnpore. Dreadful massacres of British men, woman and children took place and it was only after some fourteen months of bitter fighting that the mutiny was suppressed and the British authorities were able to emerge from their nightmare, older – sadder and very much wiser.

CHAPTER SIX: TECHNOLOGY, TRANSPORT AND EXPLORATION

A grand opening

Defeat by Napoleon III's France in 1859 was a great blow to the Austrian emperor Franz Joseph and, in an effort to restore morale and reflect 'the greatness of the Austrian Empire', he decided to rebuild much of central Vienna to match the changes taking place in Paris during the 1860s. One of the most important additions – and close to the heart of all true Viennese – was the new opera house, which was opened on 25 May, 1869, with a performance of Mozart's *Don Giovanni*. Tickets fetched unheard-of prices, and everybody who was anybody was in attendance at the first performance. But even before the lights went down and the opera began it was obvious that something was seriously wrong in the design of the new theatre. Voices were raised in many parts of the auditorium. People found they could not see the stage. In the third and fourth galleries – where many of the most prominent Viennese were seated – they could only see the rear quarter, and most of the action would take place below them as if in a downstairs room.

As the lights dimmed for the first time the celebrated actress, Charlotte Wolter, stepped onto the stage dressed as the Spirit of Vienna and began a prologue, hymning the virtues of the city and of the empire. Unfortunately, at the last moment, the public censor had objected to certain political references and had cut out chunks of her text so that what she said made no sense at all. Catcalls were now heard, joining the complaints of the many who could not see Fraülein Wolter and could not make out anything she was saying. Next a grand procession, representing all the nationalities of the empire living in harmony, descended a magnificent staircase. The orchestral conductor, meanwhile, struck up the overture for the opera and the lights were dimmed, leaving the ladies in their national costumes to battle their way offstage in total chaos. Once the music had started the emperor slipped out of his box, no doubt pretending a whole evening of Mozart was just too much for him.

The chief architects of the opera house were very sensitive to the criticism they received. Even before the fatal first night Eduard van der Nüll and Siccard von Siccardsburg had been ridiculed for designing a building that was squat and heavy: the ordinary Viennese had dubbed it 'the sunken trunk'. The two architects had proudly topped the building with two winged horses, but critics reminded them that Pegasus had been unique and two winged horses rather missed the point. In any case, the horses were too plump and too small. Eventually the offending equines were removed and sold to an American tourist. Inside the opera house one actor wetted his finger and held it up in the air to determine which way the air was blowing in. 'Perfect breeze for sailing,' he said. But it was the first night of *Don Giovanni* that proved too much for the architects: van der Nüll hanged himself in despair, while von Siccardsburg had a heart attack and died two months later.

Huskisson and the *Rocket*

On 15 September 1830, there occurred one of the first and certainly one of the most famous railway accidents in history. During the opening of the Liverpool to Manchester Railway, the Tory politician William Huskisson fell victim to George Stephenson's locomotive the *Rocket*.

The opening of the new railway was an event of national importance and crowds of people – in their hundreds of thousands – lined the entire route from Liverpool to Manchester. For the occasion, the locomotive the *Northumbrian* led the procession, drawing a splendid carriage containing the Prime Minister – the Duke of Wellington – the Home Secretary Sir Robert Peel, and thirty other distinguished individuals. Behind them came a number of other locomotives drawing carriages filled with more than six hundred of the great and the good. The air was alive with anticipation, but when the climax came it was the purest bathos.

By about noon the grand procession had reached the Sankey Viaduct. From this high point the passengers were able to look down on the fields on either side which were packed with sightseers. The vessels on the canal had been halted to watch the locomotives pass in splendour beside them. When the locomotives reached Newton, about seventeen miles from Liverpool, they stopped to take on water and fuel, and the passengers alighted to stretch their legs and discuss their impressions of the startling new mode of transport. It was here that an accident occurred, inflicting the first fatality of the new railway age. The *Phoenix* and the *North Star* locomotives, having taken on their water and fuel, had steamed past the *Northumbrian*, which was stationary on the adjacent line, so that the Duke of Wellington and his party could review all the locomotives in the procession. Several VIPs from the state carriage were milling around the track, among them William Huskisson, lately the Chancellor of the Exchequer and the nation's foremost financial expert. The Duke of Wellington, on noticing his ex-colleague, extended his hand and Huskisson stepped forward to shake it. However, at this precise moment, the *Rocket* came into sight, travelling swiftly on the other line. A cry of 'Watch out' was heard but this only seemed to confuse Huskisson, who was elderly and somewhat infirm on his legs. As several gentlemen quickly returned to the state carriage, Huskisson found himself squashed against the side of the *Northumbrian*, unable to get into the carriage. He still had time to cross the track and avoid the locomotive but he seemed to be paralysed like a rabbit and clung to the side of the *Northumbrian* until it was too late. One of the other passengers, Mr Holmes, MP, called to him, 'For God's sake, Mr Huskisson, be firm.' But Huskisson was rooted to the spot and as the *Rocket* rushed up it caught

TECHNOLOGY, TRANSPORT AND EXPLORATION

him a glancing blow knocking him onto the track and shattering one of his thighs. He died several hours later.

The Duke and Sir Robert Peel were so shocked that they expressed a wish to return to Liverpool, but a local JP informed them that so vast was the crowd waiting at Manchester that if the locomotives did not proceed he feared an outbreak of civil disorder. Local businessmen were alarmed by this prospect and directors of the railway insisted that the journey must be completed otherwise it could shatter confidence in the new mode of transport. It was therefore decided to continue the journey, though it was a sombre party who arrived in Manchester to partake of a cold collation in the upper rooms of the company warehouses.

Cable hitch

It has been said that the British and the Americans are two peoples divided by a common language. This was well illustrated by an incident that occurred during the laying of the first transatlantic cable in 1858. Truly, it was a case of the left hand not knowing what the right hand was doing, and vice versa.

In 1857 the first attempt was made to lay a cable across the Atlantic, on the 1834-mile 'short route', from Valentia in the southwest of Ireland to Newfoundland. Unfortunately, although the cable was of sturdy construction, being reinforced with heavy-gauge wire spirally wound, it broke and another attempt had to be planned for the following year. This time the problem was not the cable but the method of linking the British and the American ends together. The plan had been for the British ship *Agamemnon* and the American ship *Niagara* to set off from their respective coasts carrying with them half of the entire cable. They would rendezvous in mid-Atlantic and there join the two ends of the cable. Unfortunately, the two cables had been manufactured by separate contractors and – amazingly – certain details of its construction had not been agreed in advance. As a result, the direction of the 'lay' of the wire armouring was different on the two cable ends, one being 'right-handed' and the other 'left-handed'. Thus to tighten one end by turning in one direction was to loosen the other. Faced with catastrophe the cable-layers botched together a link that enabled a few faint messages to reach Newfoundland from Ireland. But it was never going to last and within weeks the entire cable fell silent. The investors in this bold plan lost their £500,000 investment and it was not until eight years later that a compatible cable was run out from both sides of the Atlantic and joined successfully.

The Fonthill Follies

The British pride themselves on their individualism and their sense of the ridiculous, which may or may not help to explain why Great Britain has had more than her fair

The gothic splendour of William Beckford's 'folly', Fonthill Abbey. The great central tower, not much shorter than the spire of Salisbury Cathedral, collapsed soon after completion, but was rebuilt only to fall again.

share of eccentric persons and extraordinary buildings. These men have been responsible for the many curious 'follies' which can be found scattered throughout the country. Some of them had originally been intended to house their owners in mock-Gothic splendour or to conjure up the atmosphere of ancient Greece or Rome. Many others were merely 'follies', whims and fancies in brick and stone, which may have started as jokes but remain as permanent question marks. The greatest of British follies and a building of quite exceptional absurdity was Fonthill Abbey, brainchild of a late-eighteenth century eccentric named William Beckford.

Beckford was born in 1760 and at the age of ten received a fortune of a million pounds in his father's will, producing an annual income of £100,000, making him – by the standards of the day – a veritable Croesus among Englishmen. Yet although William had other advantages for which some men would have killed, not least among which was music lessons from the young Wolfgang Amadeus Mozart, he grew up to be a withdrawn and temperamental man, subject to fits of gross eccentricity and lavishness. He travelled widely around Europe and the Levant, never sleeping anywhere but in his own bed which he could afford to have transported wherever he went. Tired of travelling, he retired in 1790 to his estate at Fonthill, in Somerset. Here he began to indulge his tastes for building by erecting a structure of truly epic proportions, which he christened Fonthill Abbey, on account of its monastic structure and prodigious central tower. First he erected a small town nearby to house the builders he would need and then he brought in an army of architects, surveyors, masons and other artisans to begin work on the great edifice. He worked them round the clock, keeping going through the night by the light of torches, and holding off fatigue by keeping every man well supplied with liquor, so that much of the building work was actually carried out by inebriated and exhausted craftsmen. The results proved that this was a poor policy. The house took eighteen years to build and cost Beckford over a quarter of a million pounds, but with its mighty tower 273 feet high – built to rival the great spire of Salisbury Cathedral – Beckford felt it was worth every minute and every penny spent on it. Alas, it was less permanent than the Salisbury spire that has, so far, lasted some six hundred years. Beckford's tower lasted hardly that many days. So quickly had it been put together that its foundations were scarcely firm and its brickwork not yet set before Beckford was piling weight upon it in the shape of heavy beams and stained glass windows. It ended badly when the whole tower collapsed. Undaunted, Beckford gathered together his drunken workmen and ordered them to build it again.

Beckford believed that anything was possible for a man with money and that if he threw enough of his legacy at a problem it would inevitably yield. He therefore swore an oath to have his Christmas lunch in the abbey kitchen, thereby setting his workers an altogether impossible target. But they liked the sound of the bonuses he was offering and once again the tower began to climb towards the sky, again built on the flimsiest foundations. True to his oath, Beckford and his guests entered the abbey kitchen on Christmas morning and prepared to eat the splendid lunch, laid out for twelve. But towering above them were hundreds of tons of stone, brick, wood and lead, just waiting to fall on their unprotected heads if they dawdled too long over their claret and chestnut stuffing. The servants were just beginning to clear away the dishes and Beckford and his friends were passing the port when the walls of the kitchen began to gently vibrate. The occupants were able to make a clean getaway before the splendid abbey kitchen collapsed in upon itself. Beckford stood in the grounds watching a huge pall of dust rising into the sky where his fine kitchen had been.

By August 1800, in spite of these minor setbacks, Fonthill Abbey was approaching completion and by Christmas, Beckford was able to entertain such distinguished guests as Lord Nelson and Sir William and Lady Hamilton. Beckford would not have recognized twentieth-century descriptions of Fonthill Abbey as a 'folly'. It was no more a folly than he was a fool. He merely had individual taste. And now he peopled his house with a bizarre set of companions – three dogs, known as Caroline, Nephew and Lord Fartlebury, an Italian dwarf who ate nothing but mushrooms and a group of servants with strange nicknames like the Doll and the Calf.

Aware that the world did not share his individual taste, Beckford surrounded Fonthill Abbey with a wall seven miles long and twelve feet high, topped with sharp spikes. The grounds of the abbey were patrolled by armed men with ferocious dogs. Beckford preferred not to mix with the *hoi polloi*, who irritated him by asking for charity. His usual response was to turn on any beggars and give them a thorough horse-whipping, usually later compensating the victims with a pound or two for their pains. For exercise, Beckford used to ride madly around his estate in the middle of the night before throwing himself fully clothed into a green pond. Those who witnessed these weird nocturnal ceremonies were convinced that the rider was no living man and his horse nothing less than a demon steed. One man, who succeeded in reaching the front door of the abbey uninvited, was given dinner by Beckford and then as night fell told to find his own way out as he had found his own way in. The poor fellow was hunted by Beckford's dogs and ended up spending the night perched in a tree for safety.

When Beckford's finances suffered a setback as a result of losses on his West Indian estates, he was forced to sell Fonthill Abbey to an Indian merchant named Farquhar for a third of a million pounds. Within two years the great central tower collapsed once again, shooting poor Farquhar thirty feet down a corridor as if fired out of a cannon. The dust cloud produced by the tower's collapse darkened the sky for miles around. Beckford would have enjoyed the scenes of panic that followed. Little of Beckford's extraordinary house remains today to remind us of its strange owner and his eccentric tastes. But as evidence of the art of 'jerry-building' it should be preserved for the nation as a warning of what can be achieved by more money than sense.

The DDTs

In Man's constant struggle against insect-borne disease the pesticide known as DDT (Dicophane) has been in the forefront of the battle. Its successes have been numerous and DDT has been called the 'atomic bomb of the insect world'. But atomic bombs can be two-edged weapons and their fall-out can be almost as dangerous to those who use them as to those who suffer them. The same has proved to be true with DDT. When, in the early 1960s, the United Nations World Health Organisation began its campaign to eradicate malaria by using DDT in some 76 countries, a number of unexpected consequences ensued. In the first place, the chemical was not universally successful in exterminating whole insect populations, so that the survivors soon developed immunity. In fact, there are now at least 57 different types of mosquito that can swim in DDT. Secondly, the vast quantities of DDT that were sprayed randomly on marshy areas in the Third World upset the ecosystem of the area with some unlikely results. In Sarawak, the DDT not only killed mosquitoes but also destroyed the cockroaches. The local cat population, eating the poisoned cock-roaches, were themselves killed in large numbers. The result was that with no cats about, the rat population boomed. The Malaysian field-rat, which is common in Borneo, is a carrier of diseases like plague and typhus, and soon these rats overran the villages. Freed from the risk of the malarial mosquito, the villagers now faced the equally terrible threat of bubonic plague. In order to solve the problem and restore balance to the ecosystem of Sarawak, the World Health Organisation had to call on the RAF to drop cats by parachute on isolated villages in the interior. This remarkable first, known as 'Operation Cat-Drop', was less ridiculous than it seemed. It was an instant response – and a successful one – to a man-made catastrophe, just one of potentially thousands of similar human blunders that may affect mankind in the years and even centuries to come.

Aguirre and the search for El Dorado

The search for El Dorado – the legendary kingdom of gold in South America – began in the sixteenth century, within a few years of the Spanish conquests of Mexico and Peru. Conquistadores plunged into the forests of Central and South America in search of the holy lake where, it was rumoured, a prince painted in gold dived into the waters in a yearly ritual. Their hopes of finding the land of limitless gold were fuelled by the discoveries of gold and silver mines in parts of the territory conquered by Cortez and Pizarro, but El Dorado was never found and thousands of Spanish lives were lost in the search and untold misery was inflicted on the native peoples of Brazil, Peru, Colombia and Venezuela. In time the search for El Dorado, like other great – and fruitless – searches, took on a mystical significance for the explorers, yet for the expedition of Pedro de Ursúa in 1560 the search became little less than a nightmare journey into the heart of evil.

No Jacobean revenge tragedy penned by Tourneur or Webster could have created a character of such unmitigated evil as Lope de Aguirre, a man unredeemed by any human qualities and driven simply by a hatred of God and all his creations. For Catholics of the time, Aguirre stood as living proof of Original Sin and as the clearest demonstration that Satan stalked the earth in many disguises. Yet, a careful study of the sources sheds just a chink of light on the development of Aguirre's personality. In 1548 soldiers guarding the Potosi silver mines were accused of mistreating the local Indians by making them carry the Spaniards' own baggage. This was a minor offence, but a local judge decided to make an example of one of the men. The man chosen was Lope de Aguirre who, unable to pay the heavy fine, was sentenced to 200 lashes. For a Spanish soldier to be flogged in view of the Indians was a gross humiliation. Aguirre argued that he would prefer to die, but in spite of his protestations he was whipped. So fiercely did he feel the shame that he henceforth refused to ride a horse or wear shoes, claiming such things were luxuries and not for common criminals like himself. Meanwhile, Aguirre, plotted to get revenge on the judge who had humiliated him. It took him three years, following the man from city to city around the Spanish American lands, but eventually Aguirre found him in Cuzco, in Peru, broke into his house and stabbed him to death. Aguirre then escaped, disguised as a Negro, and disappeared until the time of Ursúa's expedition in 1560.

The origin of Ursúa's expedition was the arrival at a Spanish settlement named Chacha Poyas in Peru of a group of 300 Indians, who claimed to have come from Brazil. They said that they had been travelling up the Amazon for ten years, trying to escape from the Portuguese colonists there. On their journey they had encountered 'marvellous things', including a tribe known as the Omaguas, who seemed to have endless riches of gold and fine ornaments. This account reminded the Spaniards of reports by one of their own explorers, Orellana, who had passed through Omagua territory and had remarked on its enormous wealth. In Orellana's view, these Omaguas were the inhabitants of El Dorado – the land of gold. As a result the Spanish

Viceroy of Peru decided to launch a great expedition to travel down the Amazon to discover – and conquer – the land of El Dorado. It was no more remarkable, except perhaps for its size, than many such expeditions launched by the Spaniards in the years since Cortez had conquered Mexico. What made this one different, though, was the presence of one man – Lope de Aguirre himself.

Pedro de Ursúa was accompanied on the expedition by upwards of 370 Spanish soldiers and thousands of Peruvian Indians. The authorities, keen to rid their territory of particularly troublesome Spaniards, thought it wise to send them with Ursúa. This turned out to be a grave mistake. Many of Ursúa's men were little more than the scum of the colonies, pirates and discontented rebels loyal only to their paymaster and with a burning hatred of their own king. Setting out in a flotilla of boats, rafts and canoes, Ursúa left Peru via a tributary of the Amazon on 26 September, 1560. From the start Ursúa proved to be a feeble leader and alienated his followers by taking with him his beautiful and capricious mistress, Inez de Atienza.

The purpose of the expedition had been exploration and colonization, and, of course, if any gold mines should be discovered *en route*, acquisition. But Ursúa's rabble soon lost all semblance of discipline once they entered the steamy rain forests. To enliven their mood they massacred all the Indians they encountered and then began fighting amongst themselves. While this disintegration of morale was taking place Ursúa seemed content to spend as much time as possible with the lovely Inez. When he did stir himself it was to punish minor offences on the part of his men by ordering them to row alongside the Indians, while their friends mocked them. The soldiers began to complain that Inez rather than Ursúa was their real leader and they declared they were not prepared to become galley-slaves on the orders of a whore. As disease began to ravage the ranks of the Spaniards, discontent grew to rebellion. On 1 January, 1561, there was a general mutiny and Ursúa was set upon and killed. By popular acclamation a Spanish nobleman, Don Fernando de Guzmán, became the new leader. But he was no more than a figurehead, and prominent among those who selected him was Lope de Aguirre.

Aguirre did not share the usual conquistador trait of acquisitiveness and, as we have seen, he seems to have been motivated simply by the thought of revenge and the enjoyment of inflicting suffering on his fellow creatures. He had no vision of El Dorado: instead he wanted to return to Peru to overthrow the government there and defy the king of Spain. But first he needed to show a degree of caution until he had cleared his path to the top. He first persuaded Guzmán to accept the title 'Lord and Prince of Peru', which was a direct challenge to the Spanish Viceroy who had initiated the expedition. All the mutineers then signed a document agreeing to support Guzmán in attempting to seize the Spanish province by force. Significantly, while others sought justification for their actions, Aguirre sought none and signed his name 'Aguirre – Traitor'. Everyone who had shown the slightest loyalty to Ursúa was hunted down and slain by Aguirre's killers. Aguirre himself now persuaded Guzmán to abandon the search for El Dorado and sail instead down the Amazon to the coast, before returning to Peru overland with a conquering army. Guzmán was little more than putty in the hands of the self-confessed traitor and his band of ruffians and mutineers, and what followed was one of the most terrible journeys of exploration ever undertaken by man.

The beautiful Inez had transferred her affections from her dead lover Ursúa to the new leader of the expedition, but she had chosen unwisely. Aguirre was the leader in everything but name and he had no love for Inez and was determined to dispose of her at the first opportunity. Little things began to play on Aguirre's mind and what annoyed him most was the amount of space in the boat that the lady's bedding took up. On 22 May, on an island in the middle of the Amazon, Aguirre's patience ran out. First he ordered his followers to kill Guzmán and while this was being done he sent two others to dispose of Inez. This they did with a pathological fury that would have made any watching Indians wonder who were the real savages in the forest. As one eyewitness wrote, 'One stabbed at her and the other took her by the hair and gave her over twenty sword thrusts.' A general massacre now ensued in which Aguirre's thugs killed all who had been loyal to Guzmán. The place of execution was thereafter known as the 'town of the butchery'.

Lope de Aguirre now took command in person, surrounding himself with a guard of fifty or more of the most heartless killers. With these men he turned the journey down the Amazon into an unparalleled horror. Avoiding the Omagua Indians – who though they might have had gold might also have had the means to protect it –

A still photograph from Werner Herzog's film *Aguirre: Wrath of God*, with Klaus Kinski portraying the evil Spanish conquistador, Lope de Aguirre, a man so embittered that he challenged not only his king but God himself.

Aguirre drove onwards night and day towards the sea. Killings were a daily event, often at Aguirre's whim. As his paranoia began to grow he would suspect even his most loyal followers and order them to be stabbed or garrotted. During the river journey he ordered at least 140 of the Spaniards to be executed, as well as hundreds of the Indians who had not already deserted and taken their chance with the cannibal tribes in the rainforest. If Aguirre saw more than two soldiers talking together at one time he assumed they were plotting against him and he ordered his guard to have them executed. To lighten his boats he ordered all the remaining Indians – Christians from Andean Peru to whom the Amazon rainforest was as alien as to the Spaniards – to be marooned on an island at the mouth of the Amazon. When some of his men questioned this order they too were executed.

In July 1561, Aguirre's boats reached the Atlantic. He ordered a landing on the island of Margarita, off the coast of Venezuela. At first the Spanish inhabitants were pleased to see their fellow countryman but, true to form, Aguirre killed their governor and conquered the island. Building up his forces to attack Peru, he landed on the mainland of South America and prepared to march across the Andes to fulfil his ambitions. But as he moved inland, many of his followers began deserting and as news of Aguirre's arrival spread, royal troops began to close in on him. With paranoia now so severe that his right hand almost doubted what the left was doing, Aguirre wrote a letter to King Philip II of Spain, challenging him and accusing him of all sorts of crimes against his loyal servants in South America, finally signing it 'Lope de Aguirre, the Wanderer'. It was his final Will and Testament. As the royal troops closed in on him, Aguirre killed his own daughter in a fit of desperation, to prevent her falling into the hands of the enemy and being forever known as the daughter of a traitor. He was finally shot by his own men, before being beheaded and his body quartered. Even in death he was defiant. As the first arquebus ball hit him in the chest, Aguirre sneered 'That was not well aimed.' When the second ball hit him he nodded approval, 'That has settled the matter.' It was a grisly end to yet another abortive search for El Dorado. Until Spain began to exercise some effective control on her conquistadores, more and more such pointless expeditions would take place in pursuit of the chimera that was El Dorado. And by sending the dregs of colonial society to carry her flag into the lands of the South American Indians, Spain was committing an atrocity against the Christian values that she claimed to champion.

Martin Frobisher and the Northwest Passage

Since the time of Columbus it had been the ambition of English mariners and explorers to find a sea route to China and the Indies that did not involve the long voyage around Africa. The English were having to make up for a slow start, for in the century after Columbus's voyage Spain and Portugal had claimed a virtual trading monopoly of the world, with the Spaniards predominant in the Americas and the Portuguese in Africa and the East. It would prove difficult – almost impossible – for

English ships to break into these markets. Their only solution was to find a route to the northeast around the northern coast of Russia or to the northwest, around what we know today to be the arctic regions of Canada. The perils of either route were considerable but the rewards they offered could make the risks well worth taking. And it was the promise of financial reward rather than simply the love of exploration that made Martin Frobisher undertake three voyages to the north of Canada in search of the way to the riches of the Indies. Eager for a slice of this 'eastern promise', Queen Elizabeth I and most of her wealthy courtiers put their money into Frobisher's voyages. But they expected a high return and what they got was anything but that.

Martin Frobisher was neither a Devonian 'sea dog' in the tradition of Sir Francis Drake nor a foppish admiral in court finery, he was a blunt, dour Yorkshireman, who called a spade a shovel and knew his way around a black pudding. Years later, in 1588, when he and a few doughty mariners stood between England and the power of the Spanish Armada, he was not averse to threatening to lend Sir Francis Drake a box on the ears if he dodged off any more in pursuit of prize money like a 'dog sniffing a bitch'. As a contemporary wrote of him, Frobisher 'had in him not only greatness but a human quality which made men curse him and love him, grumble at him and toil for him'.

Frobisher is unfairly cast as the fool. Many others would have made the mistake he made wasting the queen's money, his crew's lives and his own good name. But others would have covered their tracks better. Frobisher, however, was not a man who looked for excuses, and so the world laughed at him. And England's derelict roads – at least those around Portsmouth – were paved with gold for a short while.

Frobisher undertook his first voyage to find the Northwest Passage with just two small, 50-ton barques. He sailed in the *Gabriel* and reached what he hoped was the channel leading to Asia, naming it Frobisher Strait (it was, in fact, an inlet on the south of Baffin Island). On landing he found evidence of marcasite – a mineral containing 'fool's gold' – and took a good sample with him back to England, where analysts found what they believed to be gold ore. This sparked an immense interest in his second proposed voyage and there was no shortage of financial sponsorship, the queen herself putting up much of the money to finance the expedition. In 1577, with the grand title 'Admiral of the Seas', awarded him by the queen, and with the support of the newly formed Cathay Company, Frobisher sailed once again to the arctic region of Canada. This time he planned to collect a great deal of ore, before sailing through the Frobisher Strait to Cathay. In appalling conditions, and facing the danger of being crushed by icebergs, he reached the Frobisher Strait, again encountering resistance from the local Eskimos. He and his men mined 200 tons of ore and also took several Eskimo hostages, who were taken back with them to England, where they were presented before the queen. On his return he received a tremendous reception, more – one suspects – on account of the potential riches to be found in his ore than for his Eskimo prisoners. The analysts again vouched for the value of his ore, claiming to find evidence of both gold and silver.

The third – and last – voyage was financed by the queen and many of her courtiers.

This time – in 1578 – Frobisher took as many as fifteen ships, bearing the hopes of the most influential men in the kingdom. But all their hopes were to be dashed. He returned with 1300 tons of ore. However, by this time, the queen's analysts were having second thoughts. They had concluded that Frobisher – not they, of course – had fallen victim to 'fool's gold'. And the huge quantities of rock for which his men had braved the North Atlantic gales was just so much rubble, fit only to mend the roads. The 'bubble' of speculation burst. Many courtiers had had their fingers burned very badly and the queen wore a red face for weeks. The Cathay Company went bankrupt and everyone blamed Martin Frobisher, accusing this simple, brave Yorkshireman of being a cheat. The queen even demanded the return of the gold chain she had given him at the start of the third voyage, refusing to speak to him or see him again.

Frobisher was ruined. He returned to privateering, seizing Spanish ships when he could and burning with a sense of injustice. It was not until the war with Spain burst into life after 1585 that he found that his country still needed him. In the fateful Armada campaign of 1588, it was Frobisher in the largest of the English ships, the *Triumph,* who was in the thick of the fighting around Portland, twice single-handedly driving off four Spanish galleons. Only in the afterglow of victory did Elizabeth I forget the financial disaster of Frobisher's three voyages and remember the courage of the dour Yorkshireman, knighting him for the part he had played in repelling the Spanish invaders.

The unthinkable *Titanic*

The loss of the liner *Titanic* in 1912 may have been the result of a series of blunders by both her captain and members of the crew. Descriptions of the great ship as 'unsinkable' were quite absurd and may have introduced an element of complacency that was inappropriate in view of the dangers she faced from icebergs and pack ice. The ship's loss on its maiden voyage became a human tragedy of enormous proportions as a result of inadequate safety regulations.

In 1912, the *Titanic* was the largest ship in the world, more than twice as large as the biggest battleships being built at that time. Fully loaded its displacement was over 52,000 tons and it was able to carry 3000 passengers, with a crew almost as large. Its seven miles of deck and acres of staterooms enabled the rich passengers of Europe and the United States to travel in the greatest luxury back and forth across the Atlantic. However, in an 'unsinkable' ship, as the *Titanic* was supposed to be, the disastrous decision was taken to limit the number of lifeboats to be carried. At that time, all British vessels over 10,000 tons were required to carry just sixteen lifeboats. For the *Titanic* this meant that she had space for only 1178 of the 2207 people she was carrying on her maiden voyage. This was understandable – if hardly forgivable. The ship's owners would have stressed the fact that safety measures needed to be discreet: the mere presence of lifeboats is a reminder to the passengers that their lives are always in peril on the high seas. Moreover, a full complement of lifeboats would have taken up space that could be used for elegant promenades, deck tennis and other more worthwhile social activities. However, as a result, the *Titanic* carried only enough lifeboats to carry one person in two of all those aboard.

On 14 April 1912, the *Titanic* began her maiden voyage from Southampton. It was an event of national importance and the ship carried some very important guests, including J. J. Astor and his wife, the Countess of Rothes, Alfred Vanderbilt, two members of the Rothschild family, a Guggenheim and Charles Ismay, chairman of the White Star Shipping Line and proud owner of the *Titanic*. As they crossed the North Atlantic they encountered a lot of ice, in fact so much that the ship closest to her, the *Californian,* closed down her engines and drifted through the hours of darkness in the pack ice. But the *Titanic* sped on at 22 knots, seemingly oblivious to the threat of icebergs. The *Titanic*'s master, Captain Smith – an elderly seaman of enormous experience, who had been brought out of retirement for this special event – was clear in his mind that icebergs were not going to impede him in making a fast Atlantic crossing.

At 11 p.m. on the night of 14 April, Captain Lord of the *Californian* noticed the lights of a ship in the distance, travelling at high speed. One of his officers told him, 'It's the *Titanic*.' Lord was apprehensive. He had been forced to stop by pack ice and was alarmed to see the *Titanic* driving on at full speed. He told his wireless operator, Cyril Evans, to contact the *Titanic* with a warning. However, the senior Marconi operator on the great liner was far too busy sending telegraphs for the passengers, including advice to stockbrokers, social greetings to friends and relations. Unhappy at being bothered by the warning message from the lowly *Californian*, he replied with the words, 'Keep out. You are jamming me.' Evans took the rebuff in good heart, shrugged his shoulders and closed down his wireless, prior to having a snooze. Captain Lord, in his cabin, also fell asleep.

The sea was as still as a sheet of glass as the *Titanic* sped onwards through the darkness. Visibility was very good and the ice was clearly to be seen all around the ship. The *Titanic*'s wireless operator now received a warning from another ship, the *Mesaba*, saying 'We have seen much heavy pack ice and a great number of bergs also field ice.' Once more he disregarded the message and returned to his job of sending passenger's telegraphs. He did not pass the message on to the bridge and so the warning went unheeded. Suddenly, on the *Titanic*'s bridge, the first officer sighted an iceberg, dead ahead. He ordered 'Stop and Full astern' but it was already too late. It was impossible to stop a ship that size so quickly: it would have taken more than three minutes and a quarter of a mile of sea room to have avoided the berg. The *Titanic* never had a chance. The iceberg hit the bow of the liner, ripping a hole nearly three hundred feet long and breaching three watertight compartments. It was a fatal wound.

For most passengers on deck the incident was more exciting than frightening. They stood gazing at the towering icepack and picked up shards of ice, while others grew bored and returned to their games of cards in the staterooms. But far below the passenger decks, in the belly of the ship, the water was pouring into the engine rooms.

The 'unsinkable' luxury liner *Titanic*, photographed on trials in Belfast Lough. Complacency and inadequate safety regulations turned the ship's collision with an iceberg on her ill-fated maiden voyage into a human catastrophe.

Captain Smith, once apprised of the damage, spoke to Thomas Andrews, Managing Director of Harland and Wolff, who had built the *Titanic*, to ask what could be done. Arnold was pessimistic. He knew that once three watertight compartments had been breached the ship was doomed. Yet for some time there was no panic, as the ship remained stable, the bands played, drinks were served and people enjoyed what for many of them were to be their last moments of life.

At last the *Titanic*'s wireless operator showed a sense of urgency and sent out appeals for help. For hundreds of miles in all directions stunned wireless operators aboard a dozen boats heard the incredible news: the unsinkable *Titanic* was holed and sinking. Those ships that heard turned towards the stricken liner and sailed to the rescue, yet they were too far away. Only the *Californian*, with both captain and wireless operator asleep, was close enough to offer real assistance and they were oblivious to the catastrophe. An apprentice on board the *Californian* did approach the captain with the news that he had seen rockets in the sky – they were the *Titanic*'s distress signals – but at the last moment his courage failed him and he did not dare to wake Captain Lord. It was the *Titanic*'s last chance. Now her passengers were truly on their own.

The women and children on board the *Titanic* were being placed in the lifeboats. Only now did many realize that there were far too few boats to rescue everyone. Yet the owners had followed the Board of Trade Regulations and had provided the minimum cover of 16 lifeboats for an emergency. The men had to stand and watch as their wives and children were lowered into the icy darkness, while they had to stay behind, facing almost certain death in the sea. In the background the ship's band played ragtime tunes and many of the passengers ordered a fresh round of drinks.

In the allocation of lifeboat places it was later noted that of the survivors, 63 per cent of first class passengers had been saved, 42 per cent of second class and just 25 per cent of third class. Britain still had a very rigid class system, even when it came to emergencies. Just 711 people survived the disaster, all of them escaping in the boats available. Everyone left on board the Titanic went with her to the bottom of the North Atlantic, victims of the very 'unsinkability' of the great liner.

DAMMING WITH FAINT PRAISE

The Aswan Dam on the River Nile, begun by Egypt's President Nasser with such a diplomatic 'bang' in 1956, looks increasingly likely to end with a 'whimper', in the form of an ecological disaster for the country that built it. What started as a prestige project of vital importance to a man determined to stamp his leadership on the Arab world has, through the incompetence of the planners, been transformed into a catastrophe of startling proportions for the Egyptian people. Any political gains that Nasser might have felt he gained from the Suez fiasco and the humiliation of Britain and France in 1956 can now been seen as merely transient in comparison with the permanent damage done to the Egyptian economy which depends on the Nile waters for its existence.

As every schoolchild knows, Egypt is the 'gift' of the River Nile. The ancient civilization that grew up on the banks of the river was dependent on the annual flooding of the river which spread fertile silt over the flood plain on either bank. Beyond that, even today, Egypt is desert. And without the annual flood even Egypt's fertile areas would return to desert.

During the 1950s the Egyptian government made plans to replace an existing dam system at Aswan in the extreme south of the country, almost astride the tropic of Cancer, with a new High Dam, which would be able to maintain steady river levels throughout the year and provide hydroelectric power for dozens of new industries. It was an enormously prestigious scheme and the Egyptian leader, Gamel Abdul Nasser, received promises of financial and technical aid from both Britain and the United States. However, when the western powers learned that Nasser was purchasing Soviet arms to use against Israel and had mortgaged Egypt's cotton crop to pay for them, they withdrew their promise of aid for the dam. President Nasser faced humiliation in the eyes of his fellow Arabs and struck back at Britain by nationalising the Suez Canal, which had hitherto been run by a company in which Britain and France held majority shares. The subsequent Suez Crisis led to military defeat for Egypt but also failure for Britain and France, who were forced to evacuate Egypt after an abortive attempt to seize control of the canal. Once the political crisis subsided, Nasser looked to the Soviet Union for the money and expertise to build the Aswan High Dam and they obliged, duly completing the project in 1971. As a result of the dam a huge lake – Lake Nasser – was created south of Aswan in Nubia. It seemed that the dream of thousands of years had been achieved in a matter of a decade and a half. Egypt derived enormous short-term benefits in terms of increased production of cane sugar, cotton and maize, and the building of new industries producing fertilizer, steel and textiles. But this economic and industrial revolution would not be achieved without a price.

One wonders how much attention was paid by the men who planned the Aswan Dam to consulting those who would be most affected by it. It is a common fault among experts and élites that they are often remarkably ignorant of the 'live' issues involved in their planning. In board rooms, hi-tech

The Aswan Dam, the construction of which began in the aftermath of the Suez War of 1956, gave President Nasser of Egypt high hopes of increasing the fertility of his country's desert lands. Instead, as a result of inadequate planning, the dam has turned out to be an ecological disaster.

presentations, statistical charts, projections, video and virtual reality constructions can take the decision-makers so far away from mundane realities that their decisions may have consequences which they never intended and which could have been avoided by closer consultation with those directly affected by their planning. This, unfortunately, was to happen in the case of the Aswan Dam.

The planning that went into the dam in the later 1950s must have taken into account many important factors, such as the cost, the length of time it would take to build the dam, the availability of labour – both skilled and unskilled – materials, transportation, the accommodation and welfare of thousands of workers and many, many other considerations. In addition, the political and economic consequences of the dam – two factors which were almost indivisible – would have been high on the agenda for those who put up the money and those who spent it. In the case of the Aswan Dam there were social decisions to be taken as well, like the

disruption of the lives of the people of Nubia by the huge lake that would be created. There were also cultural concerns like the flooding of the temples of Abu Simbel, which were eventually lifted above the level of the waters and repositioned. The questions that needed to be asked of the planners seemed almost endless, yet to fail to ask them was to risk a historical and ecological disaster.

Once the euphoria created by the completion of the new dam died away, the awkward questions that had been overlooked began to be asked again. But by this time it was too late to incorporate them in the planning process. The mistakes had already been made, and they had been set in concrete. The first disappointment was the realization that the hydro-electricity produced by Lake Nasser would not, as had been predicted, supply enough electricity for all Egypt's domestic needs. It produced a lot, of course, but certainly not enough to provide an exportable surplus. The reason for this was that it had been necessary to achieve a balance between controlling irrigation, producing hydroelectricity and maintaining spare capacity for flood control. Consequently, the waters could only be used to create enough hydroelectricity for half Egypt's needs. In addition, and this is something the planners should have allowed for, because the River Nile was no longer flooding the lands of Egypt and leaving behind alluvial silt, it was necessary to manufacture artificial fertilizer to replace it. As a result, a proportion of the electricity generated was needed to power these new fertilizer factories. Furthermore, the planners did not give enough thought to where the previously vital alluvial silt would go once it was prevented from enriching the flood plain of Egypt. The outcome of the new dam was that the silt remained on the bottom of Lake Nasser, year by year reducing its depth and its capacity to store water. The time will come when the lake will be so silted up that it may return to desert. A further difficulty is that the damming of the Nile now prevents the rich 'alluvial soup' from reaching the Mediterranean so that the micro-organisms that were contained in the Nile water no longer nourish the sardines and anchovies upon which many Egyptian fishermen depend for their livelihood. Even more harmful has been the salination of the Egyptian soil which is no longer washed annually by the Nile flood and is, in consequence, less fertile than it had been in the days before the dam was built. For this reason also, the new Egyptian fertilizer industry is having to work to replace natural fertilization rather than bringing fertility to new areas.

One of the most serious human consequences of the Aswan Dam has been the increase in snails in the new irrigation system. The snails carry small liver flukes that in turn carry the disease bilharzia. The flukes enter the bodies of people working in shallow waters through the soles of the feet. Although not always fatal, bilharzia is debilitating and reduces resistance to other diseases. It had been a problem in Egypt since ancient times, but since the building of the Aswan Dam the incidence of the disease among the Nile population has increased to an alarming extent – it has been estimated that a third of all Egyptians suffer from it to a greater or lesser degree.

The ecological disasters that have followed the building of the Aswan dam constitute a historical blunder on the part of those who planned the entire project. In the 1950s decisions on the scheme were taken for purely political or economic reasons and the long-term consequences for Egypt's people were neglected. Perhaps it was asking too much of President Nasser, emerging bloodied but triumphant from his conflict with the Israelis as well as Britain and France, to think a generation ahead. In his struggle to gain supremacy in the Arab world the Aswan Dam was the kind of symbol that was worth short-term sacrifices. But the ignorance of the president and his planners has created medium-term problems and threatens to have disastrous long-term consequences for the Egyptian people years after Nasser's own ambitions have ceased to have any relevance for his country. Egypt was traditionally the gift of the River Nile, but the Aswan Dam has been a gift as well, this time from a team of short-sighted planners and a few ambitious politicians eager to echo Shelley's Ozymandias: 'Look on my works, ye Mighty, and despair!'

GOVERNMENT HOT AIR

Although the First World War had given the impetus to the development of civil as well as military aviation, it still seemed unlikely that aeroplanes would ever be large enough to carry large numbers of passengers on inter-continental flights. This market seemed ready-made for the airship, which could cater for those who preferred to fly in comfort rather than travel by sea, risking bad weather on the way. The vast bulk of the airship enabled her to compete with the transatlantic liner, matching her stateroom for stateroom and offering a unique view of the world into the bargain.

The airship seemed particularly well-suited to a country like Britain, with her far-flung empire in which long-range but luxurious travel would be much in demand. As a result, during the brief period of the first Labour Government in 1924, a plan was put forward by the then Secretary of State for Air, Lord Thompson, to build two enormous airships. One of the great vessels would be built by the state-owned Royal Airship Works at Cardington in Bedfordshire, and the other by the privately-owned Airship Guarantee Company, a subsidiary of Vickers, at Howden. It was secretly hoped by Thompson and his political colleagues, that the state-built R101 would outperform its privately manufactured 'sister', the R100. But the R101 had problems right from the start, having design faults that were concealed by its engineers in an attempt to placate their political bosses. It was a formula for disaster.

On completion in 1929, the R101 was an enormous structure, a 740-feet-long balloon coated in the skin linings of a million ox intestines. She was designed to carry a cargo of sixty tons and 100 passengers in the height of luxury. Distance was no object and R101 would cruise the skies in serene splendour, held up by the enormous buoyancy provided by her five million cubic feet of hydrogen gas. Critics did point out that helium gas would have worked just as well and was much safer than hydrogen, but the government was eager to count every penny and observed that hydrogen was far cheaper.

The fear in the minds of R101's designers was that although, on paper, the airship should be capable of achieving her specifications, this might not be the case in practice. The indications were that the R101 might have trouble lifting herself, let alone heavy cargo and passengers, from the ground at all. A million pounds of taxpayers' money had gone into building the R101 and by 1929 the designers were facing the prospect of complete failure. How would they be able to explain the apparent incapacity of state-owned industry to Lord Thompson, when the news from Vickers was that their R100 had been built quicker and cheaper, and what is more, worked to specification. It looked like private industry had put one over on the state system and this was causing harsh words in high political circles.

The designers at Cardington found themselves under pressure from the Air Minister, who wanted to know when the airship would be ready to make its maiden flight. He had already decided that R101 would fly from England to India. Lord Thompson was due to take up the post of Viceroy and he felt

it would be somehow symbolic if he were to appear from the sky, as if sent by God himself to rule the subcontinent. But the designers had discovered a snag: the R101 was too heavy. The brilliant Barnes Wallis at Vickers had made bold but inspired decisions on the structure of the R100 which the more earth-bound men at Cardington had been unwilling to do. As a result they had used the safer diesel engines on the R101, even though they were eight tons heavier than those used on the R100. In addition, the power-steering machinery for the rudders was enormously heavy, far more so than in the R100. The Cardington men had simply got their calculations wrong. In the air the steering of the R101 proved very light and the steering machinery quite excessive.

The first test flight of the R101 was quite alarming. Stripped of all inessentials, with no cargo and no passengers, the airship rose into the air like Dumbo testing out his ears for the first time. It was slow and cumbersome, particularly as the engineers could not get all the engines working at the same time. To make matters worse the gas bags moved in flight, rubbing themselves against the girders and making holes, through which the gas escaped at a rate of a thousand cubic feet an hour. One of the inspectors at Cardington, Frank McWade, was deeply unhappy about the R101 and wrote to the Air Ministry, expressing his doubts. In his view, the airship should not be allowed to have a certificate of airworthiness. Deprived of such a certificate R101 would not be allowed even to take off carrying passengers. Somewhere in the Air Ministry McWade's report was lost. Lord Thompson was never told of his own inspector's doubts.

At Cardington, R101's designers thought they had come up with the answer: they would cut the airship in half and insert a new forty foot long extension to hold enough extra gas to provide the buoyancy the airship needed. It was a desperate remedy. Lord Thompson, meanwhile, was insisting that the airship be ready for his trip to India in October 1930. The designers did what they could but they should have been more honest with him. The R101 was simply not ready – and probably never would be – for such a long voyage. There were just too many technical problems. Had the airship been required to get a certificate of airworthiness from anyone other than the men who built her, she would never have been allowed to fly at all.

On 4 October 1930, the R101, its crew of 48 and

The remains of the British airship R101, which crashed near Beauvais on its maiden flight in 1930. Doubts already existed about the viability of the airship as a form of transport and the failure of R101 ended research on airships in Britain.

its passengers, including Lord Thompson, took to the air on the first stage of its flight to India. Yet it nearly did not happen. The long-awaited Certificate of Airworthiness, without which she would not have been allowed to fly, was released by the Air Ministry only minutes before take off. Lord Thompson's baggage was in keeping with the importance of the occasion. He took with him two cases of champagne and an enormous Persian carpet. Perhaps it was his aerial lifeboat.

That evening the weather was foul: windy and with rain sheeting down. As the R101 passed over London, she was hardly making more than twenty-five miles an hour. Although there was every reason to turn back to Cardington, the decision was made to fly on through the gale. The staterooms were nearly empty, with just six passengers rattling around like peas in a whistle. The R101 was flying at just 1500 feet and as she passed over France she was hardly making any headway against the strong wind. The strain was too much for the airship and she began to lose height. As the passengers were preparing for bed one of the crew cried out that they

were nearly down to roof level and that he had just seen the spire of a church. In fact, it was Beauvais Cathedral and the R101 was flying far too low – just 500 feet above a line of hills. At the front of the airship the outer covering of the airframe tore loose and gas poured out of two of the gas bags, causing the nose to dip suddenly. With a crunch the airship hit the top of a hill and crumpled into a wreck. The hydrogen gas ignited and the whole structure was consumed in a great pall of fire. Incredibly, six crew members were thrown clear, but the rest of the crew and all the passengers died in the terrible conflagration. The French police and firemen on the ground could do nothing to help. The fire had been so intense that the steel girders of R101 were glowing white hot in the darkness. The first news of the disaster was received at the Air Ministry in Britain when one of the survivors, electrician Arthur Disley, showing true British sang-froid, telephoned the ministry from a neighbouring house. It was a bizarre moment in the circumstances. The loss of the great airship marked, for Britain, a dramatic end to a doomed concept.

INDEX